CONTENTS

ANIMALS PAGES 66–113

EARTH PAGES 114–149

TECHNOLOGY PAGES 150–185

SPACE PAGES 186–215

SCIENTIFIC CONCEPTS

From biology to geology to nanotechnology, there are many different branches of science. No matter what you are interested in—whether it is exercise, cooking, butterflies, trees, fish, stars, meteors, climate change, musical instruments, or robots—you can investigate the science behind it. Practice the scientific method, design experiments, and learn more about force, gravity, and motion. Find out about atoms, elements, and molecules and how they serve as the building blocks of matter.

TIME
FOR KIDS

SCIENCE
ALMANAC

TIME FOR KIDS SCIENCE ALMANAC

PRODUCED BY

DOWNTOWN BOOKWORKS INC.

PRESIDENT Julie Merberg
EDITORIAL DIRECTOR Sarah Parvis
EDITORIAL ASSISTANT Sara DiSalvo
SENIOR CONTRIBUTORS Beth Adelman, Jacqueline Ching, John Glenn, Allyson Kulavis, Susan Perry, Jenny Tesar
SPECIAL THANKS Lorin Driggs, Krissy Roleke, Lynn Messina, Stephen Callahan, Patty Brown
DESIGNED BY Georgia Rucker Design

TIME FOR KIDS

PUBLISHER Bob Der
MANAGING EDITOR, TIME FOR KIDS MAGAZINE
Nellie Gonzalez Cutler
EDITOR, TIME LEARNING VENTURES
Jonathan Rosenbloom

Time
HOME ENTERTAINMENT

PUBLISHER Richard Fraiman
VICE PRESIDENT, BUSINESS DEVELOPMENT & STRATEGY
Steven Sandonato
EXECUTIVE DIRECTOR, MARKETING SERVICES
Carol Pittard
EXECUTIVE DIRECTOR, RETAIL & SPECIAL SALES
Tom Mifsud
EXECUTIVE PUBLISHING DIRECTOR Joy Butts
DIRECTOR, BOOKAZINE DEVELOPMENT & MARKETING
Laura Adam
FINANCE DIRECTOR Glenn Buonocore
ASSISTANT GENERAL COUNSEL Helen Wan
ASSISTANT DIRECTOR, SPECIAL SALES Ilene Schreider
SENIOR BOOK PRODUCTION MANAGER
Susan Chodakiewicz
DESIGN & PREPRESS MANAGER
Anne-Michelle Gallero
BRAND MANAGER Jonathan White
ASSOCIATE PREPRESS MANAGER Alex Voznesenskiy
EDITORIAL DIRECTOR Stephen Koepp
EDITORIAL OPERATIONS DIRECTOR
Michael Q. Bullerdick

SPECIAL THANKS Christine Austin, Jeremy Biloon, Jim Childs, Rose Cirrincione, Lauren Hall Clark, Jacqueline Fitzgerald, Christine Font, Jenna Goldberg, Hillary Hirsch, Suzanne Janso, Raphael Joa, David Kahn, Amy Mangus, Robert Marasco, Kimberly Marshall, Amy Migliaccio, Nina Mistry, Dave Rozzelle, Adriana Tierno, Vanessa Wu

BRANCHES OF SCIENCE

Science is the field of knowledge that systematically studies and organizes information and draws conclusions based on measurable results. Traditionally, scientists have classified their fields into three branches: **physical sciences, earth sciences,** and **life sciences.** Today, **social sciences, technology,** and **mathematics** are also included. Each branch has many fields of study. Some are included here. Some are yet to be developed.

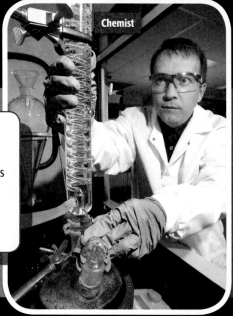

Chemist

PHYSICAL SCIENCES explore the properties of
energy and matter, as well as their relationship to each other. **Physics** seeks to explain how the universe behaves through the workings of matter, energy, and time. **Chemistry** is the study of chemical elements and how they interact on an atomic level. **Astronomy** is the study of space and its galaxies.

Botanist

LIFE SCIENCES explore the nature of living things.
Biology covers the study of how living things evolve, reproduce, thrive, and relate to one another. Medical research and development, and fields like **neurology** (the study of the brain) are included. **Botany** focuses on plants, **zoology** on animals, and **microbiology** on microscopic organisms.

guess what?
The word zoo is short for zoological garden.

The Wide World of Zoology

There are many different types of zoologists (zoh-ol-uh-jists). Some study a particular type of animal. Others study whole ecosystems. Some study animals in the wild. Others work with animals in zoos.

• **CONSERVATION BIOLOGISTS** study how to control and manage animals in their natural habitats.

• **ECOLOGISTS** study the relationship between animals and their environment.

• **ENTOMOLOGISTS** study insects.

• **ETHOLOGISTS** study animal behavior.

• **HERPETOLOGISTS** study amphibians and reptiles.

• **ICHTHYOLOGISTS** study fish.

• **MALACOLOGISTS** study mollusks (such as snails, oysters, and clams).

• **MAMMALOGISTS** study mammals.

• **MARINE BIOLOGISTS** study ocean animals.

• **MICROBIOLOGISTS** study microscopic animals.

• **ORNITHOLOGISTS** study birds.

EARTH SCIENCES

EARTH SCIENCES focus on the Earth and its composition and structure, as well as the processes that helped form it. **Geology** is the study of Earth's inner rock formations. **Geography** is concerned with the study and mapping of Earth's terrain. **Oceanography** focuses on the oceans and their currents and habitats. **Meteorology** is the study of weather. **Paleontology** focuses on the remains of ancient plants and animals.

Meteorologist

SOCIAL SCIENCES

SOCIAL SCIENCES investigate how humans behave and live together. **Psychology** explores individual human behavior. **Sociology** analyzes human behavior in groups. **Anthropology** studies human physical traits as well as cultures and languages. **Economics** is the study of how money, goods, and businesses affect society. **Law** focuses on the rules of society, and **political science** is about governmental processes and institutions.

Psychologist

TECHNOLOGY

Engineer

TECHNOLOGY deals with the practical application of scientific knowledge. **Engineering** deals with the design and construction of objects, machines, and systems. **Biotechnology** is the application of biological processes to create medicines and vaccines and to alter food and crops. **Computer science** focuses on meeting industrial needs by creating computers and new software. In **nanotechnology** (often shortened to nanotech), scientists work with microscopic materials, such as atoms and molecules.

MATHEMATICS

MATHEMATICS differs from other branches, because it deals with concepts rather than with physical evidence. Its focus is on understanding numeric relationships, analyzing data, and predicting outcomes. **Arithmetic** uses only numbers to solve problems, while **algebra** uses both numbers and unknown variables in the form of letters. **Geometry** is the study of two- and three-dimensional shapes. **Calculus** involves the computation of problems that contain constantly changing measurements. Nearly all sciences use mathematics.

Mathematician

A METHOD to the Madness

The **scientific method** is a set of steps that all scientists follow to create and conduct experiments. Here are the basic steps:

ASK A QUESTION.
Do you have any particular questions about the world around you? Begin by reading up on something that interests you. Are you concerned about beach erosion? Or curious about plant growth? Do you wish you understood more about the weather? Maybe you would you like to test a product to see how well it works. After doing some research, come up with a question you would like to answer. For example, is dish liquid more effective in warm or cold water?

DO RESEARCH ON THE TOPIC.
Investigate your topic and find out what similar experiments have been done. With lots of background information, a person can make a stronger hypothesis, or prediction.

FORM A HYPOTHESIS.
A hypothesis is a prediction based on what you have observed and read about. Hypotheses are usually put in this format: "If _____, then _____, because _____." For example, "If I put a can of soda in the freezer, then it will explode, because there is a lot of water in soda and water expands when it freezes."

TEST THE HYPOTHESIS WITH AN EXPERIMENT.
Before beginning an experiment, come up with a complete list of the materials you will need and then gather them. Write down each step in the experiment and follow them faithfully. Record your observations in writing and in pictures, wherever possible. Make sure to change only one variable (see pages 12–13) in your experiment.

PRACTICE MAKES PERFECT

Scientists must perform experiments many times, in exactly the same way, to make sure their results are valid. This is the only way to know for certain that a set of results is consistent.

Discoveries Made By Mistake

It's okay if an experiment does not yield the results you are expecting. It happens to scientists all the time, and it helps them to focus their question even more precisely. Many important discoveries have come from scientists making mistakes in their laboratories. Here are some products that have been devised by accident.

- Potato chips
- Saccharin, an artificial sweetener used in low-calorie or sugar-free products, such as sugar substitutes, chewing gum, toothpaste, candy, and diet sodas
- Vulcanization, which is the process of heating rubber with sulfur in order to make the rubber stronger and more flexible. Car tires are made with vulcanized rubber.
- Plastic

- Mauveine, the first human-made synthetic dye
- The pacemaker, which is an electrical device used to keep a heart beating at a normal rhythm
- Teflon, a nonstick material used to coat pots and pans
- Penicillin, an important antibiotic medicine

ANALYZE THE RESULTS. What happened in your experiment? Think about the data you collected during your experiment. To clarify what you've learned, put your findings into a graph or chart.

DRAW A CONCLUSION. Did the results of your experiment support your hypothesis? If not, come up with a new hypothesis and try the experiment again. If your hypothesis was proven correct, did the experiment raise questions or issues that you may want to explore in a follow-up experiment?

SHARE YOUR FINDINGS. When professional scientists complete an experiment, they will often publish a paper or article about their work and what they've found. You can do the same. Communicate your results to others. Science fair participants often make display boards to exhibit the hypothesis, research, process, data gathered, and results of a science experiment.

Science Experiments

Performing an experiment is a great way to illustrate scientific concepts and learn more about topics that interest you. Scientists observe specific things in the world and come up with rules to explain why things happen or how certain things are related. They use **variables** to design experiments that will make clear a cause-and-effect relationship in nature. A variable is one aspect, trait, or condition that can be changed in an experiment.

For example, to test which kind of packing material is the most effective, you might design an egg-drop experiment. In the experiment, you will place uncooked eggs into boxes filled with packaging materials and drop them from a particular height. There are several possible variables, such as the amount of packaging material used, the type of packaging material used (balled-up paper, Bubble Wrap, packing peanuts), and the height from which you drop the box. In an experiment, you can only accurately test one variable at a time. That means that all other aspects of the experiment should be exactly the same.

≋ Observation is key to a successful experiment. Use all of your senses to make observations during an experiment. Tools such as microscopes, magnifiers, telescopes, scales, measuring tapes, and thermometers can be very helpful when viewing and measuring changes.

INFERRING VS. PREDICTING

A prediction is a statement about what might occur in the future. When scientists make predictions, they use their knowledge and observations to make educated guesses about what they think will happen under a certain set of circumstances. An inference is a statement about what someone believes has already happened. It is the logical leap from what you have observed before to what you believe has happened. For example, if you see your friend kick a soccer ball and then hear the sound of breaking glass, you may infer that your friend kicked a ball and that it broke a window. If you see your friend lining up a shot while facing a window, you may predict that your friend will hit the window.

Some experiments take place over days, weeks, or even years.

VARIABLES

The **independent variable** is the thing you change in an experiment. There are lots of possible variables in experiments, such as height, weight, speed, heat, coldness, wetness, dryness, amount, softness, hardness, and color. The independent variable is responsible for the **dependent variable.**

Place four eggs (all four should be Grade A, extra-large eggs from the same supplier) in four identical packages (all using the same amount of Bubble Wrap). Drop each package from a different height to see if the result changes. In this case, height is the independent variable. Whether or not the egg breaks depends on the height.

To test the effectiveness of different types of packaging material, place one egg each in four boxes that are all the same size and made of the same material. Leave one box unfilled as a **control.** Fill one of the boxes with balled-up paper. Fill the next with Bubble Wrap. Fill the last box with packing peanuts. Make sure to pack each of the boxes as full as you can. Drop all four boxes from the same height. Here, the type of packaging material is the independent variable.

WHAT'S A CONTROL? The **control** sets the standard for an experiment. Each of the results of the experiment can be compared with the control. In the packing-material experiment on the right, the box with no packing material is the control. Drop the box with no packing material from a height of 8 feet (2.5 m) and record your results. You may find that the egg breaks. Then, when you drop the Bubble Wrap–filled box from the same height and the egg does not break, the control helps you to infer that it was the Bubble Wrap that helped the egg stay whole.

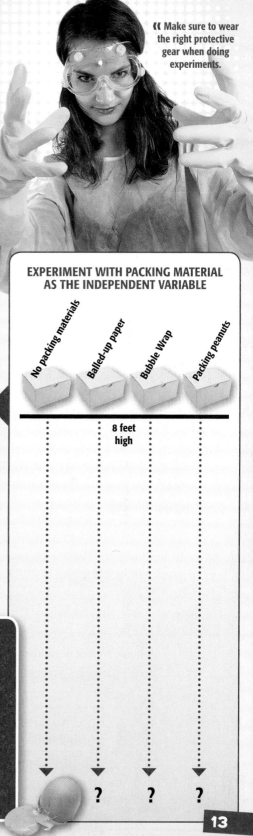

« Make sure to wear the right protective gear when doing experiments.

EXPERIMENT WITH PACKING MATERIAL AS THE INDEPENDENT VARIABLE

No packing materials

Balled-up paper

Bubble Wrap

Packing peanuts

8 feet high

? ? ?

FORCE AND MOTION

Born in 1642, **Sir Isaac Newton** made many significant contributions to the fields of science and mathematics. He is most famous for his **three laws of motion** and introducing the world to his **laws of gravity.** In 1686, Newton published *Principia*, his greatest and most comprehensive work. This book was the result of 20 years of observation, study, and thinking about matter and how it moves. Today, we call this scientific field **physics.** *Principia* began with a set of definitions that physicists still use today.

⌃ LARGE MASS: The Earth has a mass of approximately 13,169,533,694,000,000,000,000,000 pounds (5,973,600,000,000,000,000,000,000 kg).

MATTER: anything that takes up space

❮❮ SMALL MASS: This 11-year-old girl has a mass of approximately 75 pounds (34 kg). This is how many identical 11-year-old girls would equal the mass of the Earth: 177,000,000,000,000,000,000,000.

MASS: the measure of a quantity, or amount, of matter

MOMENTUM: the quantity of motion, which is the product of velocity (speed) and mass

FORCE: an action applied upon a body, or object

INERTIA: the tendency of an object at rest to stay at rest, and an object in motion to stay in motion

CENTRIPETAL FORCE (SEN-*TRIP*-IH-TUL): an attraction toward the center of something (as in gravity)

❮❮ This golf ball will stay where it is until a person hits it with a club, a strong wind begins to blow, or another force acts on it.

> The sun's gravity is so strong that it pulls on the planets, which have smaller masses, and holds them in its orbit.

Guess what?
Without gravity, some dangerous bacteria become stronger. This was discovered during experiments conducted in space.

Guess what?
Gravity on Earth is not entirely even. Because the globe isn't a perfect sphere, its mass is distributed unevenly. Uneven mass means slightly uneven gravity.

GRAVITY

Force is a push or a pull. **Gravity** is the force of attraction between objects—such as the sun and anything near it. The sun's powerful gravitational force pulls objects toward its center. This keeps all of the planets in our solar system orbiting around the sun. Earth has its own gravitational pull. Earth's gravity is the force that keeps our feet on the ground and makes apples fall from trees to the ground below.

MASS = GRAVITATIONAL PULL

Anything with mass has a gravitational pull. The more mass an object has, the greater its gravitational pull. This is why objects weigh less on the moon than they do on Earth. The moon is only about $1/4$ the size of Earth, so its gravitational pull is also about $1/4$ as strong as Earth's. This means that a person who weighs 100 pounds (45 kg) on Earth would weigh only 25 pounds (11 kg) on the moon.

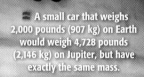

A small car that weighs 2,000 pounds (907 kg) on Earth would weigh 4,728 pounds (2,146 kg) on Jupiter, but have exactly the same mass.

MASS IS NOT THE SAME AS WEIGHT

The weight of an object depends on how much gravity is pulling on it, but no matter how much the gravitational pull varies from one place to another, the mass of an object stays exactly the same! An astronaut living on the International Space Station weighs less in orbit than on Earth, but his mass remains the same.

NEWTON'S LAWS

Sir Isaac Newton

Sir Isaac Newton made observations about the world that have held up since he published them in the 1680s. He described the relationship between force and motion in a way that works for objects on Earth and objects in space, and for both living things and nonliving objects. His three laws of motion are still used today to explain how planets remain in orbit, why a ball rolling in the grass eventually comes to a stop, and why seat belts help to keep car passengers safe.

When a rocket lifts off, hot gas and exhaust shoot downward. That downward force creates an equal reaction in the opposite direction, causing the rocket to shoot upward!

FIRST LAW OF MOTION: THE LAW OF INERTIA Objects at rest tend to stay at rest, and objects in motion tend to stay in motion.

SECOND LAW OF MOTION: THE LAW OF ACCELERATION Force is required to make something move, or accelerate. More work is required to move something heavy than to move something light.

THIRD LAW OF MOTION: THE LAW OF ACTION AND REACTION For every action, there is an equal and opposite reaction.

NEWTON'S CRADLE

There is a toy named after Newton. Made up of a group of balls of the same size and weight hanging from a frame, a Newton's cradle illustrates the law of conservation of energy. When one ball is pulled upward and allowed to fall, it bangs into the other balls and comes to a full stop. But its energy is transferred from one ball to the next and the ball on the opposite end immediately swings out.

10 LITTLE-KNOWN FACTS ABOUT SIR ISAAC NEWTON

Newton was born prematurely and not expected to live.

Newton was born into a farming family. When he was 17, his mother insisted he return from school to run the family farm. Thankfully, his uncle successfully persuaded his mother to let him attend Trinity College, which is part of the University of Cambridge, in England.

Trinity College

According to an often-told story, Newton was sitting under a tree when an apple fell and hit him on the head. This event supposedly inspired Newton to formulate his theory on universal gravitation. Newton himself said that he was staring out a window in his house when he saw the apple fall from a tree.

Newton was forced to take a two-year break from his studies when Cambridge was shut down during the Great Plague.

» During the Great Plague, doctors often wore masks with beaks that were meant to keep out infected air. Scientists now believe that the plague was transmitted by flea bites, not infected air.

Newton was elected as a member of Parliament in 1689. He served for exactly one year.

Newton was fascinated with religion and studied the Bible.

Newton made most of his discoveries between the ages of 21 and 27. He was very secretive and didn't share many of these discoveries until much later in his life.

Newton owned more books about history than any other subject.

In 1696, Newton became a warden of the London Mint, which was the government organization in charge of producing money. At the time, many criminals were engaged in counterfeiting, or making fake money. Newton was given the tough task of stopping counterfeiters.

Newton was very interested in alchemy. Alchemists believe there is a chemical process by which base metals, such as lead, nickel, or iron, can be turned into gold. He was never successful in this endeavor—and no one else has been either!

BUILDING BLOCKS OF MATTER

If something takes up space, it is called **matter.** All matter is made up of **atoms.** Dogs, pizza, rivers, insects, air, flowers, chewing gum, and jellyfish are all matter and are made up of atoms. Matter can exist in four different states: **solid, liquid, gas,** or **plasma.**

⚈ Artificially created plasma is used in some high-definition TVs, but matter in a plasma state is very rare on Earth.

Aluminum atom

ATOMS ARE MADE OF PARTICLES

An atom is made up of three particles.

The **NUCLEUS,** or center, of an atom contains **protons** and **neutrons.** The number of neutrons in an atom is usually equal to the number of protons in an atom.

One or more **electrons** orbit, or spin around, the nucleus.

- **Protons** are particles that have a positive (+) electrical charge.

- **Electrons** are particles that have a negative (-) electrical charge.

- **Neutrons** have a neutral charge, or no electrical charge.

The opposite charges of protons and electrons cause an attraction between these particles. This attraction keeps the electrons spinning around the nucleus.

Guess what? Atoms are tiny. They are so small, they cannot be seen with the human eye.

INTRODUCING ELECTRICITY

Electrons are always in motion. Sometimes they travel alone, and sometimes they travel in groups. When a large number of electrons travel together, we call this a "flow of electrons" and this gives us electricity. For more on electricity, see pages 20 and 160–163.

History of the Atom

In the 5th century B.C., a Greek philosopher named **DEMOCRITUS** developed the idea of atoms by asking an important question: If a person breaks a piece of matter in half, and then in half again, and again, is there a point at which the matter cannot be broken any further? Democritus assumed that at some point, matter would be broken into the smallest bit possible. He called these bits, or particles, atoms. And his assumption was correct. If a lump of gold were repeatedly broken in half until there remained only one atom of gold, breaking that atom would mean the pieces left over were no longer gold. Unfortunately for Democritus, no one agreed with him at the time. It took more than 2,000 years for the scientific community to begin questioning the structures of matter once again.

«« Democritus

In 1897, English physicist **J.J. THOMSON** discovered the electron, and proposed a model for the structure of an atom. Thomson knew that electrons had a negative charge, and thought matter must have a positive charge.

⌃ Thomson's model of an atom looked like raisins stuck on the surface of a lump of cookie dough.

In 1905, **ALBERT EINSTEIN** wrote a groundbreaking paper explaining how an atom can release electrons when it absorbs particles of light energy. He called the phenomenon the photoelectric effect, and, in 1921, he won the Nobel Prize in Physics for his work on this subject.

Guess what?
Utilizing Albert Einstein's work on the photoelectric effect, scientists and engineers have developed solar panels, which use the power of sunlight to generate electricity.

In 1911, New Zealand–born scientist **ERNEST RUTHERFORD** performed an experiment to investigate the inside of an atom. The results of the experiment were not what he was expecting, but they helped him develop a new model for the structure of the atom. Rutherford's model showed negatively charged electrons orbiting a positively charged nucleus, much like planets orbiting a sun.

In 1912, a Danish physicist named **NIELS BOHR** improved upon the atom model and discovered that electrons can orbit only at certain distances from the nucleus. Bohr also found that atoms give off and absorb energy when their electrons jump into a different orbit around the nucleus.

In 1932, English physicist **JAMES CHADWICK** discovered the neutron.

19

The Power of Electrons and Molecules

Electricity, also called **current electricity,** is the collective energy of many electrons traveling together.

Static electricity is also generated by electrons but in a very different way from current electricity. If an object picks up extra electrons, it becomes negatively charged. A negatively charged object will **attract** positively charged objects and **repel,** or push away, other negatively charged objects. If you rub a balloon on your head, it will make each strand of hair negatively charged, so they repel one another. The result? Your hair stands up on your head.

guess what?
Scientist (and Founding Father) Benjamin Franklin didn't discover electricity, but he did prove that lightning is a form of electrical energy.

guess what?
Electricity travels at the speed of light—more than 186,000 miles (300,000 km) per second!

When electricity jumps through the air, from one object to another, we call this **arcing.** A small spark and a bolt of lightning are both examples of arcing. While a spark can measure up to 3,000 volts, lightning can measure up to 3,000,000 volts—and lightning lasts less than one second!

CONDUCTORS AND INSULATORS

The flow of electrons, called a **current,** can only occur through certain materials. These materials are called conductors because they conduct, or carry, electricity. Metal and water are very good conductors. Plastic, glass, wood, rubber, and other materials that do not conduct electricity well are called insulators. This is why wires are made out of metal and covered in plastic.

KITCHEN SCIENCE

Conductors and insulators come in especially handy in the kitchen. To boil water, you probably use a metal pot or kettle, because metal is a good heat conducter. Heat passes easily through metal, and the pot gets hot quickly. Many pots and kettles have plastic handles. Because plastic is a good insulator, it stays cool to the touch. That's why you can touch the plastic handle of a pot without burning yourself. Oven mitts and potholders can also be used to protect hands from hot things. That's because they are made of fabric, a good insulator.

Molecules

When two or more atoms become **bonded,** or joined together, they form a **molecule.** Molecules can form into chaotic clusters, organized rows, or long chains, called **polymers.** The term "polymer" comes from the Greek words *poly,* which means "many," and *meros* meaning "part."

≈ Human-made polymers show up in many products, including the synthetic fiber used to make nonstick coatings on cookware and some of the body armor worn by soldiers and police officers.

BONDING CHANGES EVERYTHING

If atoms of two or more elements bond together and form a molecule, a new substance is created that can have completely different chemical properties from the elements themselves. The addition of just one atom can make a big difference!

Hydrogen and oxygen are invisible gases, but when **two hydrogen atoms** bond with **one oxygen atom,** they form a molecule of **WATER,** a colorless, tasteless liquid.

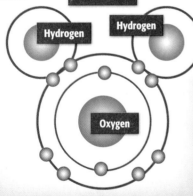

A WATER MOLECULE

Hydrogen

Hydrogen

Oxygen

When **two hydrogen atoms** bond with **two oxygen atoms,** they form the molecule we call **HYDROGEN PEROXIDE.** Hydrogen peroxide may look like water, but it's actually a powerful cleaning agent that is toxic to drink.

Guess what?
The hydrogen peroxide sold in the grocery store and used for treating minor cuts is heavily diluted with water and other liquids to make it a weak solution. Highly concentrated hydrogen peroxide is so powerful, it has been used as rocket fuel!

COMPOUND MOLECULES

When two or more different elements form a molecule, it is called a **compound molecule,** or just a **compound.** Water and hydrogen peroxide are compounds. Table salt is also a compound. It is made from the atoms of the elements sodium and chlorine. When two oxygen atoms bond together, they form a molecule, not a compound, because they are both the same element.

HALOGENS

The elements fluorine, bromine, chlorine, iodine, and astatine are called halogens. The word *halogen* comes from Greek and means "salt makers." When a halogen combines with a metal, a salt is formed. There are many different types of salt other than sodium chloride, which is commonly known as table salt. Some salts are extremely toxic, and others are even combustible, meaning they can explode. Luckily, table salt is safe.

It's Elemental

Elements are the building blocks of all matter. They are pure chemical substances so tiny they can't be divided into any other substances.

WHAT MAKES AN ELEMENT?

- All elements are made up of only one type of **atom.**

- All the atoms in a single **element** have the same number of protons.

- The number of protons in an atom determines its **atomic number.** For example, aluminum is a metal with an atomic number of 13. This means that any atom with 13 protons is aluminium and has all of the same properties as aluminum.

- So far, 118 different elements have been identified.

THE PERIODIC TABLE

The periodic table is an organized chart of all known elements. Each box in the table shows the name, symbol, atomic number, and atomic weight of a single element. Reading from left to right, the elements are listed in order of their atomic weight, from 1 (hydrogen) to 118 (ununoctium). Notice how the table also uses color to link related elements.

HOW TO READ THE TABLE

- The chart arranges the elements into seven rows, or **periods.**

- The first element in any period is highly **reactive.** That means it easily combines with other elements.

- The last element in a period is almost entirely **nonreactive.**

- There are 18 vertical columns called **groups,** and they make up "families" of elements with similar qualities. For example, all of the elements in group 18 are gases.

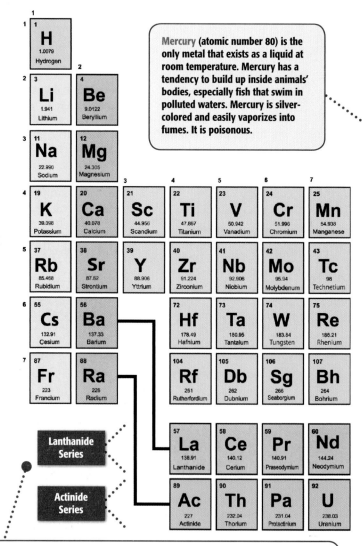

Mercury (atomic number 80) is the only metal that exists as a liquid at room temperature. Mercury has a tendency to build up inside animals' bodies, especially fish that swim in polluted waters. Mercury is silver-colored and easily vaporizes into fumes. It is poisonous.

Squeezed into spaces between groups 2 and 3 are the transition elements. These are metallic elements that chemically resemble one another very closely. One of these groups is called the Lanthanide Series, or Rare Earth Series, and the other is called the Actinide Series.

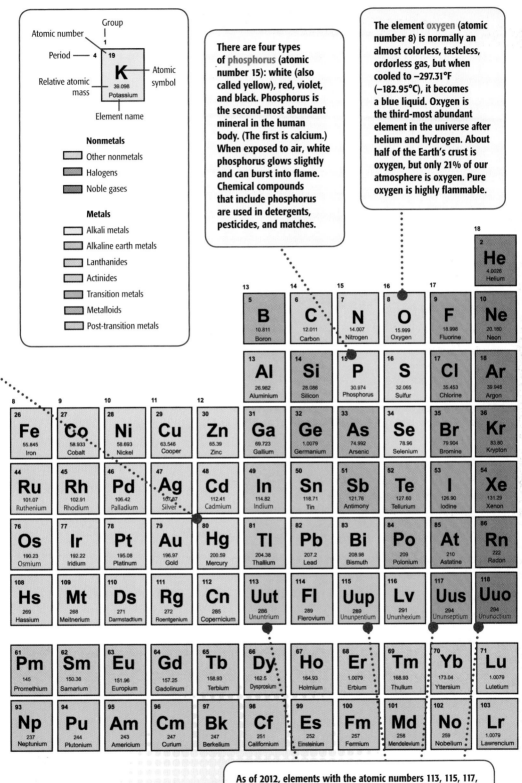

Group

Atomic number

Period — 4

Relative atomic mass

1

19

K

39.098
Potassium

Atomic symbol

Element name

Nonmetals
Other nonmetals
Halogens
Noble gases

Metals
Alkali metals
Alkaline earth metals
Lanthanides
Actinides
Transition metals
Metalloids
Post-transition metals

There are four types of phosphorus (atomic number 15): white (also called yellow), red, violet, and black. Phosphorus is the second-most abundant mineral in the human body. (The first is calcium.) When exposed to air, white phosphorus glows slightly and can burst into flame. Chemical compounds that include phosphorus are used in detergents, pesticides, and matches.

The element oxygen (atomic number 8) is normally an almost colorless, tasteless, ordorless gas, but when cooled to −297.31°F (−182.95°C), it becomes a blue liquid. Oxygen is the third-most abundant element in the universe after helium and hydrogen. About half of the Earth's crust is oxygen, but only 21% of our atmosphere is oxygen. Pure oxygen is highly flammable.

As of 2012, elements with the atomic numbers 113, 115, 117, and 118 were not yet confirmed and given official names.

23

An Elementary Hero

It was the Russian scientist **Dmitry Ivanovich Mendeleyev** who realized that "if all the elements be arranged in order of their atomic weight, a periodic repetition of properties is obtained." By this, he meant that if arranged properly and by atomic weight, elements with similar properties and characteristics would fall together. Elements that sit next to one another on the periodic table share certain qualities.

Dmitry Ivanovich Mendeleyev

FILLING IN THE BLANKS

Even though Mendeleyev's periodic table, published in 1869, had gaps where one might expect to see an element, it proved to be extraordinarily accurate. It turns out those gaps were not mistakes—those elements just hadn't been discovered yet! There were some instances when Mendeleyev had a hard time placing certain elements. In most of those cases, it was because what was known about the element at the time was incorrect. When more accurate information became available, those elements fit perfectly.

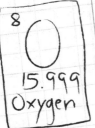

8
O
15.999
Oxygen

How Did He Do It?

Mendeleyev wrote the names of the elements and their atomic weights on a series of cards. Then he arranged and rearranged the cards until he created an order that made sense to him.

FROM TAKING X-RAYS TO DATING FOSSILS

Some elements emit, or give off, invisible particles. These substances are radioactive. Scientists found that radioactive materials and elements can be used to carry out many important tasks. Here are a few.

- Take X-rays
- Measure the heat of distant stars
- Determine the age of fossils
- Track ocean currents
- Determine the size of underground oil wells
- Sterilize medical equipment
- And even preserve food!

A Life Dedicated to Radiation

Marie Curie won the Nobel Prize in Physics in 1903 (a prize shared with her husband, Pierre Curie) and the Nobel Prize in Chemistry in 1911 for her research with radioactive elements. She was the first scientist to win both prizes.

Marie Curie

Born in Warsaw, Poland, in 1867, Marie Curie studied all compounds containing known radioactive elements, including uranium and thorium. She discovered that it was possible to exactly measure the strength of the radiation from uranium and that the intensity of the radiation is proportional to the amount of uranium or thorium in a compound. In short, the bigger the lump of uranium, the more radioactive it will be. Her most revolutionary discovery was that an element's ability to emit radiation did not depend on the arrangement of the atoms in a molecule. Instead, this ability was linked to the interior of the atom itself.

AWARD-WINNING DISCOVERIES

Marie Curie found that some compounds had stronger radiation than uranium and made the following hypothesis: There must be an unknown element in the compound that gave off stronger radiation than uranium or thorium. Her work was so interesting to her husband that he stopped his own research on crystals and joined the "detective work." In 1898, this research led the Curies to discover two new radioactive elements, radium and polonium, named after Marie's home country, Poland.

Physical Changes vs. Chemical Reactions

When an ice cube melts, the water in the cube goes from being a solid to being a liquid. It changes state, but the material is still water. This change in appearance is called a **physical change.**

≈ An ice cube melting is not a chemical reaction. The water is changing temperature, but the molecules remain the same.

Have you ever seen someone make a craft volcano erupt using baking soda and vinegar? That "eruption" isn't caused by magic. It is the result of a simple **chemical reaction.** In chemistry, a reaction happens when two or more molecules interact and change into something else. New substances are formed during chemical reactions.

《 The burning of a match is a chemical reaction.

Some chemical reactions, such as burning matches, produce heat. The explosion of fireworks is caused by a chemical reaction. In another kind of chemical reaction, two or more simple compounds combine to form a more complicated one. For example, a chemical reaction takes place when oxygen bonds with hydrogen to form water.

《 There is copper in the coating of the Statue of Liberty. When it is exposed to oxygen in the air, this coating turns green. It's the result of a chemical reaction called oxidation that happens when copper combines with oxygen.

Rust is a chemical reaction. When iron combines with oxygen in the atmosphere, a new, bright orange compound is created.

Guess what?
Cutting an onion causes a chemical reaction that releases a type of acid that rises into the air as a gas. That's why cutting onions makes some cooks cry.

Chemistry at Home

There is a lot of chemistry in baking. Cookbooks provide specific instructions for measurements of ingredients, steps to follow, and the time and temperature needed when baking. Just like any chemistry experiment, baking requires precision.

Baker's yeast is an ingredient that reacts with sugar to create a gas. The gas resulting from this chemical reaction allows dough to rise and become light and airy. If a baker does not follow a recipe exactly, the food may look or taste horrible.

>> The little holes in bread are made by gas bubbles formed in the chemical reaction that takes place during baking.

MIXTURES

Mixtures are combinations of molecules that are not chemically joined or changed. The molecules can be separated out of the mixture at any time. Salt water is a mixture of salt and water. When the water evaporates, the salt is left behind.

Painters and lighting designers study the mixture of color, also called color theory, but light and paint don't create the same colors when mixed together. Mixing blue and yellow paint will make green, but mixing blue and yellow light will create white light with a hint of either blue or yellow. Understanding how colors blend and mix is an important skill for these artists.

Guess What?
Every day, hundreds of thousands of chemical reactions happen in your body to help keep you alive, digest your food, and move your muscles!

TYPES OF SCIENTISTS

Do you like to look for fossils? Are you fascinated by butterflies? Have you ever wanted to prevent people from getting sick? No matter what your interests are, there is a possible career in science for you. Below are some neat scientific specialties that you might want to check out.

A **SEISMOLOGIST** studies earthquakes.

A biologist who focuses on butterflies is called a **LEPIDOPTERIST.**

CRIMINOLOGISTS study criminals and the causes of their behavior within a society.

To learn more about the lives and cultures of prehistoric people, **ARCHAEOLOGISTS** analyze human-made objects and other artifacts left behind.

An **EPIDEMIOLOGIST** is a scientist who examines diseases and how they spread.

GENETICISTS focus on genes and the traits that living things get from their parents.

IMMUNOLOGISTS focus on the immune systems of all living things. An organism's immune system protects it from diseases and infections.

A scientist who learns all about glaciers and ice is a **GLACIOLOGIST.**

MINERALOGISTS are experts in the chemical and physical makeup of minerals.

NEUROSCIENTISTS study the human nervous system and how it works. (For more on the nervous system, see page 42.)

PALEOBOTANISTS focus on the biology and evolution of prehistoric plants.

Forever Young (and Squeaky)

Scientists have found a way to reverse aging in **mice.** They hope that this kind of research will help them devise better treatments for age-related illnesses.

Recent Scientific Breakthroughs

Scientific fields are always changing, as people make new discoveries and draw new conclusions. Here are a few recent revelations in fields ranging from archaeology to medicine.

100,000-Year-Old Art Kit Found in South Africa »

Archaeologists recently found evidence that early humans were painting 100,000 years ago. Two kits for mixing and forming ochre, a reddish pigment used for painting and dyeing, were found in a cave in South Africa. This discovery proves that humans were creating art 40,000 years earlier than we had previously thought. This **color-dye kit** is also evidence that early humans participated in long-term planning and knew enough basic chemistry to successfully mix compounds.

Online Gaming for Good

In 2008, scientists created a video game called **Foldit** to see if online gamers could help them detect patterns in some microscopic structures found inside the human body. It took gamers only 10 days in 2011 to solve a puzzle that has baffled scientists for about 15 years. Researchers hope to use the new information to develop drugs to fight deadly viruses.

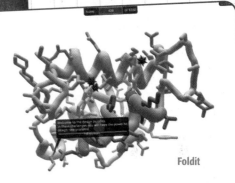

Foldit

Microscopic Cleanup Crew

After an earthquake and tsunami damaged a nuclear power plant in March 2011, scientists looked for new ways to clean up spilled radioactive material. They found microscopic organisms, such as bacteria and algae, that were able to remove radiation from the ground.

Roaches to the Rescue?

Natural antibiotics were found in the brains and central nervous systems of **cockroaches** and locusts. In early testing, these antibiotics were able to kill some bacteria that are often deadly to humans. One day, a roach brain might mean the difference between life and death for a person.

HUMANS

From the immune system's amazing ability to fight off infection to the brain's many fantastic functions, the parts that make up the human body are incredible. This chapter is chock full of interesting information about organs and body systems, nutrition and exercise, doctors and their specialties, and kooky medical practices of the past.

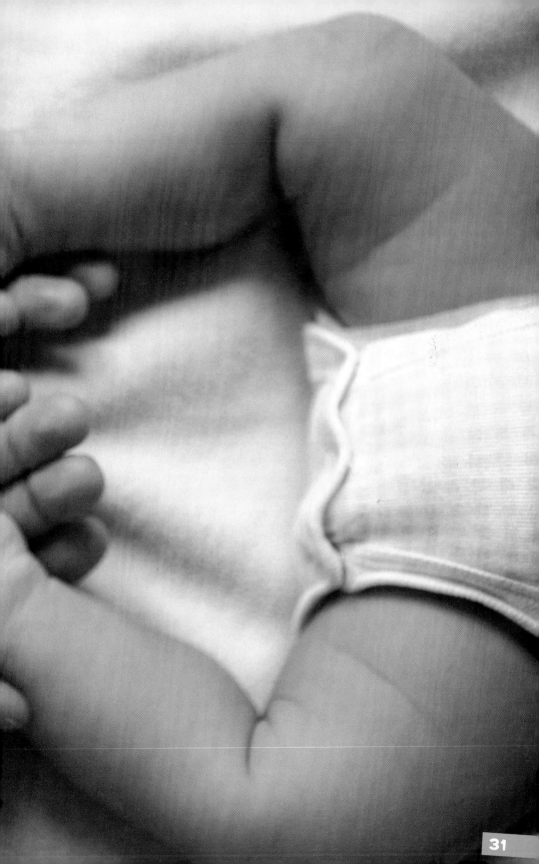

Your Body, Your Health

Your body is an amazing thing. It's made up of trillions of **cells.** No one knows exactly how many cells are in the body. Besides, the number constantly changes. New cells form; others die or are destroyed.

More than 200 kinds of cells are found in the body. Each has a specific function. Salivary gland cells make saliva. Some nerve cells pick up information from outside the body; other nerve cells carry this information to the brain. Heart-muscle cells are different from stomach-muscle cells. Fat cells are different from blood cells.

Cells are the tiniest structure in the human body. In fact, most cells are microscopic. But there is a single nerve cell that extends all the way from your spinal cord to your toes. It is incredibly long and has many branches. This means messages can be sent quickly between the spinal cord and toes.

Groups of cells form larger structures (**tissues**), which build even larger structures (**organs**), which build the different systems that work together to keep the body functioning. The **body systems** consist of organs such as the liver, kidneys, and heart that have their own special functions. Even your skin is an organ!

⋛ Sweat gland cells make sweat.

⋛ Stomach cells

BUILDING BLOCKS OF THE BODY

STRUCTURE	DESCRIPTION	EXAMPLES
CELL	The smallest unit in your body	Red blood cells, tear-producing cells, cold-sensitive nerve cells
TISSUE	A group of cells of one or more types	Connective tissue (such as ligaments and tendons), muscle tissue, nerve tissue
ORGAN	A group of tissues	Brain, heart, stomach, kidney, eye, skin

WHAT IS THE BODY MADE OF?

LARGEST ORGAN	The skin. It accounts for about 12% of a person's weight.
LARGEST INTERNAL ORGAN	The liver. An adult's liver weighs 2.5 to 3.3 pounds (1.1–1.5 kg).
LONGEST BONE	The thighbone, or femur. It grows to an average length of almost 20 inches (50.5 cm).
SMALLEST BONE	The stapes (*stay*-peez), the innermost of three tiny bones in the middle ear. It is only 0.07 inches (1.8 mm) long.
LARGEST MUSCLE	The gluteus maximus, found in each buttock
LONGEST MUSCLE	The sartorius, which crosses the front of the thigh
HARDEST MATERIAL	The white enamel that covers the crown of each tooth
MOST COMMON CELL	Red blood cells. An adult body contains about 25 trillion.
MOST COMMON SUBSTANCE	Water. It makes up about 70% of a person's weight.

STEM CELLS

Stem cells are unspecialized cells. They cannot make you grow hair or digest food or sense light. But they can develop, or differentiate, into various kinds of cells. For example, stem cells in the skin develop into different kinds of skin cells. Stem cells in bone marrow form new blood cells.

Stem cells can renew themselves. They can make exact copies of themselves over and over again until something triggers them to differentiate. Scientists are working with stem cells to learn how to make some stem cells turn into skin cells to help people who have suffered from burns, or grow into organs such as livers or kidneys to help patients whose own organs are failing. Doctors can use stem cells to treat some kinds of cancer. In the future, stem cells may also be used to treat other diseases.

About 1,000 stem cells magnified 400 times by a powerful microscope

Protein and the Body

Next to water, protein is the most plentiful substance in your body. Protein is essential for growth and repair. It is the main building material of the body. Muscles, skin, blood, and most other parts of the body are made from protein. Meat, fish, cheese, eggs, and other foods that come from animals are rich in protein. But many plant-based foods, such as beans, nuts, seeds, and wheat, also are sources of protein. Most Americans eat much more protein than they actually need. Excess protein is often stored in our bodies as fat.

Guess what?
Your eyes are almost finished growing by birth, but your nose and ears never stop growing.

The Skeletal System

The skeletal system is made of two kinds of tissue: **bone** and **cartilage.** Bone is a hard tissue. Cartilage is a flexible tissue that forms parts like the nose and ears. Cartilage also covers the ends of bones within joints. The skeleton has four main functions. First, it supports the body and gives it shape. It works with muscles to help the body move in different ways. Second, it protects other organs in the body from injury. For example, your skull protects your brain. Third, bones store important minerals such as calcium and phosphorous, releasing them into the bloodstream when the body's other organs need them. Fourth, bone marrow, found in cavities in bones, produces blood cells.

Most people have 12 pairs of ribs. A person's ribs protect the soft internal organs such as the heart and liver.

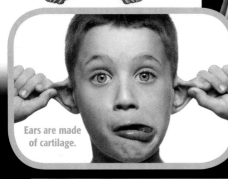

Ears are made of cartilage.

GROWING, GROWING, GROWN!

At birth, a baby has more than 300 bones. By the time the child has reached adulthood, she'll have 206 bones. Where do those additional bones go? Some bones fuse together, making one bone where there had been two. Some bones grow a lot during a person's lifetime. Just think how short a baby's arms and legs are compared with the limbs of an adult. The longest bone in your body is the thighbone, or femur. It's about one-fourth of your total height. It keeps growing as long as you do. Your spinal cord, however, stops growing when you are about 5 years old.

The Muscular System

The body contains three kinds of muscles. **Skeletal muscles** are attached to—and move—the bones. **Smooth muscles** line the digestive system and help move food and water through it. **Cardiac muscle** cells are found in the heart. They pump blood through the heart to other parts of the body. Some muscle movements are voluntary, like when you move your hand to pick up and clench a ball. Other muscle movements are involuntary. That means that they work without a person thinking about it. Smooth and cardiac muscles are involuntary muscles.

≈ Your heart muscle beats about 70 times a minute. Your eye muscles are busy too. They move more then 100,000 times a day.

The Reproductive System

This system is responsible for producing sperm cells in men and egg cells in women. During reproduction, the sperm cell and the egg cell combine to form an embryo, which eventually becomes a human baby.

THE HUMAN LIFE CYCLE

STAGE	TIME
EMBRYO	Conception to end of 8th week
FETUS	9th week to birth
NEWBORN	Birth to 4 weeks
INFANT	4 weeks to 2 years
CHILD	2 years to puberty
ADOLESCENT	Puberty to 20 years
YOUNG ADULT	20 to 40 years
MIDDLE-AGED ADULT	40 to 65 years
SENIOR CITIZEN	65 years to death

The Integumentary System

The **skin** is the main organ of the integumentary (in-*teg*-yoo-*men*-ta-ree) system, which also includes **sweat glands, oil glands, nails,** and **hair.** Sweat glands in your skin help the body cool itself. The skin's oil glands keep the body from drying out. Nails provide defense, and hair provides protection and warmth. Skin covers the body, protects your insides, and helps keep out germs. It helps your body stay at the right temperature. It aids with removing waste from the body. And it provides you with lots of information about the world around you.

Close-up view of a person's skin

LIVING LAYERS

The skin has three main layers. The outer layer, or **epidermis,** is the layer you see. Underneath are living cells. The living cells divide rapidly, creating new cells. The new cells push upward, replacing the dead cells above them. Under the epidermis is the **dermis.** It is much thicker than the epidermis. It contains tough, stretchy material that keeps the skin firm yet flexible. It also contains many specialized cells and structures, such as sweat and oil glands and hair follicles. Tiny blood vessels bring blood to the dermis. The blood supplies the cells with food and oxygen and carries away waste products. Below the dermis is the **subcutaneous layer,** which acts as a cushion, helping to protect inner organs when a person falls down or bumps into something.

THICK 'N' THIN

- The thickest skin is on the palms of your hands and the bottoms of your feet.
- The eyelids and lips have the thinnest skin.
- The scalp has the most hair follicles—more than 100,000!
- There are no hair follicles on the palms of your hands and the soles of your feet.

WHAT'S HAPPENING IN HEALTHY SKIN

The SURFACE of the epidermis consists of tough, flat, dead cells.

HAIR

PORE

Many cells in the EPIDERMIS are made of keratin, the same material in hair and nails.

BLOOD VESSEL

SEBACEOUS (OIL) GLAND

The DERMIS contains millions of tiny nerve endings.

SWEAT GLANDS produce sweat.

HAIR FOLLICLES make hair.

The SUBCUTANEOUS LAYER consists mainly of fat and helps to insulate the body.

ARTERY

VEIN

FAT TISSUE

NERVE ENDINGS respond to touch, pain, itchiness, pressure, heat, cold, and other sensations. Nerve fibers carry information from the skin to the brain.

Guess what?

Dead cells are constantly flaking off the surface of the skin. Every minute, a person loses about 30,000 to 40,000 dead skin cells. An average person sheds about 40 pounds (18 kg) of skin in a lifetime!

Skin graft

« When doctors perform a skin graft, they remove an area of healthy skin from somewhere on a person's body and transplant it to an injured area. Spray-on skin requires the removal of fewer healthy skin cells and may cover a larger portion of an injury with fewer complications.

SPRAY-ON SKIN

Scientists are able to make artificial skin to help people who have burns and scars. Today, doctors can remove a postage stamp–size skin sample and use it to quickly generate new skin cells. This type of skin is then sprayed on!

The Cardiovascular System

The cardiovascular system, or circulatory system, is made up of the **heart, blood vessels,** and **blood.** Its job is to circulate blood throughout the body. Blood contains oxygen, hormones, and nutrients that cells need to grow, work, and repair themselves. Cells take in these products and give off carbon dioxide and other waste materials. The kidneys and certain other organs remove the waste from the blood.

THE HUMAN HEART

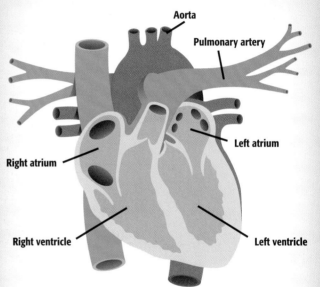

Aorta

Pulmonary artery

Left atrium

Right atrium

Right ventricle

Left ventricle

Guess what?

If all the blood vessels from a human body were laid end-to-end they would stretch more than 60,000 miles (96,500 km).

ONE-WAY STREETS

Blood vessels carry blood in one direction. Arteries are vessels that carry blood away from the heart. Veins carry blood toward the heart. Tiny vessels called capillaries connect arteries with veins. Movement of materials in and out of the blood takes place through the thin walls of the capillaries.

The heart has four chambers. The upper chambers (atria) receive blood as it enters the heart. The lower chambers (ventricles) pump blood out of the heart. The pulmonary artery carries oxygen-poor blood from the right ventricle to the lungs. There, the carbon dioxide is released and oxygen is picked up. The oxygen-rich blood then flows to the left side of the heart. The left ventricle pumps this blood into the aorta–the body's largest artery.

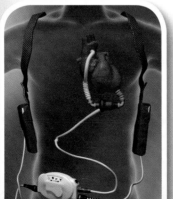

❝ In the past, when someone's heart failed, that person died. Now, doctors may perform a heart transplant or implant a pump that acts like a mechanical heart (like the one pictured). The pump is powered by a battery pack worn by the patient. The battery is attached to a cable that runs through the person's abdomen!

The Respiratory System

To stay alive and release energy from food, cells need **oxygen.** The respiratory system supplies your body with oxygen. Breathing is the most familiar part of respiration. It carries air into and out of the lungs. The lungs are made up of millions of tiny balloonlike structures called alveoli. Each alveolus is surrounded by capillaries. Oxygen moves from the alveoli into the blood in the capillaries. At the same time, carbon dioxide moves from the blood into the alveoli.

HUMAN LUNGS

People have two lungs, which take up most of the space in the chest. The lung on the right side of the body is larger. The lung on the left is smaller, which leaves room for the heart.

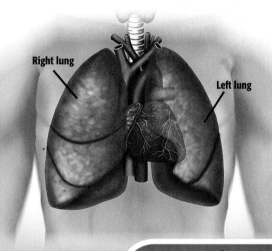

Right lung

Left lung

≋ The air that travels through your respiratory system picks up heat from the body. That's why the air that you push out of your lungs is warm.

FOOD, OXYGEN, AND EXERCISE

Burning the energy you get from food requires oxygen. You take in oxygen through your lungs. The oxygen passes from the air in your lungs into your blood. The blood then carries the oxygen to all the cells in your body. When your body needs to burn food rapidly, it needs more oxygen. This explains why you take deeper, more frequent breaths when you are running than when you are sitting. Your heart also beats faster when you are active. It has to work harder so the blood can quickly get oxygen to the cells.

The Digestive System

The digestive system takes in and breaks down, or digests, foods and liquids. Digestion turns large food particles into tiny, simple particles that can pass into the bloodstream. Digestion takes place in the **digestive tract.** This is a long, continuous tube that begins with the mouth.

WHAT HAPPENS WHEN WE EAT?

Saliva in the mouth begins breaking down food.

Food travels down the esophagus to the stomach.

Food, liquids, and digestive juices mix together in the stomach. Protein digestion begins in the stomach.

Before fat can be digested in the small intestine, it must be dissolved, or broken into tiny droplets. The liver creates bile, a liquid that helps to break down fat.

The pancreas produces digestive juices containing enzymes that help to break down carbohydrates, fats, and proteins.

Bile is stored in the gallbladder, then flows from there into the small intestine. After the fat is dissolved, enzymes digest it.

A lot of water is used during the digestion process. Water is then reabsorbed in the large intestine.

Protein digestion is completed in the small intestine. Digestion of carbohydrates and most fats takes place in the small intestine as well.

Waste is passed out of the body through the rectum.

Guess what?
Digestion begins even before a person puts food in his or her mouth. Just smelling food can trigger the production of saliva in the mouth.

Guess what?
At 20 feet (6 m) long, the small intestine is actually a lot larger than the large intestine. The large intestine is wider, but only about 5 feet (1.5 m) long.

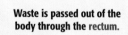

HOW LONG DOES IT TAKE?

Various factors determine how long food stays in the digestive tract. Large meals take longer to digest than snacks. Meals containing a lot of fat take longer to digest than a meal that is mainly carbohydrates. Also, if you swallow a big chunk of food without chewing it properly, the stomach needs to spend more time churning the food and mixing it with chemicals.

PART OF THE DIGESTIVE TRACT	TIME FOOD SPENDS THERE
MOUTH	5 seconds to 2 minutes
ESOPHAGUS	3 to 5 seconds
STOMACH	1 to 6 hours
SMALL INTESTINE	2 to 9 hours
LARGE INTESTINE	2 to 3 days

THE SCOOP ON POOP 'N' STUFF

BURPS (also called belches) are gases expelled from the stomach through the mouth.

BARF (vomit) is liquid and solid matter that comes up from the stomach and is expelled through the mouth.

FARTS (flatulence) are gases produced in the intestines and expelled through the anus at the bottom end of the digestive tract.

POOP (feces) is undigested food and other solid and liquid wastes that pass out through the anus.

GET PLENTY OF FIBER

Fiber, also known as roughage (*ruff*-ij), is an important part of a healthy diet. It is plant matter that your body cannot digest. What's so good about eating something your body cannot break down? As it passes through your digestive system and out of your body, it helps food move through the digestive system. It also makes it easier for waste to move out of the system. Foods such as avocados, split peas, black beans, raspberries, artichokes, and bran flakes contain a lot of fiber.

» Bran flakes

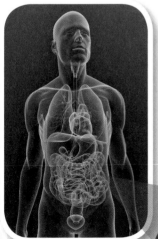

The Urinary System

The main organs of the urinary system are the two kidneys. They remove waste from the blood, including excess salts and other chemicals. They produce liquid called urine. The urine moves out of the kidneys and into the bladder through tubes called ureters. It is then excreted from the body when the person urinates.

❰❰ Kidney beans are shaped just like the kidneys in the human body.

The Nervous System

Think of your nervous system as "control central." Its job is to control body functions. It tells structures what to do and when to do it. The nervous system has two parts. The **central nervous system** includes the brain and the spinal cord. The **peripheral nervous system** consists of nerves that connect the central nervous system with other parts of the body. Nerves carry messages to or from the brain. The messages are in the form of electrical signals. Some signals travel along nerves at more than 200 miles (320 km) per hour!

THE BRAIN

The brain of an adult weighs about 3 pounds (1.5 kg). Each part of the brain has specific functions. The **cerebrum** is the largest part of the brain. It makes up about 80% of the brain's weight. It controls memory, reasoning, and voluntary muscles. When you play a video game, solve a math problem, kick a soccer ball, or high-five your friend, you are using your cerebrum. The cerebrum has four lobes: the **frontal, parietal, occipital,** and **temporal lobes.**

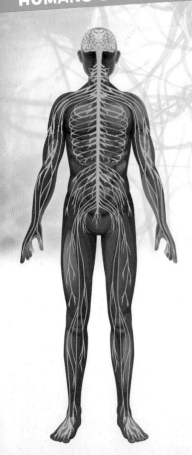

Guess what?
The messages your brain sends are kind of like the electrical signals that race through a computer.

The **frontal lobe** deals with intellect, problem solving, emotions, and the creation of memories. It helps control voluntary movements of certain body parts.

The **parietal lobe** gathers and processes information from your senses. It helps control eye and arm movements.

The **temporal lobe** helps process sounds, including speech. It helps form long-term memories.

The **occipital lobe** handles vision. It's also the part of the brain where dreams are formed.

The **brain stem** connects the brain to the spinal cord. It controls involuntary body functions, like breathing, digestion, and blood circulation.

The **cerebellum** controls balance, coordination, and movement. When you stand on one foot, walk on the balance beam, or aim the perfect free throw, your cerebellum is in charge.

Guess what?
The left side of the brain controls the right side of the body. The right side of the brain controls the left side of the body.

» Balance is controlled by the cerebellum.

THE SENSES

Everything you know about the world around you comes to you via your sense organs. Your **eyes** see your best friend; your **nose** smells cookies baking; your **ears** hear running water; your **fingers** tell the difference between paper and plastic. When a change is detected by a sense organ, an impulse is sent along a nerve, usually to the brain. The brain processes the information and determines a response.

PICKING UP THE SIGNALS

SENSE	BODY PARTS
SIGHT	Eyes
HEARING	Ears
TOUCH	Contact, pressure, and pain cells in the skin
TEMPERATURE	Heat and cold cells in the skin
TASTE	Taste buds on the tongue, palate, and upper esophagus
SMELL	Olfactory cells in the nose
BALANCE	Semicircular canals in the inner ear

BRAIN FREEZE!

Eat ice cream too quickly, or gulp down a cold drink and—oops!—you've got brain freeze. Also known as an ice-cream headache, this brief pain can develop when something cold touches the roof of your mouth.

« Your sense of taste depends heavily on your sense of smell. When you have a cold and your nose is stuffed up, you cannot smell food—and it seems as if the food has no taste.

QUICK REFLEXES

The brain is usually involved in responding to changes in the environment. But not always. Hitting the tendon just below the knee causes the leg to suddenly kick—a reaction known as the knee jerk. When the tendon is hit, a signal rapidly travels along a nerve to the spinal cord—and just as rapidly travels back to the leg muscles. This reflex is important. It helps a person keep his or her balance without conscious thought.

The Endocrine System

The organs of the endocrine system are called **glands.** **Hormones** are chemicals made in tiny amounts by endocrine glands. Hormones are sometimes called chemical messengers. They are carried to various parts of the body, where they regulate certain activities. There are more than 50 human hormones. For example, cells in the thyroid gland produce the hormone thyroxine. This hormone regulates how cells use energy. Other cells in the thyroid produce calcitonin, which helps regulate the amount of calcium in the blood.

PUBERTY

You have grown a lot since you were born. You'll grow still more before you become an adult. There will be other changes too.

The period of time during which the body completes its growth is called puberty. Puberty begins at different ages for boys and girls. And the bodies of boys and girls change in different ways. These changes are triggered by hormones. Production of certain hormones speeds up as puberty starts. As a result, differences between boys and girls become more obvious. Girls develop breasts. Their hips and thighs become rounder. Boys develop broader shoulders, and hair begins to grow on the upper lip, cheeks, and chin. Their voice boxes grow, and their voices become deeper.

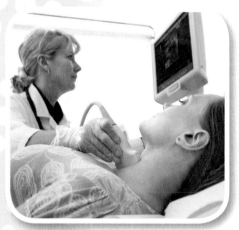

≋ The thyroid gland is in the neck. Here, a doctor performs an ultrasound scan on a woman's thyroid. Ultrasounds use high-frequency sound waves to make images of the inside of a person's body.

Guess What?
Before puberty, children average 22% body fat. By age 18, girls average 28% and boys 13%.

❱❱ Sweating is normal—everyone does it. But puberty hormones affect glands in the skin that change a person's body odor. That's why armpit sweat in teens and adults can be extra stinky.

❰❰ The same hormones that cause puberty can also result in acne, or pimples.

EVERYONE IS DIFFERENT

Puberty starts and ends at different times in different kids. Each body goes through these changes at its own pace. One 12-year-old boy may grow 3 inches (7.6 cm) taller in a year. His friend may grow only 1 inch (2.5 cm) taller—but then grow four inches (10 cm) at age 15. Girls usually enter puberty between the ages of 8 and 13. Boys begin puberty later, between the ages of 10 and 15. Growth spurts usually start and finish earlier for girls.

People are also different because of their genes, which are characteristics they inherited from their parents. Genes are the major factor determining how a person changes during puberty. If a woman entered puberty at an early age, her daughter is likely to do so too. If parents are short, their children will probably be short as well.

Guess what?
Body parts do not grow at the same pace. Hands and feet usually grow first. Then arms and legs get longer. Finally, the rest of the body catches up.

AVERAGE HEIGHTS AND WEIGHTS

At age 8, boys and girls average the same height and weight. But look what happens after puberty!

	BOYS		GIRLS	
	AVERAGE HEIGHT	AVERAGE WEIGHT	AVERAGE HEIGHT	AVERAGE WEIGHT
AGE 8	45 in. (114.3 cm)	57.2 lbs (25.9 kg)	45 in. (114.3 cm)	57.2 lbs (25.9 kg)
AGES 18–20	68–70 in. (172.7–177.8 cm)	150–160 lbs (68.0–72.6 kg)	64 in. (162.6 cm)	125–130 lbs (56.7–58.9 kg)

Guess what?
People get many of their physical characteristics from their parents. During puberty, these similarities between parents and children usually become more obvious.

Guess what?
Many humans live to be 80 years old. The highest known age ever reached by a human was that of Jeanne Calment of France. She lived to celebrate her 122nd birthday!

Unique You!

More than 7 billion humans live on Earth. Each of these humans is unique, or different from every other person. Some have dark skin; others are pale. Some are tall; others are short. Some have brown eyes; others have blue eyes.

DO YOU LOOK LIKE YOUR MOM? SMILE LIKE YOUR DAD?

You owe much of your looks and health to your biological parents. The passing of traits from parents to their children is called **heredity.** The basic unit of heredity is the **gene.** You inherit a set of genes from your father and a set from your mother. As a result, you have two copies of each gene.

The two copies of a gene may be different. Different forms of a gene are called **alleles** (a-*leelz*). Often, alleles are dominant or recessive. A dominant allele is stronger than a recessive one. If you have one of each, the dominant allele will express the trait. The recessive gene will be "hidden." For example, there is a gene that controls whether or not a person has freckles. If a person inherited two alleles for having freckles (one from each parent), the person will have freckles. If both alleles are for no freckles, the person will not have freckles. But what happens if one allele is for freckles and one is for no freckles? In this case, the freckles allele is dominant; the no-freckles allele is recessive. So the person will have freckles.

guess what?
On the tips of your fingers are patterns of ridges called fingerprints. The pattern is different on each finger. And the patterns of one person are different from those of every other person. Even identical twins have different fingerprints.

❧ The science of heredity tells us a lot about why one child may have freckles while another does not.

❱❱ Sometimes, more than one pair of genes is involved in whether or not a child inherits a characteristic from his or her parents. This seems to be true for curly hair and for whether a person is right- or left-handed.

guess what?
One study found that about 60% to 80% of the difference in height between individuals is determined by genetics. About 20% to 40% results from environmental effects, mainly nutrition.

GIRL OR BOY?

Genes are carried on structures called **chromosomes.** Chromosomes come in pairs: You get one from each parent. Each human cell has 46 chromosomes, or 23 pairs. Of these, 22 pairs consist of identical chromosomes. The 23rd pair are the sex chromosomes. These chromosomes are called X and Y. A female has two X chromosomes. A male has one X and one Y chromoome.

guess what?

How many genes does a person have? Scientists do not yet have an exact answer. But it appears that a human being has about 23,000 pairs of genes. This is more than a chicken—but less than a grape plant!

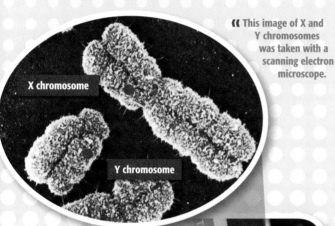

❰❰ This image of X and Y chromosomes was taken with a scanning electron microscope.

X chromosome

Y chromosome

❱❱ A scanning electron microscope uses electrons instead of light to make a hugely magnified image of something.

PUNNETT SQUARE

A chart called a **PUNNETT SQUARE** can be used to see what happens when you combine alleles from two parents. The chart also can help determine the odds that an offspring will be a girl or boy. One parent's chromosomes run along the top of the chart. The other parent's chromosomes run along the left-hand side. The four inner squares represent the possible offspring combinations. As you see, the odds of a child being a girl (XX) or boy (XY) are the same: fifty–fifty.

	MOTHER		
F		X	X
A T H E R	X	XX	XX
	Y	XY	XY

GENES AND THE ENVIRONMENT

Your genes may determine how your environment affects your health. For example, some people inherit an inability to digest certain foods. To avoid getting sick, they must modify their diets. Conversely, the environment may affect how the genes work. The food you eat and the chemicals in the air you breathe can support the genes in their work—or can interfere with their work.

About 1.5 million people in the United States are allergic to peanuts. This common food allergy may be hereditary.

Ancient Humans

The kinds of humans who lived long ago no longer exist. They died out, or became extinct. We know these people existed because they left clues called **fossils**. Fossils of ancient human bones, teeth, and footprints have been found. Remains of ancient tools, clothing, and other items also have been uncovered.

Early humans looked very different from modern humans. They were short, with small brains and apelike faces. But they stood upright, had humanlike teeth, and made simple tools. Very slowly, over many thousands of years, humans changed. They began to look more like modern humans. This gradual change in organisms is called **evolution**. Humans, like all living things, are still evolving. Humans who live 100,000 years from now will probably look quite different from the humans of today.

Guess What?
Humans are not descended from chimpanzees. But the two species share a common ancestor—one that lived an estimated 5 million to 8 million years ago. Genetic studies show that chimps share 96% of our genetic material.

Guess What?
No matter what you see in the movies, remember: Humans and dinosaurs did not live at the same time. Dinosaurs died out about 65 million years ago, long before even the earliest human ancestors appeared on Earth.

DO YOU HAVE NEANDERTHAL GENES?

Neanderthals were a form, or species, of humans that lived in Europe and the Middle East between 30,000 and 200,000 years ago. Recent genetic studies show that Neanderthals and humans mated with one another. As a result, all modern humans except Africans have about 1% to 4% of Neanderthal in them.

Mural depicting Neanderthals

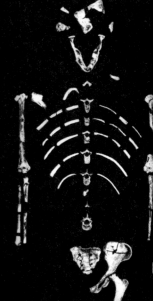

The remains of a 3.2-million-year-old being, known as Lucy

40,000-year-old cave painting in India

Major Milestones

Humans and their ancestors have changed significantly in the last 6 million years. Scientists can tell a lot about how an animal or human gets around by looking at the formation of the hip bones and the spine. They believe that by about 4 million years ago, human ancestors were walking upright. Slowly, over the course of the next 2 million years, the bodies of early humans became better suited to walking upright and for long distances. The shape of the spine bones found in the fossil record showed a kind of curving that would have acted as a shock absorber to cushion the impact on the body of walking and running. Seeing the longer leg bones and changes to the hip socket also helped scientists to draw these conclusions.

DISTANT RELATIVES

People living today are *Homo sapiens*. This species first appeared in Africa about 200,000 years ago. Three other kinds of human ancestors lived at the same time as *Homo sapiens*, but they eventually died out. Over time, *Homo sapiens* developed better hunting and fishing techniques and were able to capture and cook more varieties of prey. They began to create pottery and decorations and to make clothing out of animal hides. They traveled over large areas, spreading into Australia and Europe. By about 40,000 years ago, humans were creating cave paintings. Musical instruments came about 5,000 years later. By 17,000 years ago, *Homo sapiens* were the only kind of human left. Modern humans had migrated to the Americas by about 15,000 years ago, and shortly thereafter, began to grow crops and herd animals.

➤➤ Scientists hold what they think are 2.3-million-year-old tools.

Fire and Pictures

The ability to make fires and use them for warmth and cooking was incredibly important to human evolution. Researchers say that human ancestors were using fire by about 800,000 years ago. By about 400,000 years later, they were building and living in shelters. Archaeologists have uncovered artifacts that indicate that early humans drew symbols using sticks and pigment about 250,000 years ago.

TOOL TIME

The first evidence of human ancestors using simple tools is about 2.6 million years old. The introduction of handheld axes would have been a significant change for early humans. These axes could be used for cutting meat or carving wood. Archaeologists have unearthed handheld axes that are about 1.6 million years old. It was not until more than 1 million years later, scientists say, that people began using spears to hunt large animals.

We Are What We Eat

Food provides the body with the nutrients it needs to grow, repair itself, and keep healthy. These nutrients include carbohydrates, proteins, fats, vitamins, and minerals.

Carbohydrates are the body's main source of fuel. Your body breaks down carbohydrates into glucose (blood sugar), which travels through your bloodstream and supplies your cells with energy. Simple carbohydrates, which are found in fruits, soda, candy, and table sugar, are digested quickly. Complex carbohydrates (fiber and starches), which are found in rice, bread, whole grains, pasta, and vegetables, take longer for the body to digest. **Proteins** are mostly found in meat and dairy products, but can also be found in beans, nuts, seeds, and other foods. For more on proteins, see page 33.

Fats and oils (which are liquid fats) are found in butter, bacon, nuts, salmon, many cheeses, and sausages. Fats are a source of energy but are high in calories and increase the level of cholesterol in the body. Fats also provide essential fatty acids, which are chemicals your body needs for certain processes, such as proper growth of the nervous system. Good sources of essential fatty acids are fish, leafy vegetables, walnuts, and sunflower seeds.

KEEP IT DOWN

Cholesterol is a fatlike substance found in your cells. It is an essential part of the membrane that surrounds a cell. It's also needed for the production of certain hormones and other compounds. But a high level of cholesterol in the blood is not good. It increases people's risk of heart disease. There are two kinds of cholesterol:

HDL High-density lipoprotein, which is "good" cholesterol

LDL Low-density lipoprotein, which is "bad" cholesterol

For good health, limit the amount of fat and cholesterol in your diet.

TOP 5 CEREALS WITH THE MOST SUGAR

Eating breakfast is very important. But be careful. Many cereals may seem "magically delicious" because they contain an unhealthy amount of sugar. Here are the cereals with the most sugar.

1. **Kellogg's Honey Smacks:** 56% sugar by weight
2. **Post Golden Crisp:** 52%
3. **Kellogg's Froot Loops Marshmallow:** 48%
4. **Quaker Oats Cap'n Crunch's Oops! All Berries:** 47%
5. **Quaker Oats Original Cap'n Crunch:** 44%

SOURCE: Environmental Working Group

Guess what? One cup of Honey Nut Cheerios has more sugar than three Chips Ahoy cookies.

Vitamins and minerals are micronutrients—nutrients needed in very tiny amounts. They play many roles in maintaining good health. For example, vitamin A (found in carrots, pumpkins, and spinach) promotes good vision, and vitamin B_{12} (found in meat, fish, and dairy products) is important for the formation of red blood cells. Potassium (found in potatoes, bananas, and papayas) helps your nerves and muscles function properly.

Vitamin Tips

Eat **SUPERFOODS**, such as beans, blueberries, broccoli, oats, oranges, salmon, soy, and spinach. They have few calories and lots of the helpful nutrients.

Try **FORTIFIED FOODS**, which are foods with extra vitamins and minerals added in. Vitamin B_3 is commonly added to breads, vitamin D to dairy products, iodine to salt, and calcium to fruit juices.

too sweet

Sugar is a major culprit in weight gain, diabetes, and tooth decay. Limit the amount of sugar in your diet, and beware of "hidden sugars." These are sweeteners used in processed foods and drinks. Sucrose, dextrose, polydextrose, fructose, corn syrup, mannitol, galactose, sorbitol, and xylitol are examples of sugars you might see when you look at a food label.

HEALTHY MEAL CHOICES

Apples, lettuce, tomatoes, eggs, and steaks are examples of "fresh" or "whole" foods, which often have more health benefits than processed foods. They are grown in orchards or greenhouses, or raised on farms. Breakfast cereals, hot dogs, doughnuts, and canned soups are examples of processed foods. They are produced using manufacturing methods that turn raw ingredients into packaged goods. Artificial ingredients such as flavors, sweeteners, and preservatives are often found in processed foods.

Always read the nutrition labels on packaged food. And remember that the labels show the amount of carbohydrates, fat, and nutrients in a single serving. If there are three servings in a bag of chips and you eat the whole thing, you must multiply all of the values by 3.

Choose **MyPlate**.gov

To help people make healthy eating choices, the U.S. government developed MyPlate, which uses an image of a plate to show how much of each food group you need each day. Notice that half the plate consists of fruits and vegetables!

Exercise Burns Calories

To stay alive, the cells of your body constantly burn energy. They burn energy, in the form of food calories, when you're walking, eating, studying, dancing, watching TV, and even when you're sleeping.

The process by which your body burns calories in order to maintain itself is **metabolism.** The speed at which calories are burned is called the **metabolism rate.** It constantly changes. You burn fewer calories when you are sleeping than when you are studying. And you'll burn a lot more when you are playing basketball or running a race. Metabolism rates vary from person to person. Men usually have higher metabolism rates than women. Age is a factor as well. Genetics, the characteristics you inherit from your parents, are also a factor: Some people naturally burn food faster than other people.

Guess what? Muscle tissue burns more calories than fat tissue, even when a body is at rest. It burns a lot more calories during exercise.

>> People who are muscular have higher metabolism rates than people who have a lot of body fat.

CALORIES

You can tell how many calories a food has by looking at the nutrition label. Several factors determine how many calories a person should consume. People who are very active burn a lot more calories than folks who spend the day in front of a TV or computer. Young, growing people need more calories than old people. In general, girls ages 9 through 13 need between 1,600 and 2,200 calories a day, while boys of the same age need between 1,800 and 2,600.

HOW MUCH ENERGY DO YOU BURN?

ACTIVITY	CALORIES BURNED*		ACTIVITY	CALORIES BURNED*
AEROBICS, GENERAL	103		JUMPING ROPE	159
BAGGING LEAVES AND GRASS	63		KARATE	159
			KICKBALL	111
BALLET	76		MAKING THE BED	32
BASEBALL	79		PLAYING CATCH	40
BASKETBALL	127		RUNNING	127
BICYCLING	127		SHOOTING BASKETS	71
BOWLING	48		SKATEBOARDING	79
CANOEING	56		SLEDDING	111
CHORES	48		SOCCER	111
FRISBEE	48		SOFTBALL	79
GARDENING	63		SWIMMING	95
GYMNASTICS	63		TABLE TENNIS	27
HACKY SACK	63		TAKING OUT THE TRASH	40
HIKING	95		TENNIS	111
HOMEWORK	29		TOUCH FOOTBALL	127
HORSEBACK RIDING	63		WALKING	100
ICE-SKATING	111		YARD WORK	79
JOGGING	111			

*per half hour by person weighing about 70 pounds (32 kg)

Healthy Habits

Kicking a bad habit can be tough. Sometimes, it is easiest to start by making small changes. If you want to increase your daily exercise, begin by adding a 15-minute walk to your afternoon schedule. Gradually increase this to 30 minutes every afternoon. Here are a few ideas for improved health.

Turn off the TV! The more TV you watch, the less physically active you are. And the less exercise you get, the more likely you are to develop diseases such as diabetes or heart problems. A recent study found that adults who watched an average of six hours of TV a day lived an average 4.8 years less than people who didn't watch any television.

Get those ZZZs Are you grouchy or tired during the day? If so, you might not be getting enough sleep. Here are some tips on how to improve your sleep habits:

- Go to bed at the same time every night.
- Get up at the same time every morning— even on weekends.
- Avoid big meals at night.
- Pull the plug on electronics in the bedroom.
- Sleep in a cool, dark room.
- Eliminate noise, even if it means wearing earplugs while you sleep.

Eat breakfast People who eat breakfast tend to take in more vitamins and minerals. They eat less fat and cholesterol. They aren't as likely to overeat later in the day.

WHAT DO KIDS KNOW?

TIME For Kids and KidsHealth.org polled more than 10,000 American children and found that kids are pretty smart when it comes to health-related issues. They know a lot about staying healthy and want to learn even more. Does this knowledge lead to healthy habits? In many cases, it does. Most kids (87%) say they would rather go outside and play than stay inside and watch a movie. Many (85%) are willing to try new fruits and vegetables. About 85% read the nutrition facts on their food packages at least some of the time.

Guess what?

Kids and teenagers need the most sleep: 10 to 11 hours per night. The average adult ages 25 to 55 should aim for 8 hours. People over 65 need the least amount of shut-eye: about 6 hours.

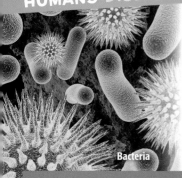
Bacteria

From Itchy Eyes to Deadly Infections

Is tree pollen making you sneeze? Are you stuck in bed with the flu? Taking antibiotics to treat an infection? If so, you're dealing with a **disease.** Diseases interfere with the proper functioning of your body. Some diseases are minor and easy to take care of. Others are extremely serious, and difficult to treat.

SIX COMMON CATEGORIES

Infectious diseases, like colds, flu, pneumonia, chicken pox, and malaria, are caused by bacteria, viruses, fungi, and other organisms. They can be transmitted from person to person.

Genetic diseases, like Down syndrome and cystic fibrosis, are transferred from parents to their child by genes.

Deficiency diseases are caused by the lack of vitamins or other essential nutrients. Examples include scurvy, rickets, and anemia.

Environmental diseases, like allergies and lead poisoning, are caused by chemical and physical agents such as smoke, dust, pollen, and radiation.

Degenerative diseases cause the gradual breakdown, or deterioration, of tissues or organs, due either to normal aging or to lifestyle choices. Examples include arthritis, Alzheimer's disease, and some cases of cancer, diabetes, and heart disease.

Mental disorders are caused by a variety of factors. Examples of these conditions are autism, attention deficit/hyperactivity disorder (ADHD), and eating disorders such as anorexia.

ANCIENT AILMENTS

Some diseases have been around for thousands of years. Ancient Egyptians described diabetes some 3,500 years ago. Cholera and diphtheria were also known in ancient times. Other diseases are of much more recent origin. AIDS was unknown until 1981, and Lyme disease was first recognized in 1975.

BACTERIA'S BAD RAP

Bacteria are everywhere, including on your skin and within your body. Indeed, your body contains about 10 times more bacteria than it does cells! But most bacteria are harmless to humans. Some even are helpful. Certain bacteria in your digestive tract help you digest food, while others prevent harmful bacteria from growing. Intestinal bacteria also make some vitamins needed by your body.

Guess what?

Scurvy is caused by a lack of vitamin C, found in fresh fruit like oranges. It was common in the 16th through 18th centuries among sailors, pirates, and passengers at sea. On ships, people often ate only salted meat and grains for long periods after all of the fresh fruits and veggies were consumed.

Vaccines to the Rescue

In 1970, more than 56,500 cases of rubella (German measles) were reported in the United States. The number dropped to 176 cases by 2000, and only 3 in 2009. The reason: vaccination. A vaccine is a medicine that protects the body against future attacks by a disease organism. Today, vaccines protect against polio, measles, mumps, rubella, chicken pox, tetanus, pneumonia, and other illnesses. Here's how they work.

≊ Doctors recommend a schedule of vaccinations for young people, from birth through age 12.

A doctor injects a person with a vaccine made of weak or dead forms of a disease.

⬇

The person's immune system targets the foreign viruses or bacteria, which are known as antigens.

⬇

The immune system creates types of proteins called antibodies that can travel through the bloodstream and destroy the antigens.

⬇

These antibodies stay in a person's system, which makes a person more capable of fighting a particular disease if he or she is ever exposed to it again. This is why most people who have had chicken pox once never get it again.

≊ Chicken pox

SUCCESS STORY

Many of the common childhood diseases of your parents' and grandparents' youth are now relatively rare.

One hundred years ago, diphtheria was one of the most feared childhood diseases in the United States. It killed more than 10,000 people every year. In the 1930s, doctors began to vaccinate children against diphtheria. Today, diphtheria is rare. Between 2000 and 2007, there were only three cases in the United States.

FROM **TIME** *FOR KIDS*

Hope in the Fight Against Malaria

By Vickie An

An experimental vaccine has been shown to protect children in Africa against malaria. In 2011, early results showed that the vaccine cuts the risk of severe infection by about half. "That's remarkable when you consider that there has never been a successful vaccine against malaria," said researcher Tsiri Agbenyega.

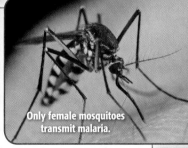

Only female mosquitoes transmit malaria.

Malaria is a disease that is spread by infected mosquitoes. Symptoms of malaria can include chills, fever, and vomiting. The disease can spread easily and quickly. While the global infection rate of malaria is continuing to drop, there are still more than 220 million new cases of malaria each year. Nearly one million people die each year of malaria. Most of these people are children in Africa.

Germs On the Move

Some kinds of germs can survive in the environment for years. Anthrax bacteria are an example. Others, such as the hepatitis B virus, may survive up to a week. Still others, such as the AIDS virus, generally die within minutes or even seconds. And some germs cannot survive outside the human body.

FIGHTING THE FLU

Influenza—"flu," for short—is caused by certain viruses. Like humans, viruses evolve, though they can do so very rapidly. This is why new flu vaccines need to be created each year. Scientists try to predict what changes are likely to occur in this year's most common flu viruses. They then create a vaccine designed to protect against the predicted viruses.

FIRST SIGNS

Some diseases develop slowly over many years. Heart disease is among these. It kills more people in the United States than any other cause. It's usually seen in middle-aged and older people. But recent studies show that the first signs of heart disease actually appear much earlier. Childhood risk factors for heart disease include:

- **High cholesterol levels**
- **Obesity**
- **Family history of heart disease**
- **Poor exercise habit**
- **High blood pressure**
- **Diabetes**
- **Exposure to cigarette smoke**

Guess what? More than 300 kinds of bacteria live in your mouth. As many as 1,000 kinds live in your intestines.

FOOD POISONING

Salmonella bacteria, which cause what is often called "food poisoning," can survive for more than a year in soil. They can contaminate vegetables and other foods. If you don't wash or cook contaminated food properly, the bacteria can enter your digestive system.

Meat, including hamburger, can be contaminated with salmonella. To prevent illness, meat should be well-cooked.

TRAVELING GERMS

METHOD OF TRANSMISSION	DESCRIPTION	EXAMPLES
DROPLETS	A person carrying germs sneezes on you.	Cold, flu
THROUGH THE AIR	You inhale air that has been exhaled by a sick person.	Cold, tuberculosis
THROUGH WATER	You drink water polluted with germs.	Cholera, hepatitis A
VIA VECTORS	A vector, or carrier, picks up the germs and carries them to you.	Malaria (*Anopheles* mosquitoes are the vectors), Lyme disease (*Ixodes* ticks are the vectors)

Prescribing Medicine

Doctors and others who practice medicine use various methods to preserve or restore health. These include such things as drugs, surgery, blood transfusions, manipulating body parts, and counseling.

Prescription drugs are given to people only on written instructions from a doctor. **Over-the-counter drugs,** like aspirin, can be bought without a prescription.

SIDE EFFECTS

Medicines have side effects. Many side effects are minor; that is, they are much less important than the benefits of the medicines. For example, many people take antihistamines to relieve the itchy eyes, runny nose, and sneezing caused by seasonal allergies, but the medicine may also make them sleepy. Some side effects can be life-threatening. Call a doctor or 911 right away if you ever get hives, have trouble breathing, or develop swelling of your face, lips, tongue, or throat after taking a medicine.

⌇ The antibiotics you might take when you have strep throat or an ear infection are examples of prescription drugs.

⌇ When you cut yourself, you bleed. Eventually the blood "dries up." That's because of blood cells called platelets. They work with other substances in the blood to make a clot, or a solid lump, that prevents any more blood from flowing out. In this way, clotting is helpful. But clots can also form inside blood vessels, which can be dangerous. If a clot gets stuck and interrupts normal blood flow, it could cause a heart attack or stroke. If a person is known to be at risk of blood clots, a doctor may prescribe an anticoagulant.

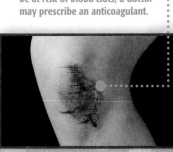

COMMON TYPES OF DRUGS

DRUG	WHAT IT DOES
ANTACID	Neutralizes acids in the stomach and intestines
ANTIBIOTIC	Destroys or inhibits bacteria
ANTICOAGULANT	Prevents blood from clotting
ANTIDEPRESSANT	Fights depression
ANTIHISTAMINE	Reduces allergic reactions
ANTI-INFLAMMATORY	Reduces inflammation
ANTIPSYCHOTIC	Reduces symptoms of serious mental illness
CHOLESTEROL REDUCER	Lowers levels of cholesterol in the blood
DECONGESTANT	Reduces congestion in respiratory passages
NSAID	Reduces inflammation and fever
STEROID	Reduces inflammation

» Opticians use a machine called a Phoroptor to figure out what eyeglass prescription a person needs.

MEDICAL TESTS

Doctors use various tests to help identify the causes of aches, pains, and illnesses. Here are a few.

AUDIOMETRY	Assesses the ability to hear
BIOPSY	Removes tissue samples—such as skin tissue—so they can be examined under a microscope
BLOOD TEST	Checks the number of blood cells; or measures levels of vitamins, minerals, sugar, cholesterol, and other substances
ECG (ELECTROCARDIOGRAPH)	Measures electrical activity of the heart
ENDOSCOPY	Lets doctors observe the inside of hollow organs and cavities
EYE EXAM	Assesses vision and eye health
GENETIC TESTING	Analyzes cells to look for abnormal genetic material
IMAGING (X-RAY, MRI, PET, ETC.)	Provides pictures of the inside of the body
SKIN ALLERGY TEST	Tests for allergies
URINALYSIS	Analyzes urine to check for sugar, blood cells, and other substances

The endoscopy, often used to examine the intestines, is the most common hospital procedure in the U.S. The procedure uses an instrument called an endoscope to light up and view a hollow organ or cavity. There are many types of endoscopies. For example, a rhinoscope is used to examine the nose, and an arthroscope is used to see the interior of a joint.

CHRONIC CONDITIONS

A chronic condition is one that persists for a long time—at least several months, and sometimes for a person's entire life. The most commonly reported chronic conditions among U.S. youngsters are asthma, learning disabilities, and ADHD.

guess what?
In the U.S., respiratory problems are the most common cause of hospitalization among 5- to 9-year-olds. Mental disorders are the most common cause of hospitalization among 10- to 14-year-olds.

MAY CONTAIN NUTS

Millions of people suffer from peanut allergies. Many of these people are also allergic to tree nuts such as walnuts and almonds. But today's methods of diagnosing the problem are not good enough to detect many cases. Scientists are working on developing more accurate methods.

Nutrition Facts

« More than 34 million Americans suffer from asthma, which can make breathing difficult.

Food labels include information about common food allergens.

I Heal the Brain

Dr. Joseph Hahn was a brain surgeon for 33 years. Now he is in charge of all the doctors at his hospital. Hahn told TFK's Kelli Plasket about his career.

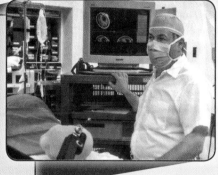

I watched my first surgery when I was just 18 years old. I was working as a hospital orderly. A doctor invited me to the operating room to watch a brain surgery. It was the neatest thing I have ever seen. I knew then I wanted to be a neurosurgeon, or a doctor who operates on the brain, spine, and nerves. After years of medical school and training, I got my first job as a neurosurgeon at the Cleveland Clinic, in Ohio. I've been there for 35 years. I am now the chief of staff. I'm in charge of all the doctors who work in the hospital's system.

SKILLS OF SURGERY

In high school, I played team sports. I had to learn how to work as part of a team and not give up when tired. These skills are important for neurosurgeons, too. We are required to concentrate for long periods of time. Many operations take four to eight hours. I once operated on a patient with a brain tumor for 24 hours!

Making a mistake can put a patient's life in danger. But surgery is rewarding. Former patients come back and tell me how grateful they are that I operated on them. Now I get to pass on what I've learned to a new generation of doctors. It's been fun. It's still fun. And I still love coming to work.

WHERE ARE THE DOCTORS?

The U.S. has about 950,000 doctors. This averages out to 3.12 doctors for every 1,000 people. But the ratio varies from one part of the country to another. For example, New York has 4.43 doctors for every 1,000 people. Oklahoma has only 2.03.

TFK GAME — WHO DOES WHAT?

Many doctors specialize in a specific branch of medicine. Match each specialty below with the body parts or issues it deals with.

1. Allergology
2. Cardiology
3. Dermatology
4. Endocrinology
5. Gerontology
6. Neurology
7. Obstetrics
8. Oncology
9. Ophthalmology
10. Pediatrics
11. Podiatry
12. Psychiatry
13. Pulmonology

a. Feet
b. Nervous system
c. Respiratory system
d. Heart, blood vessels
e. Pregnancy and birth
f. Issues of childhood
g. Issues of older people
h. Allergies
i. Mental health
j. Eyes
k. Hormones (endocrine system)
l. Cancer
m. Skin

Answers on page 216.

Guess What? A 2010 survey by the U.S. government found that 8% of U.S. children age 17 or younger had no health insurance coverage.

❮❮ Snails produce a kind of mucus or slime that has been used as medicine.

Crazy Medical Procedures of the Past

Medicine has changed greatly through the ages. Along the way, however, there have been some wacky ideas and weird practices.

⋩ Trepanation

- **Trepanation** is the practice of making a hole in the skull. Long ago, this was thought to be a way to treat headaches, epileptic seizures, and mental disorders. (And at the time, there were no anesthetics to dull the pain!)

- **Syrup of snail slime** was thought to be a fine remedy for coughs and sore throats, especially for children.

- **Bloodletting** (drawing blood from the veins) was a common medical practice from ancient times until the late 1800s. It was thought to remove illness from the body. It was recommended for more than 100 problems: everything from acne and stomachaches to cancer, diabetes, pneumonia, and convulsions.

Mummy powder was made from ground-up mummies.

- **Mummy powder** was used long ago in the Middle East to treat various illnesses. The powdered remains of poor people cost less than those of wealthy people.

- **The tapeworm diet** involved eating tapeworm eggs. These would hatch into worms that would grow in the person's intestines and consume most of the calories that the person ate. Tapeworms cause serious health problems and eventually cause the belly to extend, not shrink.

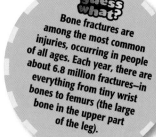

Guess what?

Bone fractures are among the most common injuries, occurring in people of all ages. Each year, there are about 6.8 million fractures—in everything from tiny wrist bones to femurs (the large bone in the upper part of the leg).

LIVING LONGER

Americans are living longer, healthier lives than ever before. A child born in 1900 could expect to live to an average age of about 49. One hundred years later, average life expectancy for a newborn was 77.5 years. There are gaps between the sexes and racial groups. Among whites and blacks, for example, white females have the highest life expectancy, followed by black females, white males, and black males.

MILESTONES IN MEDICAL HISTORY

About 2700 B.C. Acupuncture is practiced in China.

<< Acupuncture is a type of medicine in which needles are inserted in the body to reduce pain.

About 1550 B.C. Egyptian papyruses describe surgical practices and 700 different medications.

Around 430 B.C. In Greece, Thucydides reports that people who recover from the plague do not develop the disease again. This was the first observation of immunity.

Around A.D. 275 The Greek Erasistratus stresses the importance of diet and exercise in fighting disease.

Around 900 The Persian Al-Razi (or Rhazes) writes the first scientific paper on infectious diseases, describing smallpox and measles.

>> Ancient Egyptian artwork shows an injured person using a crutch.

Around 1250 Eyeglasses are invented.

1543 Andreas Vesalius, a Belgian, publishes the first accurate drawings of internal organs of the human body.

1628 William Harvey, of England, describes blood circulation.

1753 James Lind, of Scotland, explains that eating citrus fruits can prevent scurvy.

1796 The English doctor Edward Jenner develops the technique he calls vaccination.

1816 René Laënnec, of France, describes his invention of the stethoscope, a device for listening to chest sounds.

1854 John Snow, of England, shows that cholera is transmitted via contaminated water.

This painting depicts Erasistratus diagnosing a patient.

1880 French scientist Louis Pasteur and German doctor Robert Koch prove that some bacteria cause disease.

1895 In Germany, Wilhelm Röntgen discovers X-rays.

Pasteur

1899 Viruses are discovered.

1899 Bayer laboratories begins selling aspirin, the first reliable painkiller.

1921 Canadians Frederick Banting and Charles Best use insulin to successfully treat a patient with diabetes.

1928 Alexander Fleming, of Scotland, discovers penicillin, the first antibiotic.

1943 The first kidney dialysis machine, which removes wastes from the blood, is built.

1954 The first successful kidney transplant between living patients is performed in Boston.

Fleming

1962 Laser eye surgery is performed for the first time.

1972 CAT scans are developed. Other imaging techniques, including MRIs and PET scans, soon follow.

1978 The first test-tube baby is born in England.

2000 A woman's gallbladder is removed during the first robotic surgery in the United States.

Not All Illnesses Are Physical

Good mental health is as important as good physical health. It allows you to think clearly, learn new skills, develop friendships, and have self-confidence and a positive outlook on life.

Mental conditions generally start in childhood or adolescence. But diagnosis often is delayed for years or even decades.

Guess what? At any given time, one in every five young people is said to have a mental health problem.

Guess what? Physical exercise stimulates brain chemicals, helping you to feel happier and more relaxed.

Guess what? There's an old saying: "A problem shared is a problem halved." If something is worrying you, don't keep it to yourself. Talk about it with someone you trust.

Common Disorders Among Kids

ADHD (attention deficit/hyperactivity disorder) is the most common mental disorder affecting children and teens. People with ADHD behave impulsively. They have difficulty paying attention. They have difficulty behaving appropriately in school or other surroundings. ADHD is more common in boys than girls.

AUTISM SPECTRUM DISORDERS are characterized by difficulty in relating emotionally with others. Often, people with autism spectrum disorders are slow to develop language skills and have difficulty communicating with others. Autistic disorders are more common in boys than girls.

LEARNING DISABILITIES interfere with kids' ability to do well in school. The kids aren't lazy or dumb; their brains just process information differently. Dyslexia is a common problem. Kids who are dyslexic have difficulty reading. They may not recognize letters or words, or may have trouble understanding ideas. Dyscalculia is similar to dyslexia but it involves math. People with this disability may have difficulty telling time or counting, such as counting by 2s. Understanding operation signs for things like addition and subtraction may also be difficult.

GETTING THE BLUES

Everyone feels sad, or blue, once in a while. This doesn't mean the person is depressed. Depression is a continuous thing that lasts for weeks or months.

DEPRESSION is characterized by feelings of sadness and hopelessness. It can interfere with schoolwork, restrict interest in hobbies and social activities, and disrupt sleeping and eating habits.

Guess what?

National Bullying Prevention Month, observed each year in October, encourages people to raise awareness about bullying and take action to stop it. Many schools have anti-bullying programs.

BULLYING IS A BIG PROBLEM

Bullying takes many forms. It may include teasing and name-calling. It can also be physical. Bullying can happen anywhere, from the playground to the Internet. Sadly, nearly half of all kids will experience some form of bullying in school. Bullying can have serious, long-lasting effects. People who are bullied are more likely to have health problems, feel sad or depressed, miss school, and have trouble sleeping. Most U.S. states have passed laws against bullying.

You can do your part by treating others kindly and speaking out against bullying. Kids will make the biggest difference of all. Here are some things you can do:

- **Tell the bully to stop.** Make it clear that you do not approve.
- **Support the victim.** Tell people being bullied that you'll help them. For example, go with them to report the bullying.
- **Talk to an adult you trust, such as a parent or teacher.** They may help and may have ideas about how to stop the bullying.

THAT'S TERRIFYING!

Anxiety disorders are characterized by excessive fear and anxiety. The fear is out of proportion to any actual danger. For example, a person may have a fear of speaking in public, and will go to great lengths to avoid such a situation. If a feared situation cannot be avoided, the person becomes tense and may experience a pounding heart, sweatiness, nausea, and other physical problems. Some anxiety disorders are called phobias. They are irrational fears of a certain situation or object.

PHOBIA	FEAR OF
ACROPHOBIA	Heights
AILUROPHOBIA	Cats
ARACHNOPHOBIA	Spiders
CLAUSTROPHOBIA	Confined spaces
HEMOPHOBIA	Blood
HYDROPHOBIA	Water
MELISSOPHOBIA	Bees
NYCTOPHOBIA	Darkness
PHOTOPHOBIA	Light
POGONOPHOBIA	Beards
PUPAPHOBIA	Puppets
TRYPANOPHOBIA	Injections

WACKY AND WEIRD BODY FACTS

WHAT MAKES PEOPLE SWEAT?

As people exercise, their muscles change the chemical energy they get from food into mechanical energy, which is the kind of energy needed to run, jump, lift, move, swim, dance, or do work of any kind. But not all of the chemical energy in the body is changed to mechanical energy. Some of it converts to heat energy. And the body needs a way to get rid of that heat. Here is what happens.

- The blood vessels in the skin dilate, or get bigger. This lets more blood flow into the skin. Heat from the blood is lost to the air around you.

- Then nerves carry messages to the hypothalamus, which is the part of the brain that acts like the body's thermostat, telling it that the body is too hot.

- The hypothalamus sends messages to the sweat glands telling them, "Make more sweat!" As the sweat evaporates from the skin, it removes heat and cools the body.

WHERE DO FINGERPRINTS COME FROM?

Our fingerprints are all made with the same stuff—skin! And they are formed *before* a person is born. Skin is made up of many layers. As a baby grows inside the mother's womb, the top layer of skin, or epidermis (see pages 36–37), on the fingers becomes folded. Layers of skin below the epidermis stick to the epidermis and hold it in the folded pattern. This is how fingerprint patterns are formed, and the patterns remain that way for life! The ridges and lines of a person's palm are unique as well. In fact, palm prints are more commonly used to identify a suspect of a crime than fingerprints are.

The Eyes Have It!

Like fingerprints, the colored part of your eye, called the iris, has a pattern unique to you. Your left iris is even distinct from your right iris! A computerized eye scan can identify a person based on the amount and color of pigment in the iris as well as the iris's pattern of pitted depressions and raised ridges. There are 226 measurable characteristics of your iris—much more than the 35 to 50 characteristics of your fingerprint.

WHAT IS EARWAX?

The scientific term for earwax is *cerumen* (suh-*roo*-mun). It is a sticky, yellowish substance secreted by glands in the ear. It helps keep the ear canal safe in several ways. Dirt and bacteria can be trapped in it, keeping them from reaching the sensitive parts of the inner ear. Earwax also keeps the ear canal from drying out and becoming itchy. There is a chemical in earwax that combats infections.

Guess what?
Whales have earwax too!

WHY DOES HAIR TURN GRAY?

Each hair on a person's body grows out of a hair follicle. There are special cells called pigment cells in these follicles. Pigment cells generate a chemical called **melanin.** The production of melanin controls the coloring of hair. As people grow older, pigment cells die, resulting in the production of less melanin and less coloring in the hair. That's why older people have more gray or white hair than young people—although some people as young as high school age have gray hair.

HOW FAST DO FINGERNAILS GROW?

Fingernails are made of **keratin,** a type of protein fiber. It is the same substance that hair is made of. Nails rest on top of tissue known as the nail matrix. This matrix creates cells that grow and multiply. When the cells die, they harden and become the nail plate, which we think of as fingernails (or toenails). Children's nails grow much faster than those of adults. But, on average, fingernails grow about 0.12 inches (3 mm) per month. To regrow an entire nail from scratch takes about six months. Fingernails grow a lot faster than toenails. Eating a healthy diet with plenty of protein helps nails grow faster and stronger. Nails on active hands tend to grow more quickly. So, if you want long nails, start playing the piano, take up knitting or crocheting, or try learning sign language.

Guess what?
Children's nails grow about 50% faster before they hit puberty.

Guess what?
Because of the hormones released, pregnant women's nails grow faster during the pregnancy than before or after.

In humans, melanin also determines skin color. People with darker skin have more melanin than those with lighter skin. Melanin also comes into play when people get a suntan. The UV rays from the sun trigger a release of melanin in the skin, resulting in a darkening of the skin.

ANIMALS

Can you tell tell a leopard from a cheetah? Do you know how stripes help to keep a zebra safe from predators? Have you ever wondered why some animals become extinct while others thrive? From the tiniest insects to the largest creatures on land and sea, the animals found on Earth have countless cool habits, behaviors, and homes. Learn about why animals need crafty defense mechanisms, how scientists classify creatures, and which critters do jobs for people.

Six Kingdoms of Life

Scientists once divided the world's living things into only two major groups: plants and animals. But then the microscope was invented. Other types of tiny organisms (called microorganisms) were soon found to be living alongside—and sometimes inside— plants and animals. Today, scientists usually classify living things into six major "kingdoms."

Animalia The animal kingdom is the largest. It has more than 2 million species, from tiny tardigrades ("water bears"), which are only $1/500$ inch long to majestic blue whales, which are up to 100 feet (30 m) long.

Plantae This is the second-largest kingdom. Its 250,000-plus species include ground-hugging mosses and towering giant redwood trees. Plants grow by converting sunlight into energy, a process called photosynthesis. (See page 135.)

Fungi Mushrooms, mold, and mildew are examples of fungi. Although some fungi look like plants, they can't create energy from sunlight. Instead, fungi feed on the decayed remains of plants and animals.

Bacteria These single-cell creatures have the simplest structures of all living things. They are prokaryotic, which means their cells don't have a nucleus. Bacteria are found everywhere—in the air, soil, water, food, and even in the human body. Some bacteria, like those that cause food poisoning, are harmful to humans. But others are helpful.

Archaea This kingdom is made up of single-cell microorganisms that often live in extreme environments, such as near 115°F (46°C) steam vents at the bottom of the ocean.

Protista These single-cell microorganisms live in water or other moist environments. Some protists (like red algae and slime molds) act like plants and get their energy from sunlight. Others, called protozoa, act more like animals and ingest their food.

THE ANIMAL KINGDOM

There are three important ways that animals differ from other living things.

- **Animals are made up of many cells with complex structures.** That makes them different from single-cell organisms, like bacteria.

- **Animals get their energy from eating and digesting food.** That makes them different from plants, which get their energy from the sun. (There are some carnivorous plants—like the Venus flytrap—that "eat" insects. But those plants consume insects for nutrients rather than for energy. See page 137.)

- **Animals can move about from place to place.** That also makes them different from plants. But not all animals are mobile. Certain sea animals—like corals and sea squirts—remain in the same place for most, if not all, of their lives. But they still catch, eat, and digest food.

Vertebrates vs. Invertebrates

Some animals have a bony internal skeleton, including a backbone. These animals are called **vertebrates.** They include:

- **Birds,** such as bluebirds, orioles, owls, and flamingos
- **Amphibians,** such as frogs, toads, and newts
- **Reptiles,** such as crocodiles, snakes, and turtles
- **Fish,** such as salmon, sharks, and tetras
- **Mammals,** such as elephants, squirrels, killer whales, and bats

Other animals—in fact, *most* animals (at least 97%)—don't have an internal skeleton. They are called **invertebrates.** These spineless creatures are usually very small—so tiny that many of them can be seen only with a microscope. But there are some large ones too. The biggest invertebrates are giant squids, which sometimes measure more than 50 feet (15 m) long.

WARM-BLOODED OR COLD-BLOODED?

WARM-BLOODED ANIMALS (birds, mammals) are able to keep their body temperature constant. They turn the food they eat into energy that creates heat. In hot weather, they sweat, pant, or do other things to help cool their outsides and insides.

The temperature of **COLD-BLOODED ANIMALS** (reptiles, fish, amphibians, invertebrates) is the same as that of their surroundings. Because of this, they are able to be very active in hot weather but are sluggish at low temperatures. When it is hot, chemicals in their bodies react quickly to help their muscles move, but these reactions slow down as the outside temperature drops.

guess what? Turtles and tortoises are among the few animals that have both an endoskeleton, or internal skeleton, and an exoskeleton, or hard outer covering.

How Animals Are Grouped

Biologists divide the animal kingdom into different categories. The animals in each category have similar characteristics. These classification systems change from time to time, and animals are sometimes moved from one category to another as scientists learn more about them.

Lobster

PHYLUM The animal kingdom has more than 30 phyla. The best known of these phyla is **Chordata,** a name that comes from the Latin word for "cord." It includes all vertebrates, which are animals with some kind of backbone. (See page 72.) But the largest animal phylum is **Arthropoda,** a name that means "jointed leg." (See page 75.) It includes insects, spiders, crustaceans (like crabs and lobsters), and many other creatures.

Pigs

CLASS Animals in each phylum are divided into classes. Which class they are in depends on such things as how they look, act, eat, and raise their young. For example, if an animal in the Chordata phylum has fur or hair at any point in its life and raises its young on milk, it is put in the class called **Mammalia** (mammals). If it has feathers, however, it is put in the class called **Aves** (birds).

ORDER Each class of animals is broken down into orders. One of the orders of mammals, for example, is **Carnivora.** It includes tigers, raccoons, walruses, polar bears, dogs, and many other animals. All members of this group have strong jaws and teeth that are shaped in a way that enables them to tear off and eat the flesh of other animals. Carnivores also have very good senses of hearing, sight, and smell. And most give birth to their young only once or twice a year.

Polar bear

Hyena

FAMILY Orders are divided into families. In the order Carnivora, for example, is a family called **Felidae,** which includes both wild cats (like lions, hyenas, and cheetahs) and the cats that we keep in our homes as pets. All members of the Felidae family have a tail, sharp claws, and two long canine teeth, called fangs.

GENUS The next animal grouping is genus. The Felidae family, for example, includes a genus called **Panthera.** In this genus are four types of big cats: lions, tigers, leopards, and jaguars. These cats have similar body shapes, social structures, and ways of communicating. They are the only cats that are able to roar.

Tiger

Lions

SPECIES Each genus is further broken down into species. These are animals that share enough genes that they can breed and have young with each other, although they usually don't. The genus Panthera, for example, includes such species as **Panthera tigris** (tiger) and **Panthera leo** (lion).

TAXONOMY OF THE BALD EAGLE

KINGDOM • Animalia • All animals share this kingdom.

PHYLUM • Chordata • These animals have backbones.

CLASS • Aves • Birds have feathers and wings and lay eggs.

ORDER • Falconiformes • These are meat-eating birds of prey (raptors) that hunt in the daytime. Includes hawks, vultures, and falcons.

FAMILY • Accipitridae • These Falconiformes have hooked bills and usually kill the prey they eat. Cooper's hawks, tawny eagles, and red-tailed hawks are examples.

GENUS • *Haliaeetus* • This genus includes all kinds of eagles: bald eagles, harpy eagles, and golden eagles, to name a few.

SPECIES • *Haliaeetus leucocephalus* • This species distinguishes the bald eagle from all other eagles.

TAXONOMY OF THE SEVEN-SPOTTED LADY BEETLE (LADYBUG)

KINGDOM • Animalia • All animals share this kingdom.

PHYLUM • Arthropoda • These animals do not have backbones.

CLASS • Insecta • This class includes all insects. Insects have exoskeletons and six legs. Their bodies are divided into three distinct sections: the head, thorax, and abdomen.

ORDER • Coleoptera • All beetles belong to this order.

FAMILY • Coccinellidae • The beetles in this family are lady beetles or ladybird beetles (commonly called ladybugs). Most are oval-shaped and brightly colored. Most have spots.

GENUS • *Coccinella* • These lady beetles are found in the Northern Hemisphere. Most of them are red or orange.

SPECIES • *Coccinella septempunctata* • This species is the seven-spotted lady beetle, one of the most common lady beetles in North America. It's easy to identify because it is red and has seven spots.

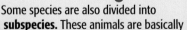

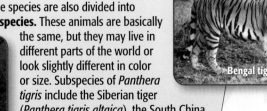

Some species are also divided into **subspecies.** These animals are basically the same, but they may live in different parts of the world or look slightly different in color or size. Subspecies of *Panthera tigris* include the Siberian tiger (*Panthera tigris altaica*), the South China tiger (*Panthera tigris amoyensis*), and the Bengal tiger (*Panthera tigris tigris*).

Bengal tiger

Siberian tiger

Types of Vertebrates

BIRDS are warm-blooded and have wings and feathers. All birds lay eggs, and most can fly (though ostriches, kiwis, and penguins cannot). Some other examples of birds are eagles, ducks, owls, pelicans, doves, peacocks, hummingbirds, cardinals, flamingos, and vultures.

- The flightless **ostrich** is the largest bird in the world.
- Scientists believe that female **peacocks** (which are called peahens) choose their mates based on the size and color of their amazing tail feathers, known as trains.
- The **arctic tern** migrates farther than any other bird, flying from its breeding grounds in the Arctic to the Antarctic and back again every year.

AMPHIBIANS are cold-blooded and begin life in the water, breathing through gills. When they are fully grown, they breathe through lungs and can walk on land. They lay eggs. Some examples of amphibians are frogs, toads, newts, and **salamanders**.

- Amphibians live on all continents except Antarctica.
- The Chinese giant salamander is the world's biggest amphibian, weighing in at well over 100 pounds (45 kg) and reaching up to 6 feet (2 m) in length.
- A group of frogs is called an army of frogs, and a group of **toads** is a knot of toads.

YUCK!

- Some Australian frogs create their own insect repellent that resembles the smell of rotten meat, roasted cashew nuts, and other scents.
- Frogs typically shed their skin about once a week—and usually eat it afterward.
- Giraffes eat the leaves of the thorny acacia tree. Extra-thick saliva protects their throats when they swallow thorns, but it also makes them drool all the time.
- Scavengers are animals that will eat any food they can find. They will eat animals that have been dead for a while, even if the flesh and meat are rotting. Jackals (wild African dogs), hyenas, rats, and vultures are scavengers.

REPTILES are cold-blooded and have lungs. Their skin is scaly. Most reptiles lay eggs. Reptiles include lizards, turtles, snakes, alligators, and crocodiles.

- An adult **rattlesnake** only needs to eat about once every two weeks.

- The **North American wood frog** actually freezes in the winter. Its heart stops beating and it stops breathing, but when it thaws out in the spring, it's still alive.

- The tongues of **alligators** and crocodiles are attached all along the bottom of their mouths. Because the tongue cannot be used to move food around, these animals swallow rocks to help them grind up the food they've eaten.

FISH are cold-blooded and live in water. They have scaly skin and breathe using gills. Most fish lay eggs. Carp, salmon, sturgeon, bettas, trout, tuna, and eels are some examples of fish.

- The **whale shark** is the largest fish. It can grow up to about 60 feet (18 m) long.

- **Flying fish** can't really fly. They have winglike fins, so when they jump out of the water, they can glide in the wind, like kites.

- Even though the **pufferfish** has a deadly toxin in parts of its body, a dish made from pufferfish (called fugu) is a delicacy in Japan. Only licensed chefs are allowed to prepare the dish.

MAMMALS are warm-blooded and, with the exception of the platypus and the echidna, give birth to live young. Mammal mothers breast-feed their young. Most mammals have hair or fur and live on land (except for porpoises, dolphins, and whales, which live in the water.)

Bats, **bears,** lions, giraffes, zebras, **cows,** elephants, guinea pigs, rhinoceroses, otters, and humans are all mammals.

- **Bats** are the only mammals that fly.

- The blue whale is the largest mammal. The African elephant is the largest land mammal.

- **Koalas,** gorillas, and chimpanzees have fingerprints that are similar to human fingerprints.

Types of Invertebrates

Sea anemone

Giant clam

Sponge

COELENTERATES

(sih-*len*-teh-rates) have stinging tentacles around their mouths. They use their mouths not only to eat with but also to eliminate waste. Examples of coelenterates are corals, hydras, jellyfish, and sea anemones.

MOLLUSKS

have soft bodies. To protect themselves, some have hard shells. Clams, oysters, octopuses, scallops, squids, slugs, and snails are all mollusks.

Slug

SPONGES live in

water and are immobile. They do not have circulatory, digestive, or nervous systems. Sponges get their food by filtering tiny organisms that swim by.

Octopus

Guess what?
Most of the sponges that people use today in the kitchen and the bathroom are created with human-made materials. But it is possible to buy natural sea sponges, derived from the cleaned, dried skeletons of these sea creatures.

Guess what?
Jellyfish have tiny stinging cells in their tentacles that can paralyze prey before the jellyfish eats it. These stings can be painful and, in some rare cases, deadly for humans. Even a dead jellyfish can sting you!

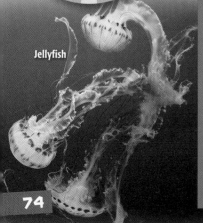
Jellyfish

TWO HALVES MAKE A BIVALVE

Some mollusks are bivalves, which means they have two shells, or valves, that are joined at one side, like a hinge. This hinge is formed by a ligament made of a tissue that decomposes after the animal dies. That's why we often find detached bivalve shells at the beach. Bivalves have a unique ability to create pearls. When a grain of sand or something else gets inside a bivalve, the mollusk will secrete layers of a mother-of-pearl coating onto the "intruder" to make it less irritating. Eventually, pearls are formed. Oysters, mussels, clams, and scallops are bivalves.

Live scallop

Scallop shells

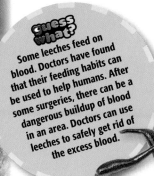
Many ocean-dwelling animals like to eat sea cucumbers. When threatened, a sea cucumber can shoot its sticky, toxic insides out of its body, harming or scaring off a predator. Afterward, it will take some time to regrow its insides.

Sea urchins are covered in pointy spikes, which help to protect their soft bodies.

WORMS

WORMS live in a variety of places, including underwater, in the ground, and even inside other living creatures. They are often cylindrical, or tube-shaped, though some are flat. Some are microscopic. Examples of worms include tapeworms, flukes, pinworms, leeches, and earthworms.

Earthworms

ECHINODERMS

ECHINODERMS (ih-*ky*-nuh-durms) live in the sea and have exoskeletons, which means that their skeletons or supporting structures are located on the outside of their bodies. Echinoderms include sea urchins, sea stars (starfish), brittle stars, sea cucumbers, and sand dollars.

Brittle star

ARTHROPODS

ARTHROPODS have bodies that are divided into different parts, or segments. They also have hard, protective exoskeletons. Arthropods include crustaceans (such as lobsters, crabs, shrimps, and barnacles), arachnids (spiders, scorpions, and ticks), centipedes, millipedes, and all insects (such as fireflies, moths, ants, mosquitoes, bees, dragonflies, and beetles).

Crab

Scorpion

MOLTING

Unlike the shells of mollusks, the exoskeletons of arthropods are complex and have moveable joints. Because these hard coverings do not grow once they've formed, arthropods periodically molt, or shed their exoskeletons. After an animal has lost its protective layer, it takes time for the new exoskeleton to firm up. The period after molting is a dangerous one, since the animal is lacking its normal defenses.

❯❯ A cicada emerges from its old exoskeleton. Often, the empty husk of an exoskeleton will remain clinging to a leaf or tree.

ANIMAL LOOK-ALIKES

ALLIGATOR

ALLIGATOR VS. CROCODILE
Alligators tend to have a wider, rounder snout than crocodiles have. Crocodiles have two teeth on their jaws that stick up over their upper lip when their mouths are closed.

CROCODILE

DAMSELFLY VS. DRAGONFLY
Damselflies have longer, thinner bodies than dragonflies. At rest, damselflies hold their wings closed. When not flying, the dragonfly holds its wings open.

DAMSELFLY

DRAGONFLY

LIGERS, OH MY!

Two liger cubs were born in a zoo in China in 2011. A liger is a cross between a male lion and a female tiger. Four days after the cubs were born, their tigress mother stopped feeding them. A dog at the zoo that had recently had puppies took over the nursing of the cubs.

Ligers—which grow into the biggest cats in the world—are rare, because lions and tigers don't crossbreed in the wild. Many scientists think zoos should not let animals of different species breed. In fact, the practice is banned in some countries.

A dog nursing the liger cubs

LEOPARD

CHEETAH

LEOPARD VS. CHEETAH

A leopard is more powerful than a cheetah, but the cheetah's body is more streamlined, so it can run faster. Cheetahs have large nostrils to help them take in lots of oxygen when they are running. Leopards have a white lining in the bottom of their eyes, which helps them see better when they hunt at night. Cheetahs have black lines from their eyes to their mouth. They hunt during the day and these dark lines absorb light, which can make bright sunlight have less of a blinding effect. Cheetahs have solid, round spots. Leopards have rosette-shaped spots that often appear in clusters.

DOLPHIN

PORPOISE

Guess What?
Porpoises are rarely seen in captivity. They are not as social or easily trained as dolphins.

DOLPHIN VS. PORPOISE

Dolphins have cone-shaped teeth, but porpoises have flat, spade-shaped teeth. Because of differences in the bones in their necks, dolphins can move their necks more than porpoises can. Porpoises have shorter beaks and are smaller than dolphins.

An officer releases a carrier pigeon in the Egyptian desert during World War II.

Llama

Animals At War and At Work

In addition to providing love and companionship, animals have been trained to do important jobs for humans. These furry and feathery friends have been taught to entertain audiences, transport people and goods, carry messages, and save lives. Carrier pigeons are known for their incredible ability to find their way home. During World War I and World War II, they carried messages back and forth between soldiers. They've also been used to get medication to hard-to-reach sick people. From 1860 to 1861, the Pony Express mail service employed 400 horses to carry saddlebags of letters 2,000 miles (3,219 km) across the United States.

Today, dromedary camels, elephants, and donkeys perform many tasks. They carry heavy loads, assist in farming, and are ridden by humans. Dogs have been used to track lost or missing people, to chase pests out of tunnels, to help hunters, and as guides for blind and hearing-impaired people. Sheepdogs can be trained to herd animals and move them to safe ground during storms. Llamas can also be fierce protectors of livestock. They will stomp on wolves and foxes that try to carry off members of the herd they are protecting. The U.S. military has trained dolphins to detect and mark the locations of underwater mines, which are explosive devices that can damage or destroy ships.

Guess What?

Bottlenose dolphins (which are actually small whales) give themselves individual whistle "names." The animals use these whistles to meet and greet other dolphins. It's a way of saying, "Hi. I'm so-and-so, and I'm friendly." Scientists believe that the dolphins choose their names when they are very young.

A member of the U.S. Navy trains a dolphin.

≋ A search-and-rescue dog climbs across the rubble of a collapsed home, looking for signs that anyone might be inside.

FROM **TIME** **FOR KIDS**

Dogs to the Rescue By Kelli Plasket

After a major disaster strikes, search-and-rescue teams race to the site. Their goal: to find and help survivors. Often, a key team member is a pooch. Search dogs are specially trained to sniff out survivors trapped in rubble.

In 1996, retired teacher Wilma Melville began the National Disaster Search Dog Foundation to improve disaster response. The foundation finds and trains dogs from shelters. Then each search dog is paired with a first responder, who becomes the dog's handler.

The foundation has trained 135 teams. Now, 73 teams are active, but more are needed. The foundation plans to open a national training center in Santa Paula, California, in 2013. "It will be like Disneyland for handlers and dogs," Melville told TFK.

A REWARDING JOB FOR DOGS

It takes a special pooch to become a search dog. The canines must be bold, focused, and driven. The dogs learn how to walk through rubble, climb ladders, and bark when they find a survivor. The dog's reward? A toy. "To the dog, this is total fun," Melville said. "They look forward to searching for victims, because that's when they get their best rewards."

≋ Ranger, a search-and-rescue dog, in Louisiana after a hurricane, reports back to his captain, announcing that a human scent has been found.

guess what?
To cool down, dogs mostly pant, but they can also sweat from their footpads.

79

Animals in Danger

VANISHED: EXTINCT ANIMALS

Earth has been home to living things for billions of years. During that time, millions of animal species have come and gone. In fact, some 99.9% of all the animal species that once lived on Earth no longer exist. They have become **extinct.**

Dinosaurs are the most famous of all extinct animals. They disappeared about 65 million years ago. Other species have become extinct much more recently—some within the past few years. In 2011, for example, the West African black rhino was declared extinct. Its disappearance from the grasslands of Africa is due to hunters, who killed the animal so they could sell its horns.

≈ The dodo bird lived on the island of Mauritius until sailors arrived. The sailors ate the dodoes, destroyed the forests the birds lived in, and brought new animals, like cats and rats, to the island. The newly introduced animals destroyed dodo nests.

Alabama beach mouse

Black bear

Hawaiian duck

ON THE BRINK: ENDANGERED AND THREATENED ANIMALS

Since 1973, the United States has had a law—the Endangered Species Act—that protects animals (and plants) that are at risk of becoming extinct. Animals needing protection are put into one of two categories. **Endangered** animals are those that may become extinct within a few years if nothing is done to help them. **Threatened** animals are those that are likely to become endangered soon.

When an animal species gets put on the endangered or threatened list, steps are taken to keep it from disappearing. People may be banned from hunting the animal, for example. Some animals in the U.S. that are on the list today are the black bear, grizzly bear, woodland caribou, black-footed ferret, Hawaiian duck, Canada lynx, Alabama beach mouse, northern sea otter, desert pupfish, and Gulf sturgeon.

Many other countries have laws designed to help save their endangered species. And several international organizations work hard to identify and rescue these animals, too. Still, many, many animal species are at risk. According to one estimate, one in four mammals, one in three amphibians, and one in eight birds in the world are in danger of extinction.

THREATS TO ANIMALS

Many things can cause an animal species to become endangered. These four factors are major threats.

LOSS OF HABITAT Millions of acres of natural habitat—the places where animals live—are lost each year due to the construction of buildings and roads, the harvesting of trees for timber, and the creation of farmlands. If an animal species is unable to find a new place to live, it will not survive.

POLLUTION Toxic chemicals and other substances can poison the water, air, or soil in an animal's habitat. The chemicals may kill the animal outright, or they may kill off other living things that the animal needs to survive.

OVERHUNTING Many animals are overhunted or overfished because of their meat, fur, feathers, shells, horns, or other body parts.

INTRODUCTION OF NEW SPECIES When an animal is introduced into a habitat where it didn't live before, it can upset the natural balance among the other animals that are already living there. For example, the introduced animal may not have any natural predators (other animals that hunt it for food) in the new habitat. It can then breed quickly and take over the habitat from other animals.

Rabbits arrived in Australia with the first fleet of settlers from England. Since then, they've contributed to the extinction of native plant species and several small ground-dwelling mammals. Today, wild rabbits eat so much of the vegetation in arid lands that the survival of animals like the bilby is threatened.

Guess What?
Bluefin tuna populations in the Atlantic Ocean have declined over 70% in the last 30 years.

Fisherman catching bluefin tuna off the coast of Spain

SAVING NEMO

Sixteen different types of fish and other sea creatures appear in the movie *Finding Nemo*. Many of them are threatened with extinction, according to a 2011 report from a group of marine scientists. The *Finding Nemo* animals most at risk, say the scientists, are sea turtles (Squirt and Crush), eagle rays (Mr. Ray), great white sharks (Bruce), hammerhead sharks (Anchor), and sea horses (Sheldon).

Overfishing is the main reason why these animals are endangered. But the destruction of the animals' underwater habitats—caused by pollution, climate change, and other factors—is also a threat. The scientists who did this study work for the International Union for Conservation of Nature, an organization that helps protect both land and sea animals from becoming extinct.

SUCCESS STORIES

Endangered animals are often saved from becoming extinct. Here are two recent success stories.

THE GRAY BAT

Millions of these insect-eating animals used to live in limestone caves throughout the southeastern United States. By the mid-1970s, however, only about 128,000 of them remained. People had disrupted and destroyed the bats' natural habitat by exploring or otherwise using the caves. In 1976, the U.S. government put the gray bat on its endangered species list. The caves in which the animals lived became protected. Today, the number of gray bats has increased to 1.5 million.

THE ARABIAN ORYX

This Middle Eastern antelope has a shoulder hump, straight horns, and wide hooves that allow it to travel easily across shifting desert sands. The last wild Arabian oryx was shot and killed in 1972. The animal was declared extinct in the wild. But a few oryxes were still living in private and public zoos. Scientists bred those animals. When they had enough oryxes, they gradually reintroduced the animal to its desert home. In 2011, scientists announced that the number of wild oryxes had hit the 1,000 mark. The animal is no longer considered endangered.

Gray bats fly out of a bat cave in Arkansas.

⌃ A biologist holds a gray bat at a survey site in 2010.

Guess what?

Endangered Japanese macaques, which live in the mountains of Japan, like to make snowballs! But they don't throw the snowballs at each other. They just roll them around and play with them. These primates are also famous for washing their food in salt water before eating it. The water cleans the food.

A group of Arabian oryxes gather together after being released into the desert in the United Arab Emirates in 2007.

FROM **TIME** *FOR KIDS*

Roaring Return

By Suzanne Zimbler

What's black and orange and growing for the first time in decades? India's tiger population! In March 2011, officials announced the results of the latest tiger count. The census tallied 1,706 tigers in forests across the Asian country—about 300 more than four years ago. "These numbers give us hope for the future of tigers in the world," said Jim Leape, international director of the World Wildlife Fund.

A tiger is released into the Sundarbans Wildlife Refuge in India. It had strayed too far into an area where people live.

TIGER TROUBLE

A century ago, about 100,000 tigers roamed India's forests. But by 2002, a count revealed that there were only 3,600 left. The number dropped to 1,411 in 2007. What caused India's tiger population to shrink so dramatically? More than anything else, experts say, development has taken a toll. People have moved into tiger territory and destroyed much of the animal's habitat.

Illegal hunting has also contributed to the decline. Poachers can demand high fees for tiger parts, which are a key ingredient in traditional Chinese medicine. The parts from one tiger can sell for tens of thousands of dollars.

A CALL TO ACTION

India's news is a step in the right direction. But while the number of tigers has increased there in the last four years, the animals' habitat has shrunk. Roads and construction projects have blocked off many tiger corridors—routes used by the big cats to go from one forest to another. "Securing these corridors should be taken up as a priority," said Rajesh Gopal, of the National Tiger Conservation Authority.

In November 2010, leaders from the 13 countries that are home to wild tigers met in St. Petersburg, Russia, to develop a plan to help the endangered cats. They set a goal to double the world's tiger population by the year 2022. Will we reach that goal? With India's tiger population on the rise and conservationists around the world focused on helping the big cats, it seems it just might happen.

Today, tigers live on just a small fraction of the land they occupied 100 years ago.

Time Line of Animal Evolution

Animals have lived on Earth for most of the planet's 4.5 billion years. But the animals that lived here millions of years ago are much different from those that are alive today. That's because animals (and plants) change, or **evolve,** over time. These changes help the animals to adapt better to their environments. That gives their species a better chance at survival. The changes are very slight. But over thousands or millions of years, they can make an animal look or behave much differently than it did originally.

Periods in Prehistory

Scientists have divided Earth's history into several different geological periods. By studying fossils (the remains of animals that died long ago) from each of these periods, they are able to tell how animals have evolved. They are also able to learn about animals that have become extinct.

PRECAMBRIAN

4.5 BILLION YEARS AGO–542 MILLION YEARS AGO

Life emerged on Earth about 3.8 billion years ago. The earliest living organisms were single-cell bacteria. They helped create oxygen, which enabled other animals to form.

The first multicelled animals, called **Ediacarans,** began to appear around 600 million years ago. The Earth had cooled down a bit by then and had oceans. Ediacarans lived on the ocean floor. They were strange creatures—not at all like modern animals. They had no head, mouth, or body parts for digesting food.

Scientists aren't sure whether Ediacarans evolved into other animals or became extinct. But other multicelled animals from the Precambrian period did evolve into modern-day animals. These include sponges, sea anemones, **jellyfish,** corals, and **flatworms.**

Modern-day jellyfish

Modern-day flatworm

CAMBRIAN

541 MILLION YEARS AGO–488 MILLION YEARS AGO

An explosion of new sea life occurred during the Cambrian period. Many of the major animal groups (phyla) that exist today got their start during this time. Scientists have found Cambrian fossils of the ancestors of today's insects and spiders. They've also found fossils of early chordates (animals with backbones). The oldest of these chordates seems to be *Pikaia gracilens*, a tiny wormlike creature that swam in the Cambrian seas.

At the end of the Cambrian period, the oceans suddenly lost much of their oxygen. Scientists don't know why this happened. But the change caused many animals, including *Anomalocaris* and *Opabinia*, to become extinct.

One of the most fearsome-looking animals of this period was the giant shrimplike *Anomalocaris*. Its eyes were perched on two long stalks, and its mouth had hooklike prongs that crushed its prey. Another bizarre Cambrian animal was the *Opabinia*. This 3-inch-long (7.6 cm) sea animal had five eyes. It also had a 1-inch-long (2.5 cm) tubular structure (a proboscis) with clawlike spines at the end. It probably used the proboscis to catch food.

Sea life in the middle Cambrian period

ORDOVICIAN

487 MILLION YEARS AGO–444 MILLION YEARS AGO

During this period, all animals still lived in the sea. Most were invertebrates. There were **nautiloids,** squidlike mollusks with beaks and long grasping tentacles. There were also hard-shelled creatures called **trilobites.** Like modern arthropods (insects, spiders, and crustaceans), trilobites had jointed legs and segmented bodies.

Trilobite fossil

guess what?
Some species of trilobites had eyes. Scientists believe they may have been the first animals to see.

Animals with backbones—mostly jawless fish—also evolved during this time. Among these were strange eel-like fish called conodonts. They had fins, teeth, and large eyes. Conodonts and many other Ordovician animals became extinct at the end of this period, probably because of changes to Earth's climate.

Nautiloid fossil

Nautiloid

487 MILLION YEARS AGO

443 MILLION YEARS AGO

Anomalocaris

SILURIAN

443 MILLION YEARS AGO–416 MILLION YEARS AGO

Eurypterid fossil

This is the period when animals (and plants) finally emerged on land. The first land animals were tiny creatures—mostly primitive centipedes and spiders.

Most animals, though, still lived in the sea. The Silurian period saw the first fish with jaws, including small, spiny sharks. **Giant sea scorpions** also roamed the oceans. They had huge eyes and powerful clawlike pincers, which they used to grab their prey. Some species were more than 6 feet (1.8 m) long, making them the largest arthropods to ever live.

DEVONIAN

415 MILLION YEARS AGO–359 MILLION YEARS AGO

The Devonian period is sometimes called the Age of Fishes. That's because many different types of fish evolved and flourished during this period. Some species began to live in freshwater lakes and streams, where they gradually developed simple lungs.

The Devonian period ended with the Earth's second mass extinction. About 70% of all animal species alive at the time disappeared. Scientists think this extinction may have been caused by sudden changes in the Earth's temperature.

Drawing of *Tiktaalik*

The *Tiktaalik* had a long crocodile-like head and strong fins, which it may have used like legs to "walk" in shallow waters or even on land. It also had nostrils on its snout, perhaps to help it breathe air. Some scientists believe that early animals like the *Tiktaalik* will provide us with clues about how and when animals left the water and began living on land.

Giant sea scorpion known as a eurypterid

Landscape during the Devonian period

443 MILLION YEARS AGO

415 MILLION YEARS AGO

359 MILLION YEARS AGO

CARBONIFEROUS

**358 MILLION YEARS AGO–
299 MILLION YEARS AGO**

The Earth warmed during the Carboniferous period. That change encouraged swampy forests to grow and spread. These forests became home to many new species of insects. Some insects developed wings and began to fly, although exactly how and why they evolved into flying creatures is not known.

The first reptiles—animals with scaly skin and that produced their young by laying eggs—appeared during this period. These animals evolved from amphibians. The earliest known reptile was a small lizardlike creature called *Hylonomus.*

The insects of this period were often huge. There were poisonous centipedes that were 6 feet (1.8 m) long and **dragonflies** with wingspans of up to 2 feet (0.6 m).

PERMIAN

**298 MILLION YEARS AGO–
251 MILLION YEARS AGO**

During the Permian period, the world was very hot and dry—conditions that are great for reptiles. Their thick, scaly skin helps them hold in moisture and lets them live in dry places.

The Permian period ended with another mass extinction, which killed off more than 90% of the Earth's animals, including the *Estemmenosuchus* and the ***Dimetrodon.***

Many of the reptiles that evolved during the Permian period were big, although not as big as some of the dinosaurs that would follow later. The *Estemmenosuchus*, a plant-eating reptile, was 13 feet (4 m) long and 6 feet (1.8 m) tall. It had a massive head with many hornlike knobs. Another strange animal of this period was the large and lizardlike *Dimetrodon*. It was a meat eater, with sharp teeth and claws. It also had a tall, sail-like flap of skin on its back, which it probably used like a solar panel to store sunlight and keep its body warm.

Dimetrodon

Landscape in the Carboniferous period

Hylonomus

Scientists unearth a nearly complete *Dimetrodon* fossil in Texas in 2010.

298 MILLION YEARS AGO

251 MILLION YEARS AGO

TRIASSIC

250 MILLION YEARS AGO–200 MILLION YEARS AGO

The Triassic period begins during a huge mass extinction, but reptiles continued to dominate the land. There were huge flying reptiles called **pterosaurs,** for example, and giant ocean reptiles called **ichthyosaurs,** with dolphinlike heads and long, toothed snouts.

Despite their size and appearance, these animals were not dinosaurs. True dinosaurs could walk on land with their feet directly beneath their bodies. But the first dinosaurs did appear during this period. One of the earliest was the *Coelophysis*, a small, light reptile that could probably run at high speeds.

Among the other animal firsts of the Triassic period were ocean corals, grasshoppers, and mammals. The earliest mammal may have been the *Eozostrodon*, a 4-foot-long (1.2 m) creature with a pointed snout, clawed feet, and a long, hairy tail.

Plaster cast of an ichthyosaur fossil

JURASSIC

199 MILLION YEARS AGO– 145 MILLION YEARS AGO

The oceans teemed with life during the Jurassic period. In addition to the ichthyosaurs, there were giant sea crocodiles called plesiosaurs, as well as modern-looking sharks and rays. Corals continued to thrive, as did sponges, snails, and mollusks.

Model of a T. rex

On land, flowering plants appeared, which led to the evolution of even more types of insects and spiders, including fleas that were 10 times larger than they are today. These ancient fleas had curved claws, which helped them hang on to an animal's fur or feathers while they sucked the animal's blood.

But dinosaurs ruled the land during the Jurassic period, which is why scientists call it the Age of Dinosaurs.

Guess what?
The T. rex and the *Spinosaurus* were both about 40 to 50 feet (12 to 15 m) long.

Spinosaurus

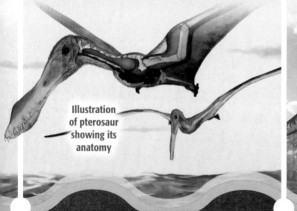

Illustration of pterosaur showing its anatomy

199 MILLION YEARS AGO

T. rex skull

Brachiosaur fossil

Some Jurassic dinos were enormous. Among the biggest were the small-headed, slow-moving, long-necked sauropods. One of these, the *Brachiosaurus*, was 85 feet (26 m) long and 52 feet (16 m) tall, and weighed up to 80 tons (73 metric tons). There were also huge meat-eating dinosaurs called theropods, such as the *Tyrannosaurus rex* (T. rex) and the *Spinosaurus.*

Brachiosaurs in a Jurassic landscape

Birds evolved from theropods. The earliest known bird, called *Archaeopteryx*, appeared during the Jurassic period. It had feathers and wings like modern birds. But, unlike modern birds, it also had a full set of teeth.

CRETACEOUS

144 MILLION YEARS AGO– 65 MILLION YEARS AGO

During the Cretaceous period, dinosaurs continued to dominate all other animals. Many new species evolved, including **triceratops.** Despite its three-horned face and massive body, the triceratops was not very menacing. It ate only plants.

Triceratops fossil

Flowering plants took off and spurred the evolution of many new types of insects, including the oldest known ants, butterflies, bees, and wasps. New types of sea creatures also evolved, including clams that stretched almost 1 foot (33 cm) wide and snakelike predators called **mosasaurs,** which sometimes grew as long as half a football field.

Model of a mosasaur

The Cretaceous period ended with another mass extinction, perhaps caused by an **asteroid** hitting Earth. All dinosaurs and many other creatures living at the time died off, never to return again.

Spinosaurus fossil

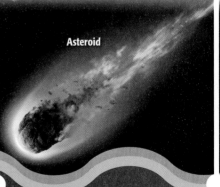

Asteroid

144 MILLION YEARS AGO

65 MILLION YEARS AGO

Paleogene
bird fossil

PALEOGENE

**64 MILLION YEARS AGO–
23 MILLION YEARS AGO**

With the dinosaurs gone, mammals began to evolve into bigger and more diverse species. Some of the mammals we're most familiar with today—such as cats, dogs, **horses,** pigs, bats, and primates—emerged during this period.

The ancestors of many modern **birds,** including ancient forms of pelicans, eagles, and vultures, also appeared in the skies for the first time. And sharks came to dominate the oceans.

Whales made their first appearance too. Scientists believe these ocean mammals evolved from land animals that took to the seas. Whales have recently been traced back to a strange Paleogene creature called a pakicetid. This now-extinct mammal, which looked like a wolf with hooves, spent part of its life on land and part in the water.

Fossilized horse and fish from the Paleogene period

 Megalodon jaws were up to 11 feet (3.4 m) wide and 9 feet (2.7 m) tall.

Megalodon teeth were much bigger than modern-day great white shark teeth.

64 MILLION YEARS AGO

22 MILLION YEARS AGO

NEOGENE

**22 MILLION YEARS AGO–
2.6 MILLION YEARS AGO**

Climate changes during the Neogene period caused many forests to become grasslands. Animals had to adapt to this change. Giraffes, bison, camels, and sheep, for example, developed specialized stomachs that helped them digest grass.

Predator animals, like cats, developed sleeker, faster bodies so they would have better chances of catching prey on the open grasslands. Sea animals were also evolving. New species included the dugong, an animal related to the modern manatee, and a huge shark called the **megalodon.** It grew to be almost 50 feet long (15 m), making it the largest shark that ever lived.

During the Neogene period, some primates evolved into hominids—apelike creatures that walked on two rather than four legs—that were the early ancestors of humans.

QUATERNARY

2.5 MILLION YEARS AGO–PRESENT

» Woolly mammoth fossil

The Quaternary period is called the Age of Humans because humans became Earth's most dominant form of life. Scientists believe that modern *Homo sapiens* evolved in Africa about 190,000 years ago and then migrated to other areas of the world.

Earth's climate has changed many times during the Quaternary period. There have been several ice ages— long stretches of time when Earth's temperatures dropped and glaciers advanced from both the North and the South Poles. During these cold periods, mammals got bigger and grew furry coats to keep warm. One such animal was the **woolly mammoth.** It looked like a furry version of a modern-day elephant, except it had smaller ears and much, much larger tusks. It also had 4 inches (10 cm) of fat under its coat to protect it from the cold. Scientists think warmer temperatures and human hunters killed off the woolly mammoth.

Artist's rendering of woolly mammoths

2.5 MILLION YEARS AGO

Humans live in the Quaternary period.

PRESENT

MIND-BLOWING FOSSILS

This drawing of the *Kairuku* is based on the fossil evidence.

During 2011, scientists made some fascinating fossil findings. Here are two of the "bigger" fossil events of the year.

A PECULIAR PENGUIN

Scientists used fossils to create the first model of a giant species of penguin that lived about 26 million years ago, during the Paleogene period. They named this prehistoric bird **Kairuku,** which means "diver who returns with food" in the Maori language. The animal's fossils come from New Zealand, the native home of the Maori people.

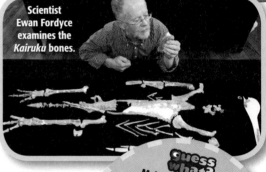

Scientist Ewan Fordyce examines the *Kairuku* bones.

Kairuku stood more than 4 feet (1.2 m) tall and weighed about 132 pounds (60 kg). That's about 1 foot (30 cm) taller and at least 40 pounds (18 kg) heavier than the largest modern-day penguin. The *Kairuku* penguin also had a longer bill and wings (flippers). Its bigger size probably helped it swim farther and deeper than modern penguins.

Guess What?

Male king penguins can store undigested food in their stomachs for up to three weeks. Scientists believe the penguins produce a chemical that kills off any bacteria in their digestive system. That keeps the food (mostly fish and squid) from going bad. Male penguins regurgitate, or spit up, food to feed chicks.

Nuralagus rex would have towered over a modern-day rabbit.

THE BIGGEST BUNNY

Paleontologists discovered the fossilized remains of a huge rabbit—the largest rabbit species ever known to exist on Earth—on the Spanish island of Minorca. The scientists named the animal **Nuralagus rex,** which means "Minorcan King of the Rabbits." It certainly had a royal size. Fossils suggest it weighed about 26 pounds (12 kg)—six times more than most modern rabbits.

But unlike today's rabbits, *Nuralagus rex* couldn't hop. Its hind legs were too short and its backbone was too rigid. In fact, this prehistoric rabbit moved in a roly-poly way—more like a beaver than a bunny. Fortunately, *Nuralagus rex* had very few predators on Minorca. Still, the species died off about 3 million years ago. Scientists aren't sure why.

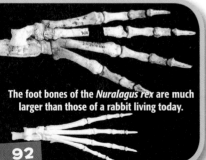

The foot bones of the *Nuralagus rex* are much larger than those of a rabbit living today.

Birth of a Baby Dino By Joe Levit

For a long time researchers wondered whether plesiosaurs—large oceangoing reptiles that lived when dinosaurs existed—laid eggs like other reptiles or gave birth to live young like whales do today. There had been evidence of live births in an ancestor of plesiosaurs, but the lack of proof for plesiosaur birth was puzzling. Now new fossil evidence suggests that the whale model is the winner.

PREGNANT PLESIOSAUR

The fossil was uncovered by Marshall University associate professor F. Robin O'Keefe and Luis Chiappe, of the Natural History Museum of Los Angeles County. It shows a fetus inside of a female plesiosaur called *Polycotylus.* Scientists examined the fossils inside the female plesiosaur and determined that they were the right size and in the right place to be a fetus and not a young animal that had been eaten by the larger animal.

O'Keefe and Chiappe suggest that plesiosaurs gave birth to live young just like modern whales. Both the ancient plesiosaur and whales of today are large animals that produce large offspring. University of Calgary professor Anthony Russell said the find is significant. "It would be hard to imagine these animals coming out onto land laying eggs somewhere."

≋ The fossilized bones of a female *Polycotylus* show that the giant reptile was pregnant when she died more than 70 million years ago.

EXCITING EVIDENCE

The uncovered fossil is now on display at the Natural History Museum of Los Angeles County. The fossil was originally discovered in 1987 in Logan County, Kansas. It had been stored in the basement of the museum until resources were available to separate the bones for display.

Unlike the typical plesiosaur image of a long neck poking out of the sea, *Polycotylus* had a short neck with a big head. The fossil is more than 15 feet (4.6 m) long and was dated to between 72 million and 78 million years ago. Though O'Keefe had seen photos of the fossil before he started working on it, he was still surprised when he first saw it. "I wasn't prepared for the emotional response I had," O'Keefe said. "You don't very often walk up to one and say, 'That is a really cool fossil.'"

≥ A plesiosaur and its young

To learn more about animals in deserts, grasslands, tropical rain forests, temperate forests, tundra, and taiga, see pages 122–125.

Home, Sweet Home

A **habitat** is the place where an animal lives. It provides the animal with all its needs, such as food, water, oxygen, and shelter. A habitat can be big, like an ocean, or small, like a puddle. Each animal species has developed special characteristics to survive in its particular habitat. For example, there are few trees or other places to hide in the grasslands, so animals live together in large groups for protection. Animals that live in cold-weather habitats often have thick fur and extra layers of fat to help them stay warm.

The Earth's habitats are always changing. Forests catch fire, for example, and rivers flood their banks. Animals must adapt to these changes if they are to survive.

« The vicuña walks on the soles of its feet and can flex its toes—factors that help it keep its balance on rocky mountain slopes.

≈ Dragonflies lay their eggs on plants or branches just beneath the water's surface.

MOUNTAIN DWELLERS

The higher up you go on a mountain, the lower the temperature drops and the thinner the air becomes. Certain sides of a mountain may get more (or less) sun or rain than other sides. All these factors influence which animals live on mountains—and where.

The **vicuña,** a distant relative of the camel, lives in the Andes Mountains of South America and is well-adapted to high-altitude living. Its lower teeth are constantly growing, enabling it to chew on tough mountain grasses. It also has a thick, soft coat that traps warm air close to its body. That protects the animal when temperatures drop below freezing at night. But one of the most important ways the vicuña has adapted to its mountain habitat can be found in its blood: It has more red blood cells than most other mammals. That means it can run and climb in the Andes's oxygen-thin air without getting too tired.

LIVING IN FRESHWATER

Freshwater habitats are lakes, rivers, and wetlands. They can be found all over the world and are home to a wide diversity of animals. Many animals in freshwater habitats spend part of their lives in water and part on land. Frogs and toads, for example, start their lives as tadpoles in water. Eventually, they grow legs and lungs and are able to leave the water and live on land. Many insects, like **dragonflies** and mosquitoes, do this too.

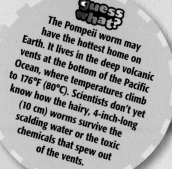
SURVIVING AND THRIVING IN THE OCEAN

On the ocean floor are huge mountains, deep valleys, and large plains. There are even volcanoes at the bottom of the sea. Animal life has been found in all these areas and at all depths.

Ocean animals have developed many fascinating ways to protect themselves from predators in the open sea. Camouflage is a popular method. (See pages 98–99.) Some slow-moving types of plankton, for example, protect themselves by being almost completely transparent, or see-through. That makes them practically invisible to predators. Other fish alter their color to blend in with their surroundings. Some fish alter their shape. For example, when the **balloonfish** feels it's in danger, it swallows a lot of water. That inflates its body and makes the spines on its skin stick out like nails.

CREATURES OF COASTS AND CORAL REEFS

A coast is where land meets the ocean. Coral reefs are underwater structures that are built by tiny living organisms called polyps. The polyps excrete an exoskeleton of calcium carbonate, which forms the reefs. Coral reefs are sometimes called "the rain forests of the sea" because they are home to such a diverse amount of life. Some 25% of all ocean animals live around coral reefs.

Coastal animals have evolved in ways that help them adjust to the ocean tides. Sea anemones open and show their beautiful tentacles only when the tide is in. Once the water has gone out, anemones close up to protect themselves from the sun. **Fiddler crabs,** on the other hand, bury themselves in the sand when the tide is high and then come out during low tide to search for food.

❝ A predator will think twice about swallowing a puffed-up balloonfish.

⤳ A fiddler crab emerges from its burrow in the sand.

STRANGE ANIMAL HOUSES

Some animals move into already existing structures, such as a knothole in a tree or a crevice in a rock. Others build their own places. Some animals even take over other creatures' homes. Here are some interesting examples of animal homes.

Guess what?
Aardvarks can dig very fast. They can make a hole 2 feet (0.6 m) deep in 15 seconds.

In Africa, Australia, and South America, some types of **TERMITES** use mud, saliva, and chewed wood to build skyscraper-like structures called termite mounds. The mounds, which can reach heights of 30 feet (9 m) or more, contain an elaborate maze of specialized rooms. Some of the rooms, for example, are used to grow a certain kind of fungi that the termites like to eat. Other rooms are used as nurseries to hatch termite eggs. Each termite mound also has a room for its queen. Most of the termites, however, live in a nest that's just under the mound.

Guess what?
Some sociable weaver nests are more than 100 years old.

The **AFRICAN AARDVARK** lives in underground burrows, which it digs out with its powerful front legs. Its burrows are often very deep—sometimes big enough for a person to sit in.

The world's largest bird's nests are built by tiny brown birds called SOCIABLE WEAVERS. They live in southern Africa. Their nests are like giant apartment buildings, with dozens of individual compartments. Each compartment is the home of a different pair of birds. Because the nests are so big, they are built only on very sturdy trees—or sometimes on telephone poles.

The **CLOWNFISH** makes its home within another animal: the sea anemone. For other fish, the sea anemone's swaying, stinging tentacles can be dangerous. But the clownfish has a mucus covering on its body that protects it from the anemone. These two ocean creatures help each other. The clownfish keeps the anemone clean by eating leftover plankton and algae. And the anemone protects the clownfish from predators.

Cool Life Cycles

Most animals have a simple life cycle. They hatch from eggs or are born live. Then they grow up. They change shape but not too much. A puppy, for example, becomes a dog. A baby turtle grows up into a bigger turtle. But some animals—mostly insects and amphibians—have a much more complex life cycle. They look and behave very differently at each stage of life. The scientific term for these big changes in body structure and appearance is metamorphosis. Some animals, like frogs and butterflies, experience a **complete metamorphosis.** For other animals, like grasshoppers, the change is slightly less dramatic. It is an **incomplete metamorphosis.**

TADPOLE TO FROG

A female frog lays her eggs in a pond or stream. A male frog then fertilizes the eggs. This process is called **spawning.**
After a week or two, the eggs hatch into tiny fishlike animals called **tadpoles.** Each tadpole has gills for breathing underwater and a tail that helps it swim. It also has a mouth, which it uses to eat algae and other tiny water plants.
After about four weeks, the tadpole begins to develop legs. The hind legs grow first, then the front ones. The tadpole also develops teeth and skin. At nine weeks, it looks like a tiny frog with a long tail.
By 12 weeks, the tadpole has lost most of its tail. It's now a **froglet**—a miniature version of an adult frog. Its gills shrink and it develops lungs instead. It starts swimming to the surface of the water to breathe air. It also starts eating insects.
By 16 weeks, the froglet has become a **frog.** Its tail has disappeared and its lungs are full-grown. It is able to leave the water and live on land.

GRASSHOPPER NYMPH TO ADULT GRASSHOPPER

A female grasshopper lays her **eggs** underneath loose soil or leaf litter.
The eggs hatch into **nymphs,** which start munching on grass and other nearby plants. The nymphs look like smaller versions of adult grasshoppers. But the nymphs have no wings. There are little buds where the wings should be.
As the nymphs eat and get bigger, they start shedding their skin, or **molting.** Each nymph molts five or six times. With each molt, the nymph's wing buds become more developed.
After about 30 days, the nymph has been transformed into an adult **grasshopper**—with a full set of wings. It can now fly, which helps it get food and escape its predators.

Camouflage as Defense

Some animals have built-in defenses that keep predators away. After all, what animal would want to chow down on a porcupine and risk getting a mouthful of quills? Or stick around after being sprayed in the eye by a skunk? Others simply avoid predators by hiding in plain sight. Many animals, like the arctic hare, have fur, skin, hair, or scales that are the same color as their surroundings, which makes them hard to see.

The patterns on some owls' feathers help the animals blend into the bark of the tree they nest in.

YOU CAN'T EAT WHAT YOU CAN'T SEE

Other animals, such as katydids, are called mimics. They have special adaptations that make them look like branches, dying plants, or other things that a predator may not want to bite into. Katydids resemble leaves, which don't look like tasty snacks to animals that eat insects. What makes katydids extra special is that they often look like old, withered, chewed-on, or unhealthy leaves. That way, even leaf eaters will overlook them.

The dead-leaf butterfly specializes in looking like unappetizing dead leaves.

Not all animals that rely on camouflage are small or defenseless. The color of a lion's hide helps it blend into its surroundings.

Here, an octopus looks like a coral reef.

ACTIVE CAMOUFLAGE

Some animals can blend into exact locations in their habitat. Cuttlefish and octopuses are two animals that can change the color and texture of their skin to mimic the exact seafloor they are resting on. Chameleons have the ability to change color based on their surroundings, though they also change their coloring to reflect mood and stress level. Often, if a chameleon is threatened, its stress level will skyrocket, and it will turn black.

Cuttlefish are masters of disguise.

Guess what?

Most sea horses rely on camouflage to stay safe, because they are lousy swimmers. They use their tiny fins mostly to keep themselves upright.

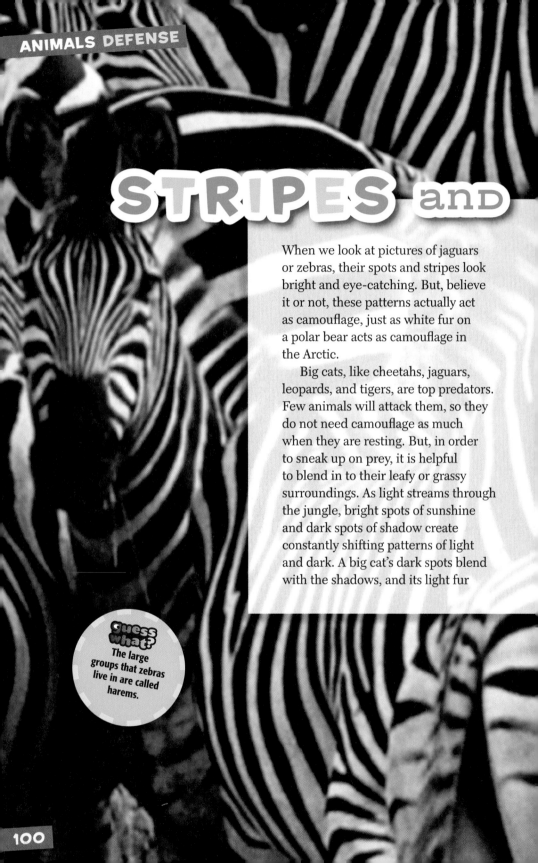

STRIPES and

When we look at pictures of jaguars or zebras, their spots and stripes look bright and eye-catching. But, believe it or not, these patterns actually act as camouflage, just as white fur on a polar bear acts as camouflage in the Arctic.

Big cats, like cheetahs, jaguars, leopards, and tigers, are top predators. Few animals will attack them, so they do not need camouflage as much when they are resting. But, in order to sneak up on prey, it is helpful to blend in to their leafy or grassy surroundings. As light streams through the jungle, bright spots of sunshine and dark spots of shadow create constantly shifting patterns of light and dark. A big cat's dark spots blend with the shadows, and its light fur

Guess what?
The large groups that zebras live in are called harems.

SPOTS

blends with sunlit grasses. It helps that the spots on big cats appear in an irregular pattern. When a tiger runs through high grass, its stripes blend into the striped patterns created by the sun on the tall, waving grasses of the grasslands.

The stripes on a zebra allow the animal to blend into the tall grass. Zebra stripes are also helpful because zebras live in herds. A lion will choose a weak-looking animal to attack and separate from the herd. But with a herd of running zebras, it can be difficult for a predator to see where one animal ends and another begins, making it is easy to loose a single animal in the crowd.

TFK GAME

PICK THE PATTERN

Can you match the pattern to the correct big cat?

1. **JAGUAR**
2. **LEOPARD**
3. **CHEETAH**
4. **OCELOT**
5. **SERVAL**
6. **TIGER**

Answers on page 216.

A.

B.

C.

D.

E.

F.

Poisonous and Venomous Animals

Some animals are poisonous. They have toxins—or poisonous substances—in their bodies. When another animal touches or bites them, the poisonous animal secretes the toxins, which kills or hurts the attacker. Other animals are venomous. They store poisonous toxins in their bodies too. But they release those toxins by biting or stinging another animal.

Poisonous animals use their toxins to protect themselves from predators. Venomous animals may use their toxins against predators or to capture prey.

POISON DART FROGS live in the tropical forests of Central and South America. They are very toxic if eaten. Some of these frogs are more deadly than others. One golden poison dart frog has enough poison to kill 2,000 mice—or 10 humans. In times past, people living in tropical forests used the poison from these frogs on the tips of their blow darts to hunt large animals. That's how the frogs got their name.

≈ Today, scientists are studying the animal's powerful poison to see if it could be used as a pain medication.

BLISTER BEETLES secrete a poison from their skin called cantharidin. If that poison gets on another animal's skin or hide, it can cause blistering. And if the poison is swallowed, blisters can develop inside the animal's body, and the animal may die. Blister beetles often crawl into hay, so horses, cattle, sheep, and other animals that eat hay are at risk of being poisoned.

» There are more than 7,500 species of blister beetles in the world. Some are more poisonous than others.

WARNING COLORS

Poison dart frogs are brightly colored. They do not rely on camouflage for safety. Instead, their colors are easy to spot and warn attackers to stay away. Other animals that have warning coloration are the black widow spider, velvet ant, coral snake, yellow jacket, blue-ringed octopus, and skunk.

The **BOX JELLYFISH**, which lives mostly in the coastal waters off Australia, has one of the most deadly venoms in the world. Each of its long tentacles contains thousands of stinging cells, which it uses to capture and eat shrimp, fish, and other small sea animals. Though the body of the box jellyfish is quite small, it can have tentacles up to 15 feet (5 m) long. Its only predator is a certain type of sea turtle that is immune to its venom.

Box jellyfish

POGONOMYRMEX ANTS

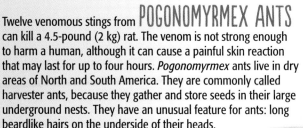

Twelve venomous stings from POGONOMYRMEX ANTS can kill a 4.5-pound (2 kg) rat. The venom is not strong enough to harm a human, although it can cause a painful skin reaction that may last for up to four hours. *Pogonomyrmex* ants live in dry areas of North and South America. They are commonly called harvester ants, because they gather and store seeds in their large underground nests. They have an unusual feature for ants: long beardlike hairs on the underside of their heads.

BLACK MAMBA

The highly venomous BLACK MAMBA snake is found in southern and eastern Africa. It can move incredibly quickly and strike with precision.

Guess what?

The black mamba gets its name from the dark color on the inside of its mouth.

DANGEROUS ANIMALS

MOSQUITOES may look harmless, but they can carry many different diseases, including malaria, yellow fever, dengue fever, and West Nile virus. Mosquitoes are responsible for an estimated 2 to 3 million deaths every year.

After a big meal, a CROCODILE does not need to feed again for a long while. A large adult can go for nearly two years between meals! This makes it a patient predator. A crocodile will lie motionless in the water and wait for the perfect moment to grab its prey with its enormous jaws. Then the croc will pull its victim into the water and spin around and around in what is known as a "death roll," until the animal has drowned.

The GREAT WHITE SHARK is one of the world's greatest predators. While some people have been attacked and killed by great whites, humans aren't the sharks' favorite dish. They eat fish, rays, sea lions, seals, and even other sharks. Great white sharks can weigh more than 4,500 pounds (2,041 kg), swim at speeds up to 43 miles (69 km) per hour, and often surprise their prey.

Strength in Numbers

Many wild animals form tight societies, such as hives and herds. Each member of the society knows its place and does its job. There are sometimes fights for the best position in the herd, but the group is usually loyal and protective of all its members. A pride of lions, for example, will cooperate in stalking and killing prey. Together the lions will drag a kill to a shady spot to share it. The dominant male usually gets the best parts, but everyone gets to eat. Chimpanzees are also good at sharing. Some animals, like bald eagles, albatrosses, beavers, swans, and termites, mate for life. These animals choose a mate and remain together as a pair.

Mothers in many species, such as bears, tend their offspring with the same devotion as human moms. (Others, such as guppies, spiders, and some rodents, will often eat their young as soon as they're born.)

Female elephants live together in groups, but males live alone.

Guess what? An elephant's trunk contains about 100,000 different muscles and can lift up to 600 pounds (272 kg). But the trunk is not all about strength. Elephants also have fingerlike structures at the tip of their trunks that they can use to grab small objects—a small branch, for example, or even blades of grass. African elephants have two of these "fingers" on their trunks. Asian elephants have only one.

Lone Rangers

Some animals are solitary. They live and hunt alone. Most of them will make exceptions during mating season and when they are raising young, but these animals are not particularly sociable.

- Green iguanas
- Jaguars
- Leopards

- Rhinoceroses
- Sharks, such as tiger sharks, great white sharks, and others

- Skunks
- Snakes
- Spiders

Guess what? Sharks are among the longest-living animals on Earth. Most live for 20 to 30 years, and some live much, much longer. Scientists believe large, slow-moving whale sharks can live up to 150 years.

STRANGE PARTNERS

An ant drinks honeydew from an aphid.

Animals often rely on another animal species for their survival. This special relationship is called *symbiosis*, a Greek word that means "living together."

APHIDS AND ANTS

Aphids are tiny, wingless insects that live on plants. They suck the sap that runs through plant stems. After they've digested the sap, the aphids release it back onto the plants through long tubes (cornicles) located on the end of their bodies. This new sugary fluid is called honeydew.

Certain types of ants like to munch on the honeydew released by the aphids. So they take care of the aphids. Sometimes, the ants gently pick up the aphids in their mouths and move them to places where there is more plant sap for the aphids to eat. Ants will also attack other insects, like ladybugs, that feed on aphids. They chase the ladybugs away.

PISTOL SHRIMP AND GOBY FISH

Pistol shrimp and gobies are undersea roommates. They share tunnel homes that the shrimp digs in the sand. The shrimp is a great home builder, but it can't see very well. The goby, on the other hand, has excellent eyesight. So the fish acts like a guard and warns the shrimp when a potential attacker is nearby.

To make sure it gets the warning, the shrimp keeps one of its antennae on the goby at all times. As soon as the goby spots a possible predator, it makes a special motion with its tail. Both the goby and the shrimp then dive into their tunnel home. They stay there until the goby sees that it's safe for both of them to come out and look for food again.

TFK GAME — USE YOUR EAGLE EYES

Draw a line from each bald eagle to its look-alike, to find out which one is the odd bird out.

Answers on page 216.

Guess what?

The loudest animal in the world for its size is a tiny European insect known as the water boatman. (Its scientific name is *Micronecta scholtzi*.) Although less than ½ inch (1.3 cm) long, the water boatman can reach volumes of up to 99.2 decibels when it sings. That's about as loud as a diesel truck. But because the insect lives in water, 99% of the sound cannot be heard by people.

DISGUSTING DINERS!

DRACULA ANTS suck the blood of their young. The adult ants chew holes in the wormlike larvae that hatch from the ants' eggs. A type of insect blood called hemolymph oozes out of the holes. The adult ants then feed on that blood. This gruesome practice doesn't kill the larvae, however. The holes eventually heal and the larvae grow up to be adult Dracula ants.

Because the **PLATYPUS** (or duckbilled platypus) is toothless, it can't chew its food like other carnivores. Instead, it grinds its food between its long, flat, bony bill. The platypus, which lives in the lakes and rivers of Australia, eats mostly shrimp and other crustaceans.

Some **MOTHS** drink the tears of elephants. Others drink the tears of horses, buffalo, deer, pigs, and even birds. The tears contain salt, water, and other substances that moths find nutritious. Not all moths wait for the eyes of the bigger animals to get wet, however. Some stick their proboscis—the long part of their mouth that they use for piercing and sucking—right into the eyeball of the bigger animal. That irritates the animal's eyes and causes it to produce tears.

The **STAR-NOSED MOLE** may be the fastest-eating mammal in the world. It can decide if something is okay to eat—and then gobble it up—within 227 milliseconds. That's because it has 22 tentacles on its face that are extremely sensitive to touch. The tentacles quickly tell the mole's brain whether something is or is not food. These speed-eating mammals dine mostly on worms and insects. They live in wetland areas of North America.

FACE THIS WAY FOR LUNCH

All cattle stand in a north-south direction while eating grass in open fields. Scientists discovered this amazing fact only recently, while studying satellite photos from around the world. They believe the cattle are responding to Earth's magnetic field. The magnetic field is an invisible electrical current that is created by huge pools of hot liquid circulating deep beneath the Earth's surface. (See page 119.) Birds and other animals use the magnetic field to help them keep from getting lost as they migrate over long distances. Scientists now believe that cattle may also have an internal magnetic compass, perhaps because the cattle's ancestors used to migrate.

The Dating Game: How Animals Find a Mate

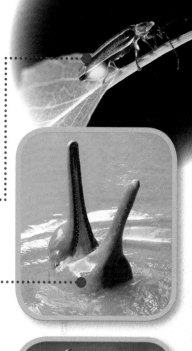

Most animals need to find a mate to produce young. And they must produce young if their species is going to survive. Animals have developed many different and unusual ways of attracting mates.

FIREFLIES use their flashlight-like tails to find their mates. The light is created by chemicals in special cells near the tip of the animal's abdomen. The male firefly blinks his tail while flying through the air. The female firefly waits near the ground. When she sees the male create a particular pattern of blinking, she flashes back with a pattern of her own. Each species of firefly has its own blinking pattern for attracting a mate.

The male **AMAZON RIVER DOLPHIN** tries to impress its future mate with weed clumps, broken sticks, or small rocks. The dolphin picks up these objects from the riverbed with its mouth, then rises up out of the water and shows them off to nearby female dolphins. Scientists have observed that the male dolphins that lift up the biggest objects tend to have the most offspring.

Male **FRIGATE BIRDS** inflate their throat sacs to attract a female mate. It can take 20 minutes or longer for the male bird to puff up the sac. When fully inflated, the sac looks like a giant, red, heart-shaped balloon. The male then shakes his head, clatters his bill, and flutters his wings to get the attention of females flying overhead.

JAPANESE CRANES court their mates with dancing. Either the male or the female may start the dance. The bird leaps into the air with its wings outstretched. The other bird then starts to slowly circle around the jumper. After a few more leaps, the birds change roles. The dance ends when the male stops and spreads his wings.

Guess what?
Frigate birds are sometimes called pirate birds because they steal food from other birds.

Guess what?
Japanese cranes mate for life. They repeat their complicated courtship dance several times a year.

Food Chains

All animals are linked together by what they eat. That linkage is called a food chain. To learn how a simple food chain works, start at the bottom and read your way up.

TOP PREDATORS
The food chain ends with the top predators. These are carnivores with few or no natural enemies. But although they may not have another animal hunting them, top predators can die if there are not enough animals further down the food chain for them to eat. For this reason, top predators never outnumber their prey.

MORE CARNIVORES
Further up the food chain are more carnivores. These animals feed on herbivores *and* other meat-eating animals.

CARNIVORES
Carnivores, or meat eaters, are the next step in the food chain. The lowest carnivores in the food chain tend to eat only herbivores. Like herbivores, they store the energy from their food in their cells.

Earthworms

HERBIVORES
Plant-eating animals, called herbivores, are the next step in the food chain. As an herbivore eats and digests a plant, the plant dissolves into tiny substances. Those substances become part of the animal's cells, where they are used for energy.

FOOD WEBS
Every animal is involved in more than one food chain. Food chains interconnect with each other within a habitat to form complex food webs. If anything breaks the food chain—if one species of animal is overhunted, for example, and disappears from its habitat—then the food web weakens. Other animals in the web may find themselves with either too little food or too many predators. They, too, may become endangered.

BREAK IT DOWN!
Decomposers are also part of the food chain. These creatures—which include fungi, insects, worms, and bacteria—help break down the carcasses of dead animals. The process returns the essential nutrients in the animals to the soil. Plants then use those nutrients to grow.

PLANTS
Food chains begin with plants. They are known as the **producers**. They make new living, organic matter—the plants' leaves, stems, roots, and seeds—from nonliving elements in the environment, such as sunlight and water. The organic matter that plants produce makes all animal life possible.

HERE'S A SAMPLE OCEAN FOOD CHAIN.
Phytoplankton < Krill < Squid < Emperor penguin < Killer whale

CATCHING PREY

Predators—animals that survive by killing and eating other animals—have highly developed senses that help them outsmart and catch their prey. They have evolved different ways of hunting.

The **BARN OWL**, which hunts at night, uses sound to find and catch its prey. It has special ears that can pick up very soft sounds, whether it's a mouse's step or a berry's fall. Those ears also help the barn owl pinpoint exactly where a sound comes from. It then dives down and grabs the animal, which it carries back to its nest to eat.

A **CROCODILE** relies on surprise to catch its prey. It will lie quietly in shallow waters with only its eyes, ears, and nostrils above the water. It waits to see, hear, or smell its prey, or perhaps even feel the vibrations in the water of a passing fish. Then it grabs its lunch.

Many **SPIDERS** use webs to catch their food. Spiders produce the sticky silk for their webs from glands in their abdomens. Spider silk is stretchy and incredibly strong. Once an insect becomes trapped in the web, the spider stuns it with venom from its fangs. The venom turns the insides of the insect into liquid, which the spider drinks.

Some spiders use their silk in other ways. The **TRAPDOOR SPIDER** digs a tunnel into the ground. At the top of the tunnel, it builds a trapdoor out of soil, plant material, and its own silk. The spider then waits inside the tunnel until an unsuspecting insect disturbs the door's silky "trip lines." At that point, the spider jumps out and grabs the insect.

Some animals, like the **WOLF**, hunt in groups called packs, which are typically six or seven related wolves. Wolf packs work together to separate a weak or old animal, such as an elk, from the rest of its herd. Once they catch and kill the elk, the wolves eat the animal together. Hunting is dangerous for wolves. Elk and other large herd animals will strike at an attacking wolf with their hooves. These strikes are sometimes strong enough to break the wolf's back.

ECHOLOCATION

A bat finds its prey by using echolocation. It sends out high-pitched sounds through its mouth or nose. The sounds bounce off objects. When the bat hears the echoes of these sounds, it can tell if the object is a moth or other insect that it likes to eat. The bat then swoops down and catches the insect.

Common poorwill

Do Not Disturb!

Some animals spend each winter in a kind of sleep called **hibernation.** It helps them survive the season's cold temperatures and limited food supplies. During hibernation, the animal's body temperature drops and its heart rate and breathing slow down. When a woodchuck hibernates, its body temperature plummets from about 98°F (37°C) to about 40°F (4°C).

≈ A bear emerging from its torpor

Because its body functions slow down so much, woodchucks go into a very deep sleep during hibernation. They are almost impossible to wake up. Scientists call these animals "true hibernators."

Winter Is for the Birds

≈ One of the few birds known to hibernate is the common poorwill. Each winter, this North American bird nestles into a space under a rock or in a rotten log and "sleeps" for 100 days. It doesn't move or eat. For centuries, Hopi Indians have referred to this bird as "The Sleeping One."

≈ A hibernating dormouse curled up next to some hazelnuts

Other animals, like bears, are light sleepers during hibernation. Their body temperature drops just a few degrees, so they wake up easily if disturbed. Scientists call this lighter version of hibernation **torpor.**

GOING UNDERGROUND

Cold-blooded animals, like snakes and turtles, also hibernate. Red-sided garter snakes, for example, coil up together in underground burrows during northern Canada's long, cold winters. When spring comes, thousands of the snakes suddenly crawl to the surface, looking for food and mates. Frogs hibernate under leaves, logs, and rocks. Some even burrow into the mud at the bottom of ponds. The mud has air trapped inside it. Hibernating frogs are able to "breathe" that oxygen through their skin instead of through their lungs.

Guess What?
A hibernating woodchuck's heart rate slows from a speedy 80 beats a minute to a sluggish 4 beats a minute. Its breathing slows from about 25 breaths a minute to one breath every five minutes.

≈ Red-sided garter snakes coming out of hibernation

GETTING READY FOR THE LONG NAP

Warm-blooded animals, like woodchucks and bears, prepare for hibernation by eating large amounts of food and storing it on their bodies as fat. While they're hibernating, their bodies turn that fat into energy to keep them just warm enough to stay alive. Some animals—like chipmunks—also store caches of nuts or seeds in the burrow where they're hibernating. They wake up from time to time during the winter, eat some food, and then go back to sleep.

Monarch Butterflies

By Elizabeth Winchester

Guess what? The monarchs we see flying around are the children and grandchildren of the butterflies that flew south.

˄ Sometimes, there are so many monarchs clinging to the trees that the bark is no longer visible.

Most monarch butterflies spend the winter fluttering above the fir trees of Mexico. "You hear a gentle whooshing sound of thousands of monarchs flying all around you," scientist Ernest Williams told TFK.

The monarch is the only butterfly known to make a two-way migration. Every fall, millions of monarchs leave Canada and the northern United States and head south to spend the winter hibernating in Mexico and California. In early spring, the monarchs head north. Females lay their eggs on milkweed plants along the way. New generations of butterflies continue the journey north.

Williams teaches biology at Hamilton College, in Clinton, New York. For a recent study, he observed monarchs in Mexico. He and other scientists found that over the past 17 years, the number of monarchs in Mexico has dropped. "The data shows a distinct and sad decline," said Williams.

PROTECTING BUTTERFLIES

Monarchs face three main threats: habitat loss, plant-killing chemicals, and extreme weather. In Mexico, people illegally cut down trees, destroying the butterflies' homes. Logging also thins the forest. This causes temperature changes that make it hard for the monarchs to survive.

In areas where monarchs lay their eggs, the use of chemicals is a big problem, said Williams. These chemicals kill milkweed plants. Female monarchs lay their eggs on the plants' leaves. Caterpillars eat the leaves. To help monarchs, Williams urges people to plant milkweeds. Some experts are not convinced monarch numbers are falling. They feel more research is needed. But all experts agree that the annual migration is a natural wonder that shouldn't be lost. "Different generations fly in two directions. How do they know which way to go? How do they end up on the same mountaintops in central Mexico?" said Williams. "It's simply amazing."

FROM TIME FOR KIDS

Guess what?
The U.S. government has spent nearly $20 million on white-nose syndrome since 2007.

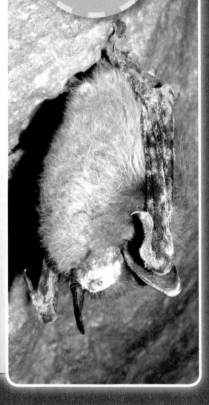

Bats, Beware! By Elizabeth Winchester

A mysterious disease has killed more than a million bats in parts of Canada and the United States. The sickness is called white-nose syndrome. It first appeared in 2006, in upstate New York.

White-nose syndrome appears to affect only bats that hibernate. Scientists believe the disease is caused by a fungus that grows on a bat's nose, wings, and ears. The fungus damages wing tissues. This may cause bats to end their hibernation early. When they wake up, they burn the fat they need to survive the winter. Unfortunately, there are not enough insects to eat in winter. With nothing to eat, the bats starve and die.

"Bats are our friends," says Tom Kunz. He is a scientist and the director of the Bat Lab at Boston University. "They help people and the environment they live in," he says. In May 2011, the U.S. government launched a major plan to help. Scientists are hard at work, looking for ways to stop—or at least slow— the spread of the disease.

Guess what?
Bats are helpful to humans. They eat mosquitoes and other insects that harm crops and carry disease.

New Frog in the Big City

By the TIME For Kids Staff

Usually, scientists search rain forests, ocean habitats, or other remote spots on Earth to find new plant and animal species. So when a new species of frog was found hopping around urban New York, you could say scientists croaked with delight.

Rutgers University science student Jeremy Feinberg heard a frog croaking in New York City and felt that something was unusual. He listened for the repeated croaking chuckle of the southern leopard frog. Instead, he heard one single cluck. "When I first heard these frogs calling, it was so different," he says. So Feinberg contacted biologist Catherine E. Newman. She compared the new frogs' DNA with the DNA of leopard frogs. DNA is a material in all living things. It is what gives them their special traits. Even though the frogs looked nearly identical, their DNA was very different.

The New York frog was from a newly discovered species. This shows that even in heavily populated urban areas, new species can be found. The new frog's habitat ranges from New Jersey to northern New York. It may even be found in Connecticut and Pennsylvania.

Fancy Feathers By the TIME For Kids Staff

What has blue-and-black feathers with a luminous shine? A crow? A dinosaur? Both, say scientists who are studying a 130-million-year-old fossil discovered in China. The fossil is that of a *Microraptor*, a four-winged, pigeon-size dinosaur. Scientists say its feathers had a sheen called iridescence (ir-ih-*des*-uhns). Bird feathers show iridescence. The dino's feathers are the earliest known iridescent color in animals. The researchers believe that the dino's tail feathers were long and fancy. That means it didn't use those feathers to fly. Instead, it used them to attract mates.

❮❮ This illustration of a *Microraptor* is based on the fossil found in China.

❮❮ The *Microraptor* fossil indicates that the dinosaur had dark, glossy feathers.

Amazing New Animals By Joe Levit

The Mekong River begins in China and runs through five other countries on its way to the South China Sea. Some of the world's most endangered species—such as tigers, Asian elephants, and the Mekong giant catfish—live in the Mekong River region. In 2011, scientists working in the area announced that they'd found more than 200 new species of plants and animals.

One of the most interesting new species is the psychedelic gecko, found only on Hon Khoai Island, off the southern tip of Vietnam. Another new lizard reproduces by cloning, or making an identical copy of, itself. The self-cloning lizard is a species made up entirely of females. No males are needed to create more members.

The wolf snake is a new snake found in a mountain region in China. It is named after the wolf because it has big fangs in both its top and bottom jaws. These snakes hunt for frogs and lizards at night.

Just because these species are new to scientists doesn't mean they are new to everyone. One monkey from Myanmar has been known to the local people in the area for many years.

All of the discovered animals live in a region that is considered rich in wildlife. Unfortunately, the area is also threatened by habitat loss, deforestation, climate change, and overdevelopment. Scientists worry that many creatures may become extinct before they can even be recognized by science in the first place.

Guess What? The Mekong River is the 10th-longest river in the world.

The psychedelic lizard sports a rainbow of lively colors.

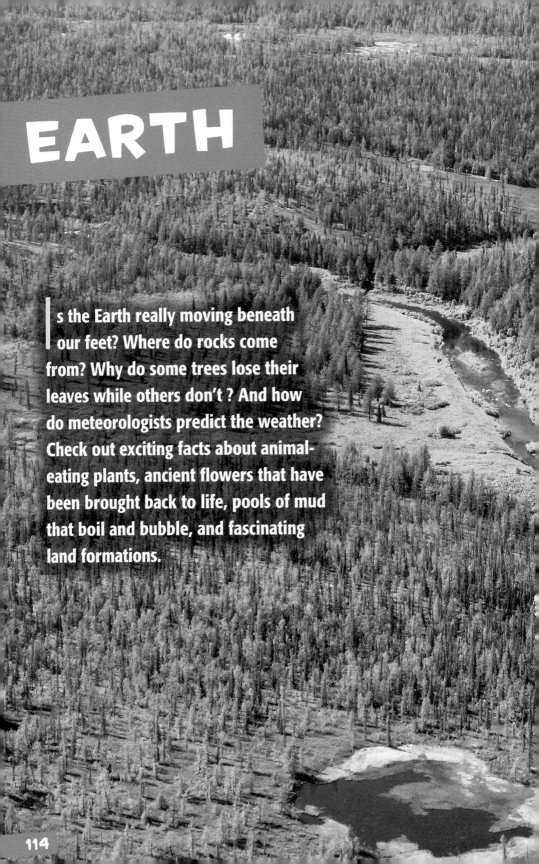

EARTH

s the Earth really moving beneath our feet? Where do rocks come from? Why do some trees lose their leaves while others don't ? And how do meteorologists predict the weather? Check out exciting facts about animal-eating plants, ancient flowers that have been brought back to life, pools of mud that boil and bubble, and fascinating land formations.

Earth's Crust

Earth is approximately 4.5 billion years old. In its lifetime, it has changed a lot. Although we do not feel the land shifting beneath our feet, it is moving.

The ground we walk on is the outer layer of the Earth, or the Earth's crust. Soon after the Earth formed, this rocky crust hardened. But the crust is not a single solid layer of rock. It's broken into many plates that move across, under, and over one another.

During a volcanic eruption, the molten rock from deep in the Earth leaks or shoots out.

Guess what? Many of the world's volcanic eruptions and earthquakes occur in a region in the South Pacific Ocean known as the Ring of Fire. Several of the Earth's plates meet in the area, which causes the quakes and the volcanic activity.

JOURNEY TO THE CENTER OF THE EARTH

CRUST On the continents, the crust averages about 20 miles (32 km) thick. In some places, it may only be a few miles thick.

MANTLE Beneath the crust is the mantle, a rocky layer that makes up about 85% of the weight of the planet.

OUTER CORE This liquid layer is made of molten rock (mostly iron and nickel).

INNER CORE The center, or core, of Earth is made up of a solid ball of mostly iron and nickel.

PANGAEA AND PLATE TECTONICS

Many scientists believe the seven continents we have today were once part of a single gigantic supercontinent, which they call **Pangaea,** a Greek word that means "all of the Earth." According to this theory, Pangaea began to break apart about 200 to 250 million years ago. Today, the Earth's crust is broken up into seven or eight major plates. There are also other, smaller plates. Volcanoes form where plates meet—both aboveground and deep underwater.

The breakup and drift of different plates is called **continental drift.** There are three kinds of drift: divergent, convergent, and lateral.

- **DIVERGENT** movements occur when plates pull apart from each other. When two plates diverge, pieces from each plate sink toward the Earth's core, forming a valley or rift.

- **CONVERGENT** movements occur when plates crash into each other and land crumples, forming trenches and mountains, such as the Mariana Trench in the Pacific Ocean and the Andes Mountains in South America.

- **LATERAL** (also called transforming) movements occur when plates move alongside each other in different directions. This sideswiping motion causes earthquakes. The San Andreas Fault in California is a place where laterally moving plates meet. That is why there are so many earthquakes there.

THE PROOF IS IN THE BONES!

Scientists have found fossils that support the theory of Pangaea. They have found the fossilized remains of animals that lived more than 200 million years ago in areas that are now separated by enormous oceans. When the animals were alive, these areas would have been right next to each other.

⌃ Scientists have found Mesosaurus fossils in southern South America and southern Africa. The Mesosaurus lived about 270 to 300 million years ago, when these two regions would have been connected by land.

The fractured hillside after an earthquake in California in 2010

Andes Mountains

Guess what?
Due to the slow movement of two of Earth's plates, the Atlantic Ocean actually becomes a few inches wider each year.

Magnets

A magnet is a special metal that attracts things made of iron or iron compounds (like steel). It has a north pole at one end and a south pole at the other. The force exerted by a magnet can pull objects to it or push them away. The north pole of one magnet is attracted to the south pole of another. This force creates a field of energy known as a **magnetic field.** (See page 119.)

⚡ Look at the iron filings all around these magnets. See how they move differently around the magnets.

SOUTH	SOUTH

Two like poles (south to south) will push away, or repel, one another.

NORTH	SOUTH

Two opposite poles (north to south) will pull, or attract, one another.

Magnets can be used to pick up some other metal objects.

Earth's Poles

Earth has two North Poles and two South Poles: geographic and magnetic. The **geographic poles** are the most northern and the most southern spots on Earth. The Earth's axis of rotation—the invisible line around which our planet spins—runs through the geographic North and South Poles. Those poles are always in the same place. The South Pole is in Antarctica, and the North Pole is in the middle of the Arctic Ocean.

The Earth also has **magnetic poles**—points where the lines of the Earth's magnetic fields come together. When the needle on a magnetic compass points to the north, it points to the magnetic North Pole, not the geographic North Pole. The magnetic North Pole is pretty far north and the magnetic South Pole is pretty far south, but both of these poles move around a lot.

Guess what?
The needle of a compass is a small magnet. It responds to Earth's magnetic field. That's how it can tell us which way is north or south.

The Earth's Magnetic Field

Earth is surrounded by its own magnetic field. This magnetic field is generated in Earth's core, where there is a solid ball of mostly iron that is about as hot as the surface of the sun. It is floating in a layer of liquid iron and spinning just a little bit faster than the rest of the layers of Earth. The liquid iron, or outer core, is constantly moving, like water boiling in a pan. It is the complex motion of this liquid iron that generates electric currents. These currents then create Earth's powerful magnetic field.

The magnetic energy of this magnetic field protects the planet from the solar wind, a stream of charged particles that come from the sun. Without the magnetic field, these particles would strip away the ozone layer, which keeps harmful ultraviolet rays from reaching Earth's surface.

Our magnetic field is constantly moving and changing, because of the swirling and turbulent activity in the planet's core. As a result, the magnetic North and South Poles move between 6 and 25 miles (10 to 40 km) a year.

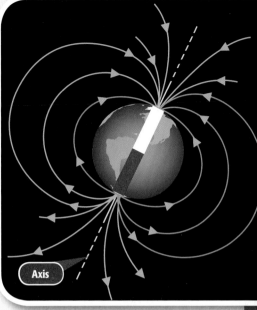

Axis

≈ Think of Earth as a gigantic magnet, with poles and a magnetic field.

Guess what?
Earth's solid inner core is about 70% as wide as the moon.

≈ Sea turtles migrate through the open ocean, where there are no visual landmarks to help point them in the right direction. Scientists believe they rely on signals given off by the planet's magnetic field to get to their destinations.

MAGNETIC SOMERSAULTS

Scientists who study bands of magnetism in rock layers know that sometimes the magnetic poles flip, and then north becomes south and south becomes north. These magnetic-field reversals do not come at regular intervals, so nobody knows when the next one will happen. The last one was 780,000 years ago. The magnetic-field flip, when it happens, takes a few thousand years to complete. During that time, magnetic lines of force near Earth's surface become twisted and tangled, and magnetic poles pop up in weird places. For example, a magnetic South Pole might pop up in Brazil, or a North Pole in Indonesia. Compasses would probably not be helpful during the switchover. Otherwise a change in Earth's magnetic field would not affect humans in a major way. However, scientists believe that some migratory animals use magnetic fields to orient themselves. These species, such as sea turtles, may be affected by a shift in the magnetic field.

A volcano erupts behind Rampino, during fieldwork in Hawaii in 1997.

FROM TIME FOR KIDS

Volcanoes Are His Business

By Ariella Pultman

Getting close to active or erupting volcanoes can be dangerous. But for Michael Rampino, it's all in a day's work. Rampino is a volcanologist (vol-ka-*nol*-uh-jist), a type of geologist who studies volcanoes and how they affect the planet. Rampino has been close to red-hot lava flows in Hawaii and explosive volcanoes in Indonesia. He knows when to get close to an active volcano and when to back away.

Rampino wasn't always a volcanologist. He worked for NASA for seven years. He studied rocks until he began to research climate change and the effects volcanoes have on climate. He became fascinated with the subject. "Once I started working with volcanoes," Rampino told TFK, "I was hooked."

Rampino is a professor at New York University. As part of his job, he travels to areas where volcanoes have been **active.** Rampino studies the deposits of ash and other materials from the eruptions. The ash may hold clues to what happened on Earth in the distant past. It may also help scientists predict what could happen to Earth's climate in the future. Rampino doesn't work alone. He works with a team of scientists who use computers to simulate, or re-create, the effects volcanoes have on Earth's atmosphere.

ACTIVE means they have erupted within the past few centuries and probably will erupt again.

WHY STUDY VOLCANOES?

Being a volcanologist may be hard work, but it's also fun. "It's cool traveling the world studying volcanoes," Rampino says. When he talks to students about his work, he tells them that his goal is "to understand the events that have shaped Earth's history." And if that means getting up close to the edge of a volcano, then that's just what he'll do!

CRATER This is the opening at the top of the volcano.

ASH CLOUD Ash, steam, and other gases shoot out from the volcano.

VENT Pressure forces magma up through this space, like thick toothpaste through a narrow tube.

LAVA When magma reaches the top of the volcano, the volcano erupts. Magma bursts out as red-hot lava.

Layers of hard lava and ash build up over time.

UNDERSTANDING ERUPTIONS

MAGMA This hot, melted rock collects deep inside the Earth.

Minerals and Rocks

Minerals are naturally occurring, solid substances that don't come from living things. They can be found in dirt or in water. They can form into crystals or combine together into rocks. Some minerals are made from a single element, like gold, copper, or nickel, but most are a combination of elements. Gemstones like diamonds, opals, and sapphires are minerals that are often cut and polished to be used in fine jewelry.

Rocks are made up of combinations of minerals and belong to one of three categories: igneous, sedimentary, or metamorphic.

Columns of basalt at Devils Postpile National Monument in California

- IGNEOUS rocks are made from magma. This burning-hot substance is found deep inside the Earth and cools and hardens when it reaches the air. Granite and **basalt** are common igneous rocks.

- SEDIMENTARY rocks are made from bits of larger rocks, other pieces of earth, and even seashells that get washed into riverbeds, lakes, and oceans. They settle under the water and more and more pieces are piled on top of them. Over very long periods of time, these pieces become cemented together, often in layers. **Limestone** and sandstone are examples of sedimentary rocks.

The Great Pyramid at Giza, in Egypt, is made of more than 2 million enormous limestone blocks.

- METAMORPHIC rocks are formed when either igneous or sedimentary rocks are subjected to so much heat or pressure underground that they change form. **Marble** and slate are well-known metamorphic rocks.

Guess what? Diamonds are formed only at the high temperatures and pressures that occur deep in the Earth's mantle. They are brought to the surface by volcanic eruptions.

Guess what? In January 2012, geologists (scientists who study rocks) in western Australia found small amounts of a mineral called tranquillityite, which was previously found only on the moon.

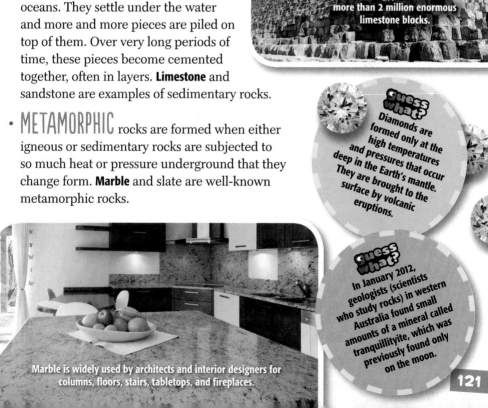
Marble is widely used by architects and interior designers for columns, floors, stairs, tabletops, and fireplaces.

Habitats and Wildlife

The landmasses on Earth consist of six different kinds of large regions called **biomes.** The environment of each biome reflects the climate, temperature, and geographical features that exist there. Within a biome are many smaller areas called **habitats.** The wildlife found in a biome has adapted over millions of years to survive and thrive in their own habitats. For example, thick-furred animals live in the Arctic, and color-changing chameleons live in lush forests filled with colorful plants. The relationship among various species of plants, animals, and other creatures within a habitat is called an **ecosystem.**

FROM TIME FOR KIDS

Back to the Future By Joe Levit

Harvard University entomologist Piotr Naskrecki is out to discover ancient secrets. To uncover them, he has hiked the world's oldest habitats. In his book *Relics,* Naskrecki describes organisms, or living things, that have remained nearly unchanged for millions of years.

"Ancient organisms often possess characteristics that make them the ultimate survivors," Naskrecki told TFK. These plants and creatures offer clues about how life existed on Earth before humans were a part of its history. Horseshoe crabs have crawled across beaches since before dinosaurs ruled. Lizards have perfected how to survive harsh climates. Insects such as katydids thrive in many types of habitats. How do they do it?

HARDY Horseshoe crabs have been around for so long because they eat almost anything, saltwater changes don't bother them, and they can even survive out of the water for up to four days.

SCARY
Generations of peacock katydids have been able to hide on the forest floor, looking like dead leaves. When hiding doesn't work, they flash their eyelike wings when a predator gets too close.

SHARP Not much bothers cycads these days. But some scientists think the plants developed their spiky leaves millions of years ago, in response to dinosaurs eating them.

COOL The ancient creature called the tuatara has many survival tricks up its sleeve. Unlike lizards, tuataras live and hunt for food in areas with cool temperatures.

SMART The Cape flat lizard perfected its defense over time. When danger is near, the animal jams itself into a crack in a rock. Then it inflates its body so it can't be removed.

BIOMES

More kinds of trees exist in tropical forests than anywhere else in the world.

TROPICAL FOREST

These habitats are near the equator. They have a significant amount of rainfall, and their temperatures do not change very much. There are two basic types of tropical forests. Rain forests have a rainy season that lasts all year. Monsoon forests have an extremely heavy rainy season, called a monsoon, which is followed by a long dry season.

Because tropical forests are so dense, many of the animals that live there rely on sound and smells rather than on sight to communicate with each other. Some of the world's loudest animals can be found in tropical forests. The loudest of all is the South American **howler monkey.** Its shrieks can be heard up to 3 miles (5 km) away. Tropical forests also have many species of animals that have developed winglike flaps that help them glide from tree to tree. An Asian lizard called the flying dragon can glide up to 50 feet (15 m) after leaping from a tree. Many insects thrive in tropical rain forests, including colorful butterflies, ants, and camouflaged stick insects.

DESERT

These habitats receive less than 10 inches (25 cm) of rain each year. When rain does come, it falls in brief and heavy downpours. Desert temperatures tend to fluctuate greatly. In Africa's Sahara desert, for example, the difference between daytime and nighttime temperatures can be be as much as 30°F to 50°F (17°C to 30°C). Not all deserts are hot during the day and covered in sand dunes. There are also "cold" deserts, like the Gobi Desert in northern Asia, where temperatures can drop to -40°F (-40°C) on winter nights.

Desert animals must be able to survive in a habitat where both water and food are scarce. The **camel** is a good example. It has humps of fat that help it survive for two weeks or more without food or water. And it has two rows of eyelashes to keep sand out of its eyes during desert storms.

⌃ Camels have big, wide feet to keep them from sinking into the desert sand.

The needles stay on conifer trees all year long, so little sunlight reaches the forest floor. As a result, forests in the taiga have few shrubs or other large plants growing under the trees.

Most trees in a temperate forest lose their leaves in the fall.

TAIGA

Winter in the taiga is long, snowy, and cold. The taiga is found in cold, northern areas of North America and Asia. There are many mountainous areas in this biome. Most of the trees in these habitats are conifer or evergreen trees, like spruces, pines, and firs. Conifer trees have needles instead of leaves and cones instead of flowers. The often-rocky ground is mostly covered with thick layers of dead pine needles.

Animals that live in coniferous forests have to survive very cold winters. For that reason, many of the mammals that live there, such as minks and wolverines, have thick fur. They often shed, or molt, some of their fur during the warm months of summer. Then they grow it back in time for winter. Some animals, like the stoat, change the color of their fur according to the season: brown (the color of tree bark) in summer and white (the color of snow) in winter. That helps them hide from predators. Elk, **brown bears,** grizzly bears, moose, caribou, lynx, and **reindeer** are other examples of taiga wildlife.

TEMPERATE FOREST

Temperate, or deciduous, forests are located in North America, Europe, and other parts of the world that have changing seasons. Temperatures in these habitats are warmer in the summer than they are in the winter. Many hardwood trees, such as maple, oak, birch, and hickory, are found in this climate. The trees and plants found in temperate forests usually shed leaves each winter, leaving a deep layer of leaf litter on the ground. All that decaying plant matter makes a great home for insects and other invertebrates.

Animals living in temperate forests must adapt to living through winter, when food is in short supply. Many of the birds and mammals in these forests, like blue jays and squirrels, bury nuts and seeds to eat during the winter. Other temperate-forest animals—like **hedgehogs,** groundhogs, and bats— hibernate during the winter.

HIBERNATION is a type of sleeping. While hibernating, the animals live on body fat built up during the summer months. Some insects hibernate, often under the bark of trees.

There is 24-hour daylight during the summer in the tundra and 24-hour darkness during the winter.

TUNDRA

It is very cold year-round in the tundra biome. The Arctic tundra region encircles the North Pole. It's an ice-covered ocean surrounded by treeless plains, where moss, lichen, grasses, and low shrubs can be found. There is hardly any precipitation—rain or snow—in the tundra. Underneath a rocky layer of topsoil is a layer of permafrost, which is permanently frozen soil that never gets soft or warm enough to cultivate plant life.

Animals have made remarkable adaptations to living in such harsh habitats. Some animals migrate to these regions only during the summer. But others, like whales, seals, and polar bears, stay even in the winter. They have an extra layer of fat—called blubber—under their skin that keeps them warm. Blubber can also be used as a source of energy when food supplies get low. Other tundra animals include **foxes,** wolves, falcons, ravens, and salmon.

During the short, cool tundra summers, some flowering plants flourish.

GRASSLAND

In this biome, grasses are the main type of plant. These areas are too dry for most trees and shrubs, but too moist to become a desert. Examples of grassland habitats include the prairies of North America, the steppes of central Asia, and the savannas of South America and tropical Africa.

Because these habitats offer animals few places to hide, many species— like **zebras** and **wildebeests** in Africa—live in large herds to protect themselves from predators. A lack of hiding places also means that the predators— animals like cheetahs— have to rely on speed rather than on stalking to catch their prey. Some other grassland animals are prairie dogs, lions, giraffes, buffalo, eagles, sheep, horses, meerkats, and coyotes.

Guess what? In Argentina, the grasslands are known as pampas.

125

Salty, Frozen, or Fresh!

There's a lot of water on Earth—about 326 million cubic miles (1.4 billion cubic km) of it. (There are more than a million gallons/3.8 million liters of water in a cubic mile.)

But you can't drink most of it. The oceans cover about 70% of the Earth's surface and have 97% of the water, and ocean water is salty. The 3% that's left is freshwater, but about 2% is frozen in the polar ice caps and other glaciers. That leaves only about 1% of all the Earth's water that is fresh and not frozen. Most of this water is underground, but some is in lakes, rivers, springs, pools, and ponds.

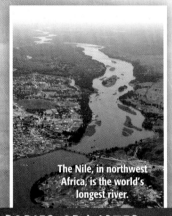
The Nile, in northwest Africa, is the world's longest river.

Guess what? The Great Lakes hold 22% of the world's freshwater.

BODIES OF WATER

One enormous body of water covers the planet. You can sail in a boat and reach every ocean without ever taking the boat out of the water. But it is generally recognized that there are five oceans: Pacific, Atlantic, Indian, Southern, and Arctic. The Pacific is the biggest and covers about ⅓ of the Earth's surface. The Arctic is the smallest and is frozen all the time, except at its edges.

A **SEA** is a branch of one of the five oceans. A sea is partially enclosed by land. For example, the Indian Ocean is divided in two by the country of India, forming the Arabian Sea on one side and the Bay of Bengal on the other.

A **LAKE** is a body of water that is completely surrounded by land. Some lakes have the word *sea* in their names, but they're really lakes. A lake filled with salt water is usually called a *sea*. The Dead Sea is one example.

A **POND** is a very small lake that is not moving and is shallow enough to support plants with roots.

A **RIVER** is a channel of moving water, traveling from a higher altitude to a lower altitude, propelled by gravity. A small, narrow river is a **STREAM**. Rivers usually end in oceans, but streams may end in a lake.

India

Arabian Sea

Bay of Bengal

Indian Ocean

WATER'S JOURNEY

Water circulates slowly through all the oceans. Heavy, cold water sinks into the northern part of the Atlantic Ocean and flows south to Antarctica. Then it flows east and north, through the Indian and Pacific Oceans, then back into the Atlantic. It takes seawater about 1,000 years to complete this trip around the world.

The Water Cycle

Water is constantly on the move as part of the water cycle. It is unique in that it can change state and exist as a solid (ice), liquid (water), or gas (water vapor). These changes occur when heat is added or taken away. Here's how the water cycle works.

TRANSPIRATION At one time or another, all the water on Earth enters the air as water vapor. About 85% of the vapor in the air comes from the oceans evaporating. But plants also add moisture to the air. Plants take liquid water in through their roots and pass water vapor out through their leaves in a process called transpiration. A birch tree gives off about 70 gallons (265 liters) of water a day. Corn gives off about 4,000 gallons per acre (37,416 liters per hectare) a day.

EVAPORATION
When the sun beats down on the water in rivers, lakes, and oceans, some of that water absorbs heat and changes into a gas called water vapor, which rises into the air.

COLLECTION
When water falls back to the surface of the Earth, it is collected in oceans, streams, ponds, and other bodies of water. Some of it soaks into the ground, where it is used by plants and animals. Eventually, it evaporates or transpires and continues as part of the water cycle.

CONDENSATION
When water vapor cools down, it returns to a liquid state, forming clouds in the sky.

guess what?
Water is the only common substance that exists as a solid, liquid, and gas in Earth's atmosphere.

PRECIPITATION
When enough water vapor has condensed, the water droplets become too heavy to float in the clouds. Water falls back to the ground as rain, sleet, snow, or hail.

The highest ocean mountain is Mauna Kea, which is in the ocean near Hawaii. It rises 33,474 feet (10,203 m) from its base on the ocean floor, but only 13,680 feet (4,170 m) of it are above sea level.

OCEAN MOUNTAINS

The ocean floor is as varied as the surface of the Earth. It has mountains twice as tall as Mount Everest and canyons six times as deep as the Grand Canyon. It has volcanoes and earthquakes too. The underwater mountains form a great mountain range, almost 40,000 miles (64,374 km) long, that weaves its way through all the major oceans.

In some places in Kazakhstan and Uzbekistan, old, rusting ships sit on dry ground that was once part of the Aral Sea.

SAVING A SEA

The Aral Sea in central Asia used to be one of the four largest lakes in the world, with an area of about 26,000 square miles (67,340 sq km). But it has been steadily shrinking since the 1960s, after the rivers that fed it were rerouted by irrigation projects. By 2007, it had declined to 10% of its original size. It split into two large lakes and two smaller ones. By 2009, two of these lakes were almost gone, and scientists now expect them to dry up completely.

In 2005, the government of Kazakhstan began work to restore what was left of the two northern lakes, together known as the North Aral Sea. Water levels have slowly begun to rise and fish are returning.

Guess what?
In the past few decades, the Aral Sea's volume has decreased by 85%.

Dry, cracked earth remains in places that used to be deep under the Aral Sea.

Glaciers are huge sheets or rivers of ice that flow slowly over the Earth.

MELTING GLACIERS

Glaciers begin as packed snow that has built up over many years. The weight of the snow eventually compresses the lower layers into ice, and gravity makes the ice flow downhill. Glaciers range in thickness from several feet or meters to 10,000 feet (3,048 meters) or more. Found in the colder regions near the North and South Poles and in mountains, glaciers scrape the ground as they move over it, changing the landscape.

As the climate warms, the ice in glaciers melts. Scientists are studying glaciers to find out how much is melting and how fast. This is important because all that melting water will eventually raise the levels of the oceans. The first major satellite study of the world's melting glaciers and ice caps was completed in February 2012 by a team at the University of Colorado at Boulder. The researchers examined measurements taken by two satellites, and found that glaciers and ice caps shed about 148 billion tons (134 billion metric tons) of ice per year from 2003 to 2010. Ice sheets on Greenland and Antarctica lost an additional 80 billion tons (73 metric tons) of ice.

Russian scientists at the Vostok station pose for a photo.

05.02.12
ст.ВОСТОК скв.5Г2
гл 3769,3м ОЗЕРО

FROM TIME FOR KIDS

An Antarctic Discovery

By Joe Levit

After two decades of start-and-stop drilling, Russian researchers in Antarctica have finally reached Lake Vostok, which has been completely covered by ice for millions of years. The lake is buried beneath ice that is 2 miles (3.22 km) thick. Its freshwater has remained untouched for the last 20 million years. At 160 miles (257 km) long and 30 miles (48 km) wide, it is similar in size to Lake Ontario in North America.

American and British teams are drilling to reach other Antarctic lakes under the ice. But according to Robin Bell, a Columbia University scientist who studies glaciers, those other lakes are smaller and younger. Bell says the age and size of Lake Vostok make it a big scientific prize. "It's like exploring another planet, except this one is ours," she said.

Scientists around the world are eager to see what the Russians find at Lake Vostok once they study water samples. Researchers want to find out what—if any—life exists in that cold and dark place. It's possible that bacteria too tiny to see might live and even thrive there. That might not seem like much, but Lake Vostok's life dates back millions of years.

"The more we learn about life, the more we learn about its ability to grow and survive and [do well] in environments that we formerly thought were too inhospitable," said David Morrison, a senior scientist at NASA's Astrobiology Institute.

Analysis of Lake Vostok will provide more information about the history of Antarctica, which many believe was part of a larger continent in Earth's distant history.

Other people think what we learn about the lake will improve our knowledge of Earth's climate and help us to predict changes to it. Mahlon Kennicutt II, a Texas A&M University professor of oceanography, believes this is very important. "A view of the past gives us a window on our planet's future," he said.

How's the Weather Where You Live?

Weather takes place in the atmosphere, the layer of air that surrounds the Earth. Weather is the state of the atmosphere at some particular place and time. When we talk about the weather, we might be talking about the temperature, whether the sky is clear or cloudy, how hard the wind is blowing, or whether it is raining or snowing.

Weather changes from day to day, and sometimes even from minute to minute. **Climate** is the weather of a specific region averaged over time. For example, a climate might be hot and dry, or cold and dry, or hot and rainy. Climates do change, but those changes usually happen over many years.

WHERE DOES WIND COME FROM?

Winds are caused by the sun's heat falling on different parts of Earth at different times of the day and year. The temperatures over water and land change at different rates during the day and night. In addition, warm air rises and cool air sinks. These fluctuations cause the movement of air in different patterns, called winds.

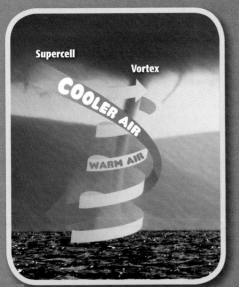

Supercell

Vortex

COOLER AIR

WARM AIR

HOW A TORNADO FORMS

Tornadoes usually form during giant thunderstorms called supercells. Winds close to the ground are weaker than winds higher up. When the two winds push on the layer of air between them, the layer rotates, or spins. It forms a horizontal tube. Rising warm air lifts the tube until it is vertical. Cooler air drops down, pulling the tube to the ground. A tornado is formed. Many are black or brown from the dust and dirt they suck up through the vortex, or center.

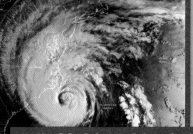

<< Satellite view of a hurricane

5 HURRICANE CATEGORIES

The Saffir-Simpson scale predicts hurricane damage by wind speed. The higher up the scale a hurricane ranks, the more damage it can do to houses and other structures in its path.

	WIND SPEEDS
CATEGORY 1	74 to 95 miles (119 to 153 km) per hour
CATEGORY 2	96 to 110 miles (154 to 177 km) per hour
CATEGORY 3	111 to 130 miles (179 to 209 km) per hour
CATEGORY 4	131 to 155 miles (211 to 249 km) per hour
CATEGORY 5	More than 155 miles (249 km) per hour

HOT IN THE CITY, COOL BY THE WATER

The air temperature of a location is affected by:

• Heat given off by the ground and rising into the air. This is why the weather in a city is often warmer than in the surrounding suburbs. Buildings and paved surfaces soak up the heat, which can raise the temperature by as much as 10°F (12°C).

• How close the area is to a body of water. Water does not absorb heat the way the ground or the pavement does, so it remains cooler. Cool water-surface temperatures result in cooler air temperatures and cooler winds above and near the water.

• The effect of warm and cold fronts as they pass through an area. (See the box on the left.)

Warm Fronts and Cold Fronts

Weather forecasters talk about fronts all the time—warm fronts, cold fronts, high fronts, low fronts. But what exactly is a front? A front is the boundary between two masses of air with different temperatures, wind speeds, and amounts of moisture. In a cold front, cooler air is advancing and pushing warm air ahead of it. In a warm front, warm air pushes into the cold air in front of it. Cold air is heavier than warm air. When a front is warm, the warmer air generally rises above the cool air. As the warm air is pushed upward, it cools quickly. If there is moisture in the air, it will probably rain.

Fronts can move quickly or slowly, depending on the difference in temperature between them. Sometimes, fronts take a long time to move. These are called stationary fronts.

COLD FRONT

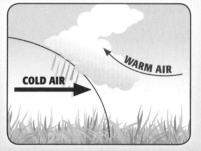

WARM FRONT

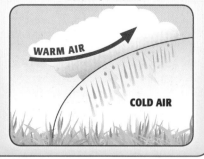

MONITORING AND MEASURING THE WEATHER

Meteorologists have many ways to monitor weather conditions, including land-based observation stations, radar systems, weather balloons, airplanes, ships, and satellites. Because no single country can constantly measure and report on conditions in every part of the atmosphere, nations cooperate to monitor the weather effectively.

THERMOMETERS measure **temperature.** The most common thermometers may contain a column of alcohol or mercury that expands in the presence of heat, or they may be digital and use liquid crystals or electricity. When it comes to weather, **air temperature** is important.

BAROMETERS measure **air pressure,** or barometric pressure, the force exerted by the weight of air molecules, which are tiny, invisible particles in the air. Clear weather is caused by high pressure; storms are caused by low pressure. Air pressure tends to decrease the higher up you go.

SATELLITES high above Earth can be used to measure the temperature and currents of the oceans, follow the progress of tropical storms and hurricanes, spot dust storms and sandstorms, and see changes in snow and ice coverings.

RADARS are instruments that determine the distance of objects and the direction in which they are moving. These can be used to track rain and snowfall.

ANEMOMETERS measure **wind speed.** Most anemometers have three cups extending from a central point. The speed of the wind is measured by how fast the cups spin.

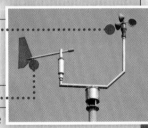

WIND VANES tell the direction of the wind.

HYGROMETERS and **sling psychrometers** measure humidity, or the amount of water vapor in the air.

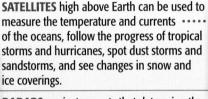

SCIENTIFIC BALLOONS

Weather balloons carry instruments and sensors that help meteorologists learn about humidity, air pressure, wind speed and direction, and temperature. They can rise nearly 20 miles (32 km) above the ground and drift more than 125 miles (201 km) before popping in the atmosphere. After the balloons burst, a small parachute opens and the instruments can float back to the ground. If you ever find one, go online to find out how to return it to the National Weather Service.

Guess What?
Human hair absorbs moisture from the air around it. In fact, it becomes longer when humidity increases. That's why some people's hair gets frizzy on humid days. Their hair gets longer and that extra length causes it to bunch up.

Predicting the Weather

Weather predictions are based on observations of current weather conditions and an understanding of how weather systems develop. After meteorologists have gathered weather data from around the world, they analyze it to make predictions, or educated guesses, about the development and movement of future weather systems. To forecast the weather, they use weather maps and mathematical models.

A mathematical model of the atmosphere is a set of equations that act just like the atmospheric processes that drive the development and movement of weather systems. A mathematical model begins with the most recent weather observations. The model uses the data to predict the state of the atmosphere for a specific time interval—for example, the next 10 minutes. Using this predicted state as a new starting point, the model then forecasts the state of the atmosphere for another 10 minutes. This process repeats over and over, until the model produces short-range weather forecasts for the next 12, 24, 36, and 48 hours.

⌃ Weather forecasts for the next 12 to 24 hours are correct more than 80% of the time. Forecasts for the next week or month are a lot less accurate.

⌃ A meteorologist points to the visual representation of hurricane weather patterns on his computer.

FAHRENHEIT OR CELSIUS?

Temperature is measured in degrees Fahrenheit (°F) or degrees Celsius (°C). These scales are different. Water boils at 212°F and 100°C. Water freezes at 32°F and 0°C. You can convert one temperature to the other with these formulas:

$°C = (°F-32) \times (5/9)$

$°F = (°C \times 9/5) + 32$

MAP IT!

Weather maps show the state of the atmosphere at a particular time. By examining a sequence of weather maps, forecasters can determine how the weather changes through time and then make predictions about the future.

DOPPLER RADAR AND THE WEATHER

The Doppler effect is the change in frequency of waves that occurs whenever the source of the waves moves relative to their observer. For example, the pitch (frequency of sound waves) of a fire truck's siren seems higher as the truck approaches you and lower as it moves away. As raindrops, snowflakes, or dust particles move through the atmosphere, the radar signals they reflect also change in frequency. A Doppler radar monitors these frequency changes and uses them to calculate the speed at which drops, flakes, or particles are advancing or moving away.

Doppler radar

General Sherman

The Plant Kingdom

There were plants on Earth long before there were animals, and animals could not live without **plants.** Plants are found on land, in oceans, and in freshwater, and currently there are about 260,000 different species of them.

To study plants in a systematic way, biologists have broken down the plant kingdom into smaller divisions, based on several characteristics. They look at whether a plant can circulate fluids (such as water) through its body or needs to absorb it from the surroundings. They also use a plant's size and height, and how it reproduces (by spores or seeds or by sending off shoots or dividing itself) as a way to classify it.

The majority of the plant species (about 230,000) are flowering plants. Most trees, shrubs, vines, flowers, fruits, vegetables, and legumes fall into this group, called angiosperms. They grow their seeds inside an ovary, which is embedded in a flower or fruit.

guess what?
The world's biggest tree is General Sherman, a giant sequoia that's 275 feet (83.8 m) tall and 102.6 feet (31.3 m) around at the base. The tree is in the Giant Forest of Sequoia National Park in the United States, east of Visalia, California. The tree is believed to be between 2,300 and 2,700 years old.

Milkweed seeds

SPREADING SEEDS FAR AND WIDE

Many of the fruits that contain seeds, such as apples, grapes, and strawberries, are things humans eat all the time. Even though we call them vegetables, cucumbers, eggplants, and pumpkins are the fruits of the plants they come from. Other fruits are not eaten by people. An acorn is the fruit of an oak tree, and cones are the fruit of pine and spruce trees.

If an acorn or a pinecone fell directly under its own tree, it would probably not grow into a new tree, because it would not get enough sunlight to grow. For this reason, many fruits are designed to travel away from their original source, where there might be less competition for water, soil, and sunshine. Tasty fruits will be eaten by animals who later deposit the seeds elsewhere, in their droppings. Samaras, the fruit of the maple tree, float on the wind like little helicopter propellers. Chestnut trees, cockleburs, and burdock plants produce burrs that stick to animals' fur and people's clothing and are carried away. When milkweed seeds are ready to grow, milkweed pods burst open. The seeds inside the pod are attached to a silky material, which is carried away in the wind.

Samaras

IT'S EASY BEING GREEN

Chlorophyll gives plants and leaves their green color. During the spring and summer, the leaves on many deciduous trees have lots of chlorophyll (*klor*-o-fill) and are green. In the fall, the leaves are exposed to less sunlight and the chlorophyll absorbs less light energy. The chlorophyll begins to break down, and the leaves lose their green color. The fall colors we see were in the leaves all along but were covered up by the chlorophyll.

When an animal eats a plant, the animal's digestive system breaks down the glucose (which is stored as starch) in the plant to release the stored energy. The animal's body then uses that energy to move, grow, and stay alive.

TURNING SUNLIGHT INTO ENERGY

Plants cannot live and grow without photosynthesis. Photosynthesis is the process plants use to make food. Plants need three ingredients for photosynthesis: carbon dioxide, water, and light.

THE STEPS OF PHOTOSYNTHESIS

Carbon dioxide (CO_2) from the air enters plants through stomata, which are holes in the leaves of plants. Water (H_2O) from the soil enters plants through roots.

Light from the sun (or from special lamps) shines on leaves, which contain structures called chloroplasts (*klor*-o-plasts). Chloroplasts contain a green pigment, chlorophyll, that absorbs light energy.

The plant uses the light energy to split molecules of water into hydrogen and oxygen.

The plant gives off oxygen through its leaves as a waste gas. Most of the oxygen we breathe is released as waste by plants and algae during photosynthesis.

The hydrogen released during photosynthesis bonds with substances in the chloroplasts. This creates energy the plant can use to continue the process when there is no light.

The plant combines carbon from the carbon dioxide in the air and hydrogen from the water to produce glucose. Plants use some glucose for energy. They store extra glucose as starch.

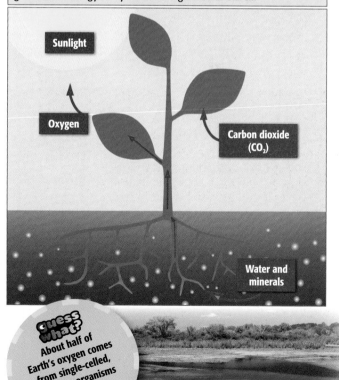

Sunlight

Oxygen

Carbon dioxide (CO_2)

Water and minerals

Guess what? About half of Earth's oxygen comes from single-celled, plantlike organisms called algae.

135

Deciduous tree in winter

Evergreen trees in winter

≈ Pine needles

Guess what? The world's oldest recorded living tree is a 9,550-year-old spruce in the Dalarna province of Sweden.

To Shed or Not to Shed?

Some trees are **deciduous,** which means they shed their leaves every year (the word *deciduous* means "fall off"). Some trees are **evergreens** and never drop their leaves. In the spring, deciduous trees grow thin, broad leaves that capture the sunlight needed for photosynthesis. (See page 135.)

But if the trees kept their leaves all winter, the water in them would freeze, damaging the leaves. So deciduous trees and plants shut down all photosynthesis in the autumn and lose their leaves. They seal the spots where the leaves were attached with a protective covering called a leaf scar. They also make a concentrated sugar solution, called sap, to keep water from freezing in their stems.

Evergreen trees have needles, which are actually tightly rolled leaves with a waxy coating. The waxy coating holds in moisture and helps protect the needles from freezing. The needles stay on all winter (although evergreens do grow some new needles every year). Deciduous trees have to spend the spring growing new leaves, but evergreens can resume photosynthesis as soon as temperatures start to get warm.

)) Leaf scar ····

PLANT CELLS

Most of a plant cell is water. A lot of that water is in the cell's central vacuole (a space with fluid inside). Cytosol, the liquid around the structures in the cell, is also mostly water. Water moves in and out of cells through tiny openings in the cell membrane. The cell wall surrounds the cell membrane. It forms a protective barrier.

Plant cells collect water in their central vacuoles. Full vacuoles press out against the cell wall. This makes the cell rigid, which helps the plant stand upright and keep its structure.

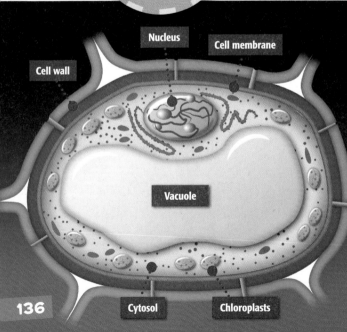

Nucleus

Cell membrane

Cell wall

Vacuole

Cytosol

Chloroplasts

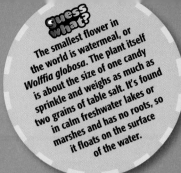

Plants That Are Not Vegetarians

Most plants get nutrients from the soil in which they grow. But some plants grow in such nutrient-poor environments that they have become predators to survive. These plants are meat eaters, and they use clever devices to trap and eat insects. Some have hollow areas that insects fall into. Some have sticky patches to trap their prey. Others knock or suck insects into a pool of digestive fluids.

SUNDEWS get their name because they have tiny drops of sticky fluid on their leaves that look like dew. When an insect goes to drink the dew, it gets caught by the plant's tentacles, which release enzymes that digest the insect's body. It takes about two days for a sundew to digest an insect meal.

Rootless **BLADDERWORTS** are found mostly in the water. They have small hollow spaces, or bladders, beneath the surface of the water, that work like vacuums to suck in and trap tiny animals. The bladderwort then secretes enzymes from special glands that break down the insects and uses them for food. Bladderworts usually live at the bottom of the shallow part of lakes, but they float to the top when it is time to flower.

PITCHER PLANTS are shaped like tall cups, or pitchers. Digestive enzymes in the bottom of the "pitcher" release a sweet nectar that attracts insects. Once the insects go into the pitcher, they are unable to climb up the slippery sides of the plant to get out. Some pitcher plants also have pointy hairs that face downward and make it even harder for the insects to escape.

When an insect brushes against one of the hairs on a **VENUS FLYTRAP** leaf, the hair sends out a small electrical charge. If the insect brushes against more hairs, the charges build up until the leaf is triggered to close, trapping the animal inside. If the leaves were to shut after only one electrical charge, then wind or raindrops would set off the snap trap.

137

The Changing Food Scene

At one time, food moved directly from farms to consumers. Today, many foods move from farms to food processors and then to consumers. Other changes have also occurred in food supplies. Medical scientists worry about the effects of food additives on people's health. Environmental scientists worry about the pollution caused by shipping food over great distances. Many people worry about the effects of genetically modified (GM) foods and try to eat organic foods instead. What does this mean for you?

≋ The USDA Organic seal from the U.S. Department of Agriculture certifies that a product is at least 95% organic.

NOTHING ADDED

Organic foods are produced as they were in the "old days." These foods are grown without the use of synthetic pesticides and fertilizers. They are processed without using radiation to kill germs and without adding chemicals, synthetic food coloring, or other food additives.

USED BY CONVENTIONAL FOOD PRODUCERS	USED BY ORGANIC FOOD PRODUCERS
Chemical fertilizers, which are chemicals added to soil to make plants grow bigger and faster	Natural fertilizers, such as manure or compost
Chemical insecticides, which kill insects	Insects, birds, and other natural methods to limit pests
Chemical weed killers	Hand weeding, crop rotation, and other natural methods to limit weeds
Growth hormones, antibiotics, and other medications to prevent disease and increase growth in farm animals	Organic feed, no medication

Chemical weed killers come in the form of sprays or powders. Some are mixed in with fertilizers.

WHO EATS WHAT?

A **LOCAVORE** eats food that has been produced locally, usually within an area of 100 miles (161 km).

A **VEGAN** eats a plant-based diet that does not include any animal products.

A **LACTO-VEGETARIAN** eats mainly plants but also dairy products.

An **OVO-VEGETARIAN** eats mainly plants but also eggs.

An **OMNIVORE** eats a diet that includes both plant and animal products.

A scientist examines hybrid potato plants.

GM foods are genetically modified. That is, they have been changed in some way that does not occur naturally. Specific genes have been introduced into the genetic makeup of the plant or animal. For example, a gene that protects against weed-killing chemicals has been added to soybeans. This makes the soybean plants resistant to the weed killers. Soybean genes also have been changed to increase the amount of oil the plants produce. GM foods promise to meet the food needs of the growing world population. But there are critics, who worry about the effects of these foods on people and the environment.

MESSING WITH MOTHER NATURE

Many farmers manipulate plants through a process called **hybridization.** A hybrid is a cross between two different plant varieties. It is made by taking the pollen from one plant and using it to fertilize another plant. The resulting seed is planted and a hybrid grows.

The idea is to end up with a plant that has the best of both varieties. Hybrids might be developed to have more fruit, better color, a sweeter flavor, bigger flowers, a nicer scent, or stronger resistance to a certain plant disease. Most plants we buy today are hybrids. Hybrids are not the same thing as GM plants, which have been altered at the molecular level using techniques such as gene cloning and protein engineering.

In an example of genetic engineering, an antifreeze gene from cold-water fish has been introduced into potato plants. These plants can survive in cold temperatures that normally kill young potato plants.

BRINGING AN ANCIENT PLANT BACK TO LIFE

In 2012, Russian scientists grew a living plant from a piece of the fruit of the narrow-leafed campion, a small, white Arctic flower. What makes that so amazing is that the fruit was 32,000 years old. It was stored by an Arctic ground squirrel in its burrow in the tundra of northeastern Siberia and lay frozen until scientists dug it up. At the time the fruit was buried, woolly mammoths and woolly rhinoceroses roamed the area.

A Russian scientist examines a specimen of the ancient plant.

◀ The world's oldest regenerated plant

THE FOUR SPHERES OF EARTH

The part of Earth that houses living organisms is called the biosphere. The layer of air and gases surrounding the planet is called the atmosphere. The hydrosphere includes all of the parts of the planet made up of water or water vapor, and the lithosphere is the rocky crust of the Earth. It includes the ground we walk on, the tallest mountains, and the deepest seafloors in the ocean.

Guess what?

Venus is an example of a planet where the greenhouse effect has gone to extremes. Scientists believe Venus probably once had large amounts of water like Earth, but it all boiled away.

The Greenhouse Effect

Burning fossil fuels creates the energy that can be used to power manufacturing plants, enable you to ride in a car, and keep the lights on in your home. (A fossil fuel is a natural fuel, such as coal or oil, that formed from the remains of living organisms.) Burning these fuels releases carbon dioxide (CO_2) and other gases into Earth's atmosphere, which is made up of layers of gases that surround the planet and protect it from extreme heat and cold.

When sunlight strikes Earth's surface, some of its heat is reflected back toward space. Gases such as CO_2 and methane trap the heat of the sun in the atmosphere, just like the walls of a greenhouse trap heat and moisture inside. In this way, gases like CO_2 and methane help keep the temperature of the planet warm enough for living things. But scientists believe that humans are producing far more CO_2 and methane than the atmosphere needs. As a result, the world is getting warmer.

Greenhouses are covered with glass or plastic, which lets sunlight in, but also traps some of the heat inside, keeping the air warm for the plants and crops inside.

ENERGY FROM THE SUN

Clouds and atmosphere absorb some sunlight.

Clouds scatter and reflect sunlight.

A small of amount of sunlight is reflected by Earth's surface.

About half of the sunlight that reaches Earth is absorbed.

CLIMATE CHANGE

Earth has gotten more than 1°F (0.6°C) warmer over the past century. That may not seem like a big difference, but even the difference of a single degree can have a devastating effect on the planet. Parts of the Arctic have warmed by 5°F (3°C) since 1950. The physical effects of climate change are visible in the Arctic.

The surface waters of Earth's oceans are getting warmer. Hurricanes, which feed on warm water, are getting stronger and more numerous.

Glaciers are melting, causing sea levels to rise. This destroys the habitat for polar bears and other animals.

Less freshwater is available as bodies of water dry out. This means humans and animals are competing for water, and there is less water available for agriculture and industry as well.

Tropical diseases are spreading into temperate regions that are becoming warmer.

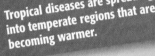

Melting inland glaciers cause an increase in flash floods, mudslides, and river flooding.

Warmer air causes wind patterns to shift, leading to climate changes around the world. Some areas are experiencing longer droughts, while others are getting too much rain and flooding. This results in a loss of crops and wildlife.

Tropical forests are drying out and changing into grasslands. This causes a loss of biological diversity and the extinction of many species.

REFLECTING SUNLIGHT

Snowy, polar regions reflect a lot of sunlight back into the atmosphere. As a result, the temperature of these snowy areas does not rise greatly. Deserts absorb a lot of the heat from sunlight and the surface temperature rises. Grasslands, forests, oceans, and cities all absorb and reflect different amounts of sunlight and heat. Clouds play a role too. Clouds reflect a large amount of sunlight back into space, preventing it from ever hitting Earth's surface. Some of the sunlight that is reflected by Earth's surface hits clouds and bounces back down to the ground.

How Cities Affect the Environment

Smog in Santiago, Chile, makes it difficult to see the mountains that overlook the city.

Cities are drier and warmer than the countryside that surrounds them. They are drier because they have storm sewers that quickly carry off rainwater and melted snow. Streams and lakes within city limits are often drained or diverted. The brick, asphalt, and concrete surfaces of buildings, sidewalks, and streets absorb more heat from the sun than a natural landscape does, and then radiate it into the air, which makes air temperature rise. Cities also generate heat from cars and trucks, heating and air-conditioning systems, and smokestacks.

The weather downwind from cities tends to be cloudier and rainier than it is upwind from them. That's because smokestacks and car tailpipes give off water vapor and tiny particles that stimulate cloud formation. The emissions from factories and cars are also the source of smog. Smog forms when sunlight causes a chemical reaction with pollutants in the air. The resulting haze of pollution travels with the wind and can affect areas outside the city.

Cars and trucks give off emissions that pollute the environment.

Guess What?
People in the United States use more than 800 million gallons (3 billion liters) of oil every day. Worldwide, more than 3.5 billion gallons (13.2 billion liters) are used each day.

Guess What?
Every gallon of gasoline burned by a typical car releases about 20 pounds (9 kg) of carbon dioxide into the atmosphere. Hybrid car engines cut carbon dioxide emissions in half.

DAMAGING RAIN

Acid rain occurs when chemicals in the atmosphere react with water molecules to produce acids. Volcanoes and lightning strikes are natural sources of acid rain. But the main cause is sulfur and nitrogen compounds from human sources, such as electricity generation, factories, and cars. Acid rain damages everything it falls on, including buildings, forests, soil, and water. Stricter controls on emissions from power plants, factories, and cars help reduce the amount of pollution in the air that causes acid rain.

The World's Worst Oil Spills

An explosion on the Deepwater Horizon oil drilling rig in the Gulf of Mexico in April 2010 killed 11 people and caused the biggest accidental marine oil spill in history. BP, which owned the rig, was unable to cap the oil well until July, and oil gushed from the broken well for more than 85 days. An estimated 206 million gallons (780 million liters) of oil spilled into the Gulf, killing thousands of birds, fish, and other wildlife and damaging the ecosystem. Scientists continue to study the area to determine the long-term effects of such a disastrous oil spill.

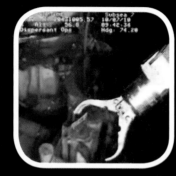

≈ Robot submarines were used to try to shut off the flow of oil after the Deepwater Horizon explosion.

The Deepwater Horizon disaster was an accident, but the largest spill ever was not. In January 1991, Iraqi soldiers tried to prevent American forces from landing in the Persian Gulf by deliberately opening up the valves at an offshore oil terminal. They ended up spilling between 380 and 520 million gallons (1.4 billion to 2 billion liters) of oil into the Gulf, creating an oil slick 4 inches (10 cm) deep that spread out 4,000 square miles (10,360 sq km).

OIL EATERS

Scientists have developed special chemicals called dispersants to aid in the cleanup of oil spills. Dispersants break up big globs of oil into smaller droplets. While some of these chemicals may harm ecosystems, the smaller bits of oil don't coat plants and wildlife the way larger oil slicks can. And the main reason for using dispersants? The smaller oil droplets are easier for oil-eating microbes to consume! In fact, scientists released a lot of tiny, genetically enhanced bacteria into the Gulf of Mexico to help gobble up oil after the 2010 spill.

Setting oil on fire is one way to keep it from spreading, but it pollutes the air.

CHEMICALS GONE WRONG

Chemical contamination of the Earth comes in different forms. The most common are agricultural pesticides (used to kill insects), herbicides (which kill weeds), and fertilizers (used to enrich the soil). There are also chemical waste products from factories, especially those that work with metals and plastics. In large amounts, these contaminants can harm people and wildlife. But even in smaller amounts, they can damage the environment.

Globs of oil wash up on a beach in the Gulf of Mexico.

Guess What?
After an oil spill, cleanup agencies and oceanographers use computer programs to predict the direction and speed of the oil's movement, based on tides, currents, and other information about the water.

DAMAGED LAND

NOW YOU SEE IT, NOW YOU DON'T

Erosion is the process by which rocks and dirt are removed from the ground surface and transported to another location. It is a natural process caused by wind, water, ice, and even the force of gravity. The ocean waves beat at the cliffs on the shore and eventually large chunks fall off, or the wind scours an open plain and carries the soil away with it.

A certain amount of erosion is natural and, in fact, healthy for an ecosystem. Excessive erosion causes serious problems, though, such as depleting soil that could be used for growing crops and clogging up waterways with sediment.

The way people use land affects how quickly it erodes. Land that is used for industrial agriculture, for example, erodes at a greater rate than land that is farmed less intensely or that is left wild. Roads are especially likely to cause increased erosion, because, in addition to removing ground cover, they can significantly change water-drainage patterns. However, improved land-use practices, planting trees around fields and roads, and not turning up the soil can limit erosion.

Waves crash against rocks with incredible force. Over time, rocky cliffs can be worn down or even broken apart by water erosion.

In the 1930s, wind erosion turned the Great Plains into a dusty area called the Dust Bowl.

FARMING FIXES

Since the agricultural disaster of the Dust Bowl in the 1930s, farmers have changed how and what they plant in certain areas. They've developed strategies such as strip cropping, contour farming, and terrace farming to help prevent soil erosion. In strip cropping, farmers alternate crops that closely cover the ground with crops that leave more soil exposed. This way, wind and rain do not move away as much soil as they would if the crops that left a lot of ground exposed were planted all together. With contour farming, crops are not planted in straight lines along a slope. Instead, the crops are planted in rows that wrap around slopes. This keeps water from flowing directly down a slope and carrying soil away. In terrace farming, tiers of retaining walls help hold soil in place. Agricultural and earth scientists continue to study erosion and develop new techniques to prevent the earth from eroding from certain areas.

CAN EROSION BUILD THINGS UP?

The rock and soil that erode always end up somewhere. So erosion in one area can actually build up another area. River deltas are one example. A delta is land that is formed where a river flows into an ocean or lake. The river carries sediment eroded from its banks and deposits it at the mouth of the river, forming wetlands and swamps.

Guess what?
The Grand Canyon was formed by erosion that took place over several million years.

DUST STORMS

Dust storms or sandstorms arise in dry regions when strong winds blow up loose sand and dirt from the ground. A sandstorm can pick up a lot of sand and unexpectedly dump it somewhere else. Dust storms, especially, can carry large amounts of dust. The leading edge of a storm may be a solid wall of dust almost a mile (1.6 km) high.

The Sahara desert and dry lands around the Arabian Peninsula are the main sources of airborne dust. Poor management of dry areas is increasing the number of dust storms, especially around the fringes of deserts.

CREEPING DESERTS

Desertification happens when land that is already dry changes into desert. Dry ecosystems are very fragile, and any extra pressure put on them—for example, from more people moving into an area, the removal of trees, or too many animals grazing—can cause them to rapidly become deserts. Dust storms are one result of overly dry land.

The most common cause of desertification is the overcultivation of dry lands, which means that people farm more intensely than an area of land can sustain. Overcultivation causes the nutrients in the soil to be depleted faster than they are restored, turning the soil into dust. Climate change is also contributing to a speedup in desertification.

Plants and trees help hold water in dry lands and prevent desertification. Their root systems also help hold the soil in place to prevent dust storms.

Dust storm

Things That Collapse

A **sinkhole** is a natural depression or hole in the Earth's surface. Sinkholes occur where the rock below the surface is dissolved by groundwater circulating through it. As the rock dissolves, caves develop underground. The land usually stays intact for a while, until the underground space gets too big. Then the land surface suddenly collapses, leaving a sinkhole.

A **blue hole** is a sinkhole with water in it. It might be in a cave or in the ocean. It gets its name from the bright blue color of the water.

Natural bridges and arches are carved by flowing water. When a river forms a loop, almost circling back on itself, a thin rock wall is created between the sections of the river. Water scrapes away at both sides of the thin wall. Eventually, the river breaks through and part of the wall collapses. The river continues to wear down the rock and enlarge the hole. In many places with a natural bridge, the river has long since dried up but the beautiful arches remain.

Blue hole in Mexico

Natural bridge in Israel

A giant sinkhole, 66 feet (20 km) wide and at least 100 feet (30 m) deep, opened up in Guatemala City in 2010.

Natural arch in Utah

Things That Boil

Hot springs are bodies of water that boil and bubble as the result of heat created by underground volcanic activity. They are just one of the neat geothermal features found around the world.

BOILING LAKES usually fill a crater formed by a volcano.

Boiling lake in Dominica

MUD POOLS can form where steam and acidic gas rise to the surface and break down rocks. The rock particles mix with water, forming clay. The clay-rich soil is heated by the escaping steam until it bubbles.

Bubbling mud pool in New Zealand

GEYSERS are a special kind of boiling spring. They occur when underground water cannot easily reach the surface and is forced through a narrow neck or opening from a larger reservoir below. The water pressure builds up, and the superheated mixture of water and steam intermittently erupts, sending a tall column of water and steam into the air.

Geyser in Iceland

Field of fumaroles in Bolivia

FUMAROLES (fyoo-muh-rolz) are steam and gas vents. The water that creates fumaroles is so hot that it turns to steam before it reaches Earth's surface. Fumaroles are common on the sides of active volcanoes as well as in geothermal fields, where temperatures are generally close to the boiling point of water. They give off gases such as hydrogen sulfide.

AMAZING ROCK FORMATIONS

DEVILS TOWER, WYOMING, UNITED STATES
This 60-million-year-old structure is made up of basalt columns formed when a volcanic eruption pushed molten lava upward. It is 867 feet (264 m) tall.

FAIRY CHIMNEYS, CAPPADOCIA, TURKEY
Ten million years ago, volcanoes deposited ash, lava, and basalt across this plateau. Wind and water carved out the lower layers of soft volcanic material, but the harder top layer of basalt remains as a cap on some "chimneys."

GIANT'S CAUSEWAY, COUNTY ANTRIM, NORTHERN IRELAND
These 40,000 interlocking basalt columns were formed in an ancient volcanic eruption 50 to 60 million years ago. The tops of the columns form stepping-stones that go from the foot of the cliff into the sea.

TWELVE APOSTLES, PORT CAMPBELL, AUSTRALIA These 12 islands were formed when the ocean eroded the soft limestone cliffs to form caves. These caves eventually became arches and then finally collapsed into stacks of rock.

STONE FOREST, KUNMING, CHINA This area was the ocean floor 270 million years ago. The water carved the limestone seafloor into channels and pillars.

WHITE DESERT, FARAFRA, EGYPT
The White Desert was once a seabed. Over time, the sediment left behind when the sea dried up turned to chalk. Then sandstorms carved the soft chalk into interesting shapes.

TECHNOLOGY

W here does energy come from? How does electricity work? Can magnets really make trains float? And what can cutting-edge robots do? Read on to learn about technology and engineering, the branches of science concerned with the practical application of scientific knowledge. And find out about cool inventions of the past and neat new devices being developed today.

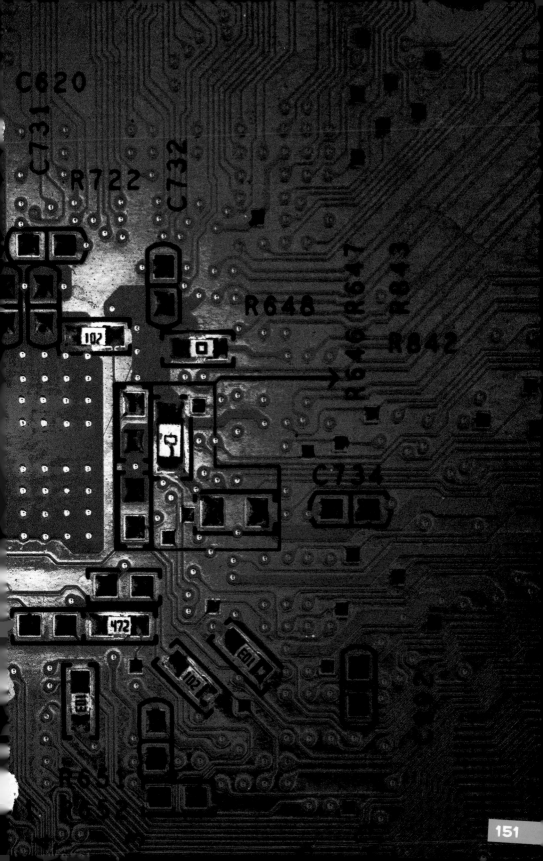

Energy Is Everywhere

Energy can be found in many different forms: in light, heat, motion, and more. There is energy in everything, even in a book sitting on a table. All energy can be lumped into one of two categories: potential energy and kinetic energy.

ENERGY ON THE WAY

POTENTIAL ENERGY is stored energy. Here are some of the many types of potential energy.

- The food we eat has lots of potential energy. As soon as we eat it, it is converted into **chemical energy.** People get the energy they need to run, jump, laugh, and breathe from the chemical energy stored in food.

- Natural gas and coal have lots of potential energy. When we burn them, they are converted to **thermal energy,** or heat.

- There is a great deal of **nuclear energy** stored in the nucleus of an atom. (See page 18.) When atoms are split at a nuclear power plant, huge amounts of energy are released.

- Some potential energy depends on the position of an object. The higher up an object goes, the more potential **gravitational energy** it has. When you let the object go, its potential energy will immediately be converted to kinetic, or motion, energy.

- Like gravitational energy, **mechanical energy** depends on position. If you stretch a rubber band as far as it can go, it has the potential to fly farther than if you'd barely stretched it at all.

≈ When the heavy ball dangling from a crane is pulled back, it has a great deal of potential energy.

TRANSFERRING ENERGY

According to the law of conservation of energy, energy cannot be created or destroyed. Instead, it changes form. When an object is held above the ground, it has potential energy. The second the object starts to fall or roll, potential energy starts to change to kinetic energy. As the object speeds up, its kinetic energy increases and its potential energy decreases. Upon impact, kinetic energy suddenly drops. The energy in the object is converted to other forms of energy, such as heat energy or sound energy. And some of the kinetic energy transfers to other objects in the impact. (See the box below.)

ENERGY ON THE MOVE

KINETIC ENERGY is the energy of motion. Moving people or objects have kinetic energy. Electrical, heat, sound, and light energy are types of kinetic energy.

- The **electrical energy** that flows from power plants, through wires, and into outlets in your home is kinetic energy.

- **Heat** is kinetic energy. Everything on Earth is made up of miniscule particles called atoms and molecules. (See pages 18 and 20.) When something heats up, its atoms and molecules begin to move faster and faster. There is motion there, even if it is microscopic and you can't see it.

- **Sound** travels as vibrations in the air. When a musician plucks the strings of a guitar, the strings vibrate and send vibrations through the air. Your eardrum picks up these vibrations and detects the sounds. Here again, there is motion in the air, even though you cannot see it.

≈ When an archer draws back the arrow on a bow, the arrow has potential energy.

≈ When the archer lets go, the potential energy in the arrow is converted into kinetic energy.

≈ When the arrow hits the target, the kinetic energy is transferred to the target. Some of it is converted to heat energy and sound energy.

Energy from Deep Within the Earth

The world relies heavily on nonrenewable sources of energy, or fossil fuels, including coal, petroleum, and natural gas. These natural resources are extracted from the Earth and converted into electricity, which is used for cooking, refrigeration, lighting and heating homes, charging computers and cell phones, and much more. Unfortunately, fossil fuels exist in limited supply and will eventually be used up entirely.

NONRENEWABLE SOURCES

Digging for coal

Coal

COAL is a hard rock made of carbon. Many millions of years ago, decaying plant matter underwent a change and transformed into coal. Coal is the largest source of fossil fuel in the United States. World coal consumption is increasing, even though coal mining and processing is one of the dirtiest forms of electricity production, causing pollution and sickness. While many scientists are focusing on developing more eco-friendly sources of energy, some scientists are trying to clean up coal production.

Guess What?
Fossil fuels provide about 90% of the energy used around the world.

Oil rigs are used to pump oil up from underwater.

PETROLEUM is found deep in the earth and has to be drilled and piped up to the surface. Like coal, it began as decaying plant and animal remains and was formed from pressure and heat over many millions of years. In its "crude" state, before it is refined, it is known as petroleum. Petroleum can be refined into oil, gasoline, or diesel fuel.

Oil pumps bring oil up to the surface.

Natural gas pipelines

NATURAL GAS was formed in the same way as coal and petroleum, except that it is the odorless by-product of the decaying matter. The colorless, odorless bubbles of gas are trapped underground and can be piped to the surface. Natural gas is used as a source of home heating as well as for grilling and cooking.

Guess what? Natural gas supplies about 23% of U.S. energy. It is found in 33 U.S. states, with the largest amounts coming from Texas, New Mexico, Oklahoma, and Wyoming.

Nuclear power plant

NUCLEAR ENERGY was developed in the 20th century. In nuclear fission, the atoms of an element, most often uranium 235, are hit with atomic particles called neutrons. The uranium atoms are split and give off lots of heat, which is used to boil water. The steam from this water powers electrical generators.

ENVIRONMENTAL IMPACT

Mining, processing, and using fossil fuels creates big environmental problems. When we burn fossil fuels, we produce large amounts of CO_2, or carbon dioxide, causing global climate change. (For more on climate change, see pages 140–141.) With global energy demand expected to grow almost 40% by 2030, scientists and engineers are in a race to find new forms of clean, renewable energy. But fossil fuels aren't going away anytime soon.

EXTRACTING NATURAL GAS

To extract natural gas from deep inside the Earth, some energy companies use a technique called hydraulic fracturing, or fracking, for short. In this process, millions of gallons of freshwater, sand, and chemicals are shot down into the earth at high pressure to break up strong shale rock and force the gas to come up to the surface. The process can supply clean, cheap energy to many homes and businesses. But it can also greatly damage the areas around the fracking sites. The water used in fracking becomes polluted and can contaminate clean water and soil. The chemicals can seep into underground water resources that are often used as drinking water, and the equipment used for fracking pollutes our air.

Many people oppose fracking.

RENEWABLE SOURCES

No single energy source will replace fossil fuels, but in the future, countries and regions will be more energy independent, which means they will produce their power locally and depend less on energy from other countries and regions. Areas with lots of sunshine or wind will be able to produce wind and solar energy. Places with strong rivers may choose to use hydropower.

WATER can produce energy called hydropower.
Water pressure can turn the shafts of powerful electrical generators, making electricity. Waterfalls and fast-running rivers are major sources of hydropower, because their natural flow creates pressure. Another way to harness hydropower is the "storage" method, in which dams are used to trap water in large reservoirs. When power is needed, the dams are opened and the water flows out. The water pressure created is then converted into energy.

Hydroelectric dam

Hydroelectric turbines

Guess what?
About 0.1% of the world's energy comes from solar power, but the industry is expected to grow to 10% in the next 20 to 30 years.

SUNLIGHT can be converted into heat and electricity.
Solar cells absorb the heat from the sun and convert it to energy. Solar power plants collect the sun's heat onto huge solar panels, which then heat water to produce steam. This steam powers an electrical generator. On Earth, cloud cover and the cycle of day and night limit the amount of solar energy that can be collected. But in the future, solar panels orbiting Earth or placed on the moon may harvest solar energy and transmit it back to our planet.

Solar panels

Solar-powered home

Wind farm

WIND farms use huge turbines to transform the power of wind into usable energy. Wind turns a turbine's giant blades, which are connected to a long shaft that moves up and down to power an electrical generator. Wind is an excellent renewable energy source. The industry is growing more than 15% a year, faster than solar power and other natural sources.

Guess What? There are 2,900 wind turbines in Iowa. That's enough to power 1 million homes!

Geothermal power station

GEOTHERMAL energy uses the heat that rises from the Earth's core, located about 4,000 miles (6,400 km) under the planet's surface. The most common way of harnessing geothermal energy involves capturing steam that emerges from deep in the Earth by way of volcanoes, fumaroles (vents in the ground that give off steam), hot springs, and geysers (fountainlike bursts of water). The steam, heat, or hot water can be trapped in pipes that lead directly to electric power plants and even to homes.

HYDROGEN is the most common element in the universe, but it doesn't exist on Earth in its elemental form. Scientists have to produce pure hydrogen from hydrogen compounds, like water (which is made of hydrogen and oxygen), methane (hydrogen and carbon), and ammonia (hydrogen and nitrogen). Up-to-date technology is being used to separate hydrogen molecules and turn the hydrogen gas into a liquid that can be used in fuel cells. Like batteries, fuel cells are energy-conversion devices that convert pure hydrogen into electricity.

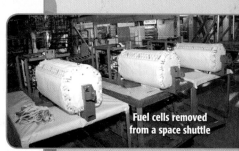

Fuel cells removed from a space shuttle

In the last decade, Honda has come out with automobiles and a scooter that run on fuel cells, and they are in the hands of a few dozen lucky customers. But there are still cost issues and technological problems to solve before they're used by the average driver. Billions of dollars have already been spent in researching hydrogen fuel cells. Why is it worth it? Because fuel cells give off no pollution and could make it so people are no longer dependent on oil for energy.

⚊ Fuel-cell–powered car

HONDA FCX FUEL CELL POWER

157

Is There a Future for Bioenergy?

Many scientists dedicate their time and energy to finding, creating, or perfecting new renewable energy sources that do not pollute the planet the way fossil fuels do. Whether harnessing energy from manure or turning algae into fuel, scientists are experimenting with energy sources derived from plants.

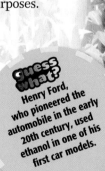
Switchgrass can yield nearly twice as much ethanol as corn. Some botanists are working to breed types of switchgrass that are even better sources of biomass energy.

WHAT IS BIOMASS?

Biomass energy, or bioenergy, comes from plant and animal matter. Biomass can be made from plants such as switchgrass, corn, soybeans, and sugarcane. It can come from the leftover scraps at paper mills and lumber mills. It can also come from manure (animal droppings) and animal fats. Biomass is different from some other forms of energy because it can be transformed into liquid biofuels.

Bioenergy is biodegradable and renewable, but the machines that convert organic matter into electricity can often be polluters themselves. So scientists are working to find ways of converting biomass into energy without releasing many pollutants into the environment or using up a lot of land that is needed for other purposes.

Guess what? Burning wood in a fireplace is one example of biomass at work. But burning wood causes pollution and destroys trees.

ETHANOL AND METHANE

Some biofuels are already in use. Ethanol is one example. Ethanol can be made from corn, wheat, barley, and other crops. In cars, ethanol is used in combination with gasoline.

Methane is another gas that can be collected for use in creating electricity. It is given off by garbage. As garbage decomposes in landfills, pockets of methane build up. Normally, the methane is released into the atmosphere. But it is a greenhouse gas (see page 140), so it contributes to climate change. When methane is collected and used for energy, it is kept from rising into the atmosphere. As of January 2012, there were 576 landfill energy projects in the United States.

Guess what? Henry Ford, who pioneered the automobile in the early 20th century, used ethanol in one of his first car models.

ENERGY FROM ANIMAL DROPPINGS?

Animal manure can also be used as a source for biomass. It can be burned or processed into a gas. In Wisconsin, 2,500 cows from three farms provide 7 million gallons (26.5 million liters) of manure a year to be converted into electricity using a machine called a "digester." Manure can be seriously stinky; in addition to the unpleasant odors, it also releases greenhouse gases into the air. Reusing manure helps to keep it from polluting the air and getting into rivers or drinking water supplies.

Guess what?

As pioneers and cowboys moved west, they used animal droppings to make fires. They called them cow pies, cow patties, or buffalo chips.

Cow pies

Algae

THE GREAT GREEN HOPE

In theory, algae is the ultimate energy source. It is one of the fastest-growing plants in the world. And it removes harmful CO_2 from the air, which can offset the CO_2 that is released when it is used as a fuel. Planting and growing corn, wheat, and other plants for use as fuel, takes up a lot of farmland that might otherwise be used to grow food. Growing algae does not. It may be 10 years before we are harvesting algae for energy on a large scale, but the U.S. government has given millions of dollars to universities and other organizations that are working to make this miracle fuel a reality.

SUNSHINE + OCEAN = ENERGY?

The oceans, which cover 70% of the planet, are the largest solar collector on Earth. Every day, the sun warms the oceans with enough thermal energy to match the energy output of 250 billion barrels of oil. Currently, harvesting this energy is not an efficient or affordable option and remains experimental. But perhaps one day soon, scientists will discover a way to trap and use the heat collected by the planet's oceans.

Electricity

At its most basic level, electricity is the flow of electrons. There are four basic units of measurement in electricity: voltage, current, wattage, and resistance.

Guess what?
Electric eels can produce strong electric shocks of around 500 volts. They do this to hunt or to defend themselves.

VOLTAGE measures potential energy, or how much force an energy source, such as a battery, has to push an electric current through a circuit. This is measured in volts.

CURRENT is the movement of electrons through the circuit. It is measured in amperes (amps). Put another way, amps tell you how much electricity is being drawn through the power cord.

WATTAGE is a measurement of total power. It is measured in watts. Multiply volts and amps to get watts (voltage x current = watts). Wattage tells you how quickly electricity is consumed through the power cord.

Guess what?
Static electricity can make your hair stand up. But did you know lightning is also an example of static discharge?

RESISTANCE is opposition to the flow of electric current. It is measured in ohms. Circuit boards use resistors to control the amount of electricity that moves through a circuit. These resistors make it possible to use dials to adjust volume or dimmers to adjust lighting.

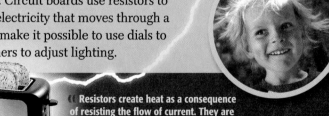

❝ Resistors create heat as a consequence of resisting the flow of current. They are a major part of heat-making appliances, such as hair dryers and toasters.

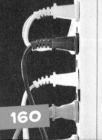

SURGE PROTECTORS

Although electric circuits use switches, transformers, and resistors to control the flow of electricity, there can still be power surges. A big enough surge can damage computers and household electronics. A surge protector works by diverting the extra electricity into the outlet's grounding wire. All modern outlets have grounding wires to protect people from electric shock.

AC VS. DC CURRENTS

As electrons flow from atom to atom (making electricity), they create a current. There are two types of currents that are used to transport electricity. **Direct current (DC)** flows in the same direction, although it can increase or decrease. Portable devices, such as flashlights and remote controls, use direct current because they are powered by batteries. **Alternating current (AC)** reverses direction periodically. Alternating current is what we get from the electrical outlets in our walls. Why? Because it's stronger and cheaper than direct current.

Unlike direct current, alternating current can be transmitted over long distances through thin wires. Direct current is relatively low in voltage. Another advantage of alternating current is that it can be changed from one level to another using a transformer, making it a more efficient mode of energy distribution. Transformers do not work with direct current.

Guess what?
Personal computers use only direct current, so one of the jobs of the charger is to convert AC to DC power.

Guess what?
AC currents run through the wires in our homes. The electrons that flow through the wires change direction 60 times every second.

CURRENT COMPETITION

Nikola Tesla, who experimented with AC power, invented a transformer that would convert DC to AC power. At the time, direct current was the standard in the United States and Thomas Edison, who is known as the father of the lightbulb, did not want anyone to challenge this. He patented a system of electricity using direct current and made his fortune with it.

To scare people from switching to the cheaper, more efficient AC power, Edison spread tales of fatal accidents caused by AC currents. He even electrocuted animals in public to show that AC kills (although DC current would too).

《 Nikola Tesla, supporter of AC power

》 Thomas Edison, champion of DC power

Circuits

We often store electricity in a "box" until we need to use it. These "boxes" are batteries, generators, and solar cells. They are the energy source of an electrical circuit. An electrical circuit is a pathway of wires that electrons can flow through in order to make a gadget work.

Circuits have to be complete in order to work. When we switch on an appliance, we are completing an electrical circuit: Electricity flows from the power lines to the outlet, through the power cord, to the appliance, and back again. This is why batteries have a positive (+) and a negative (−) end so they can carry the charge all the way around.

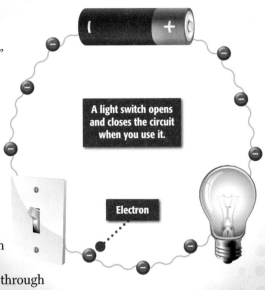

A light switch opens and closes the circuit when you use it.

Electron

Guess what?
Electrons always flow from the negative pole of a power source to the positive pole.

TYPES OF CIRCUITS

SERIES CIRCUITS

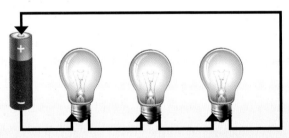

Series circuits are the simplest kind of circuit. They are one continuous loop. If there is a break or opening in the circuit at any point, electricity will stop moving. This happens often to strings of holiday lights.

PARALLEL CIRCUITS

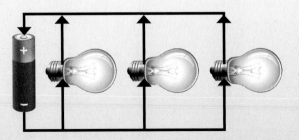

Parallel circuits are a bit more complex. The current travels along more than one path. If one light in your living room goes out, the rest will be unaffected.

Staying Safe Around Electric Currents

⤸ One side of a battery has a "+" sign and the other has a "–" sign. These symbols indicate which direction the negatively charged electrons flow out of a battery. The electricity always exits the battery from the negative side and returns on the positive side.

Electricity can only travel through certain materials. We call materials that carry electricity easily **conductors.** Metals and water make very good conductors. Because humans are mostly water, we have to be careful when working with electricity. We can handle having small amounts of electricity travel through our bodies without harming us, but too much electricity can cause serious injury.

Electricity moves at the speed of light. As electrons move incredibly quickly, they're constantly rubbing against one another. This interaction is called **friction,** and friction creates heat. Because the electrons in electricity are doing so much rubbing, they are also creating a lot of heat. This is one reason why it's important to cover wires with an **insulator.** Insulators hold in electricity and heat to help prevent accidental electrocution or fire. Glass, wood, plastic, and paper are examples of common insulators.

BATTERIES

A battery is a small container full of chemicals that can make electricity. It turns a chemical reaction **+** into electrical energy using two electrodes: an anode (the negative end) and a cathode (the positive end). An electrical current passes through a chemical medium between the electrodes. Different chemical reactions occur at each end. The reaction at the anode releases electrons, and the reaction at the cathode soaks up electrons.

The medium used to conduct electricity between the electrodes is potassium hydroxide in water. When old alkaline batteries leak acid, that acid is the potassium hydroxide. Be careful with leaking batteries, because they can irritate your eyes and skin.

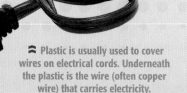

⤴ Plastic is usually used to cover wires on electrical cords. Underneath the plastic is the wire (often copper wire) that carries electricity.

ELECTRICITY SAFETY TIPS

Never use an appliance with a frayed cord. ⋯⋯⋯⋯⋯

Unplug cords by pulling on the head of the plug, not by tugging on the cord.

Keep water away from electricity and electrical appliances.

Never put anything other than a cord into an electrical outlet.

If you see that a power line has fallen down, do not touch it. Let an adult know about it.

Electrons Form Magnetic Fields

Magnets are objects that have a magnetic field that attracts metals like iron and nickel, or steel, which has iron in it. We can tell if something is magnetic by how it pulls toward or pushes away from metal surfaces. But why does it behave this way? A magnet's field comes from the movement of its **electrons.** (For more on electrons, see pages 18–21.)

Everything is made up of **atoms.** Atoms have a positively charged core, called a **nucleus,** which is orbited by negatively charged particles, the electrons. Electrons usually orbit in pairs, enough to create a tiny magnetic charge, but their magnetic fields cancel each other out. Magnetic materials have several unpaired electrons. With no opposing fields to cancel their effects, some of the magnetism remains.

≋ The iron filings around this magnet show the shape of the magnet's magnetic field.

EVERYDAY USES OF MAGNETS

Since magnets can be made artificially, in various shapes and sizes, they are used for a lot of things.

CARS	Magnets are used in the electric motors that move electric windows, and in the needles on the speedometer and other gauges on the dashboard.
TELEVISIONS (CRT, or cathode ray tubes ; not plasma TVs or LCD TVs)	Inside a CRT television, cathode-ray tubes shoot electrons toward the screen. Without electromagnets, the electrons would travel directly toward the center of the TV screen. Electromagnets placed in the neck of the tube direct some of the electrons to the edges of the screen.
COMPUTERS	Data is stored on computer hard drives that are coated with an iron material that contains tiny magnetic fields in a pattern—a code made up of north and south signals. These patterns correspond to the information being saved.

THINGS MADE WITH MAGNETS

Electric toothbrushes
Doorbells
Phones
DVD recorders
Air conditioners
Water heaters
Vacuum cleaners
Cell phones
Digital cameras
Portable music players
Elevators
Blenders
Audio speakers
Some toys

From Fortune-Telling to Navigation

Ancient Greeks observed magnetism in a lodestone. This is a piece of magnetite, a mineral that has been naturally magnetized by lightning. Around the 4th century B.C., the Chinese invented a magnetic compass that used lodestones. At first, these compasses were used for fortune-telling. Later, compasses with magnetized needles became common navigational tools on Chinese ships.

See how metal paper clips are attracted to magnetite.

Electromagnets

Some magnets, like a lodestone, are **permanent magnets.** They generally retain their magnetic properties at all times. Others are **temporary magnets.** Like magnets, electromagnets attract metal objects, but they act as magnets only as long as they are in the magnetic field of a permanent magnet or in an electric current.

Electromagnets are useful because we can turn their magnetic power on and off. That's why they're used for doorbells. When you press the button by the front door, an electromagnet makes a metal clapper hit the bell repeatedly until you release the button. If a doorbell had a permanent magnet inside, it would never stop ringing.

» In this homemade electromagnet, a nail is magnetized when it is connected to a battery, which supplies an electric current.

» When electric current flows through a wire, it creates a magnetic field. Winding the wire into a coil increases its magnetic force.

Magnets of the Future

- Maglev, or magnetic levitation, elevators will replace wheels and cables with magnets. Not only will elevators go up and down, but they'll travel left and right, using a combination of magnetic attraction and repulsion.

- Doctors will treat patients who suffer from heart disease or cancer with magnetized stem cells. (See page 33.) Nanosize magnets (extra tiny!) can be attached to stem cells, so that a magnet outside the body can guide the nanomagnets (and the attached stem cells) to the right places inside the body.

- A new kind of car may produce a magnetic field to propel its wheels. The car, as envisioned by concept designer Harsha Vardhan, would be noiseless and, best of all, emit no pollution.

- Rockets may use electromagnetic thrusters to reduce costs and improve efficiency. Such an engine could reduce travel time from Earth to Mars from two-and-a-half years to five months!

FLOATING TRAINS!

Maglev trains use very strong electromagnets to suspend trains several inches above tracks and propel them forward. There are currently maglev systems in Japan, Germany, and China. Another maglev system is supposed to be completed in South Korea in 2013. Faster than a conventional train, the highest recorded speed of a maglev train is 361 miles (581 km) per hour.

CELLULAR PHONES

Cellular phones use the same technology from great-grandpa's day. They rely on radio. A cell phone turns the sounds of a person's voice into radio waves. These radio waves are sent by the phone's antenna to the nearest cell tower, which then sends them on to the recipient's phone.

THE EARLY DAYS OF CELL PHONES

Before cell phones existed, cars could be fitted with radiotelephones that included transmitters. The first radiotelephone call from a car was made in 1946. The transmitter had to be big enough to reach a central tower. The central tower would have had only about 25 channels, so not many people could be on their mobile phones at once. Today's cell phones can make millions of calculations every second.

I hope Grandma picks up.

Hello?

Guess what?

The first handheld mobile phone was made in 1973 and weighed 2 pounds (0.91 kg). It took 10 years for the first commercial mobile phone to appear—the DynaTAC 8000x. Launched in 1983, it weighed 1.75 pounds (0.79 kg) and was 13 inches (33 cm) long. Try sticking that in your pocket!

WHAT GENERATION?

The very first cell phones were analog phones. Cell phones went from analog to digital in a short period. Digital was the second generation, or 2G, of cell phones. The 2G phones were smaller and lighter than analog phones, but were still designed to transmit only voices. The next crop of phones were called 3G (third generation). They have even greater bandwidth and can accommodate smartphones, with their Internet features and ability to download audio and video files. Data is transferred at a rate that is more than 100 times faster than 2G. The first 4G phones were released in 2010.

A 4G phone   Definitely not 4G

WHERE IN THE WORLD?

Throughout history, people used landmarks—a hill or a tall building, even the stars—to get their bearings. In the case of the Global Positioning System (GPS), created by the U.S. Department of Defense, those landmarks are very high up indeed. They are satellites orbiting 12,427 miles (20,000 km) above Earth. These satellites make two full rotations a day. It takes 24 satellites to provide global coverage. There are seven spare or deactivated satellites, as well, for a total of 31.

When someone mentions a GPS, he or she usually means a GPS receiver, which is a small device that can cost less than $100. Many cell phones and cars are equipped with a GPS receiver. A receiver works by locating four or more satellites, figuring out its distance to each, and using the information to pinpoint its exact location or track its movement. It can tell how far away the satellite is by measuring how long it takes for radio signals sent from the satellites to arrive. The more satellites the receiver can detect, the greater the accuracy.

Once the position is determined, the receiver can calculate other information, such as speed, distance to destination, and more. Receivers also have an electronic map on which the information is displayed.

Satellite phone

EYES IN THE SKY

The satellites used by GPS devices aren't the only satellites in the sky. Some satellites make it possible to transmit television signals directly to people's homes. Others provide meteorologists with information about worldwide weather patterns. Environmental scientists use data beamed down from satellites to monitor reefs, coastlines, and glaciers, and track climate change. Communication satellites allow people in remote regions to have access to news. When phone lines and power lines are damaged during wars and natural disasters, battery-operated satellite phones keep people in touch.

DISTANCE

DISTANCE

DISTANCE

DISTANCE

Guess what?
This process of pinpointing a location is based on a mathematical principle called trilateration.

The tether is a thin fiber-optic cable that can transmit video and receive instructions from operators on board the support ship.

Guess what? Nereus was designed and built at Woods Hole Oceanographic Institution.

Ceramic spheres

Fins

Aluminum frame

UNDERSEA VEHICLES

NEREUS

Thrusters

LED lights at the front of Nereus work kind of like the headlights of a car.

The batteries used in the submersible are rechargeable lithium-ion batteries, similar to the ones used in laptop computers.

Operators use a robotic arm to collect rocks and other samples.

The cameras on the vehicle can transmit high-quality images and real-time video to the surface.

Humans have explored only about 5% of the Earth's oceans. In 2009, scientists launched an undersea research vehicle, Nereus, to explore Challenger Deep, the deepest known point on the Earth's seafloor. On May 31, 2009, it reached the bottom.

Nereus has a simple design. It consists of two parts that enable it to transform from a free-swimming vehicle for wide-area ocean surveys to a tethered vehicle that can be remotely operated.

Traditional submersibles are made of metal and glass, but Nereus has an aluminum frame, which houses approximately 1,500 flotation spheres. These lightweight ceramic spheres make the vehicle buoyant and keep it upright. Each sphere is the size of a grapefruit. They can withstand tremendous underwater pressure. When dropped, these balls will break like coffee mugs, but under compression, they have five times the strength of steel. All the electronic equipment—from lighting to camera systems—is stored in ceramic housings.

Guess what? Humans have now reached both the Earth's deepest trench (Challenger Deep, 35,576 feet/10,844 m beneath the Pacific Ocean) and its highest peak (the summit of Mount Everest in the Himalayas, 29,035 feet/8,850 m above sea level).

Mount Everest

A Director's Deep Dive

Director James Cameron is best known for directing and producing Hollywood films, like *Titanic* and *Avatar*, that break box-office records. But on Sunday, March 25, 2012, he broke another kind of record. Piloting the mini-submarine *Deepsea Challenger*, Cameron set the world record for the deepest ocean dive by a single person when he traveled 6.74 miles (10.84 km) down to the Mariana Trench in the Pacific Ocean. He is the first person to visit the Trench since 1960.

On his record-breaking dive, Cameron spent three hours in the Challenger Deep, Earth's deepest spot, nearly 7 miles (11 km) under the sea. It's a dark, desertlike place with near-freezing temperatures, no sunlight, and heavy water pressure.

The sub was equipped with 3-D cameras and lights for filming the adventure for a documentary. It also had a mechanical arm for collecting samples of soil and deep-sea creatures, though there was a problem with the probe that kept the sub from collecting anything during the trip.

Traveling in the deep-sea submersible *Trieste*, U.S. Navy Lieutenant Don Walsh (left) and Swiss oceanographer Jacques Piccard spent 20 minutes at the Mariana Trench. But they could hardly see anything—their landing kicked up too much sand from the seafloor. They took no pictures.

James Cameron helped design the 24-foot-long (7 m) minisub *Deepsea Challenger*.

Guess What?

"Most people know me as a filmmaker," Cameron said during a press conference after his record-breaking dive. "But the idea of ocean and exploration has always been the stronger driver in my life."

ROBOTS

When you think of a robot, you may not immediately think of a vehicle like the Nereus (see page 168) or a space rover like Curiosity (see page 211), but that's exactly what they are. Nereus and Curiosity are machines capable of performing tasks automatically or by remote commands. Scientists, engineers, and toymakers have been designing and building robots for years. But, in 2011, a particularly impressive robot was completed.

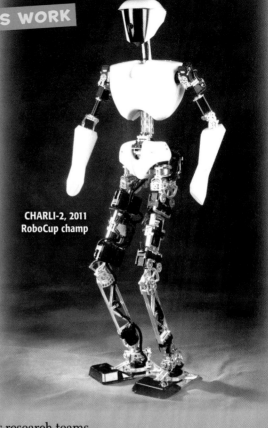

CHARLI-2, 2011
RoboCup champ

ROBO-CHAMP

CHARLI-2 is a full-size humanoid robot with special talents. And it used its skills to win the RoboCup soccer match with a penalty kick. The annual RoboCup tournament pits research teams from around the globe against each other in a sporting event. CHARLI-2, or Cognitive Humanoid **Autonomous** Robot with Learning Intelligence, was the entry created by Virginia Tech's College of Engineering. The ultimate goal of RoboCup is for scientists to build an entire team of robots that can play against the human World Cup champion team by the year 2050. Robot players are all autonomous. They feature the latest technology for running and kicking, while maintaining balance, navigating, and visually perceiving the field, the ball, and the other players around them.

> Being **autonomous** means that something can act independently and does not have to be remotely controlled.

CHARLI-2's chest cover is made of plastic.

MATERIALS MATTER

CHARLI-2 is constructed with aluminum alloy, titanium, carbon fiber, and plastic. These lightweight materials are an advantage for walking. Building a robot that is bipedal, or walks on two feet, is one of the major challenges in robotics. Even taking a single step involves dozens of postures.

MIMICKING HUMAN MOVEMENT

Humanoid robots have a movable body that uses motors to move like joints and muscles. To create the same kinds of movement as a human body can, CHARLI-2 uses rotary motors, operated by electric currents. The motors are wired into an electrical circuit that is connected to a computer that acts like a brain. Sensors such as cameras mounted in the head "see" the environment and send this information to the computer brain. CHARLI-2 is also equipped with a balance sensor, called an accelerometer, that works a lot like the human inner ear and is used to maintain

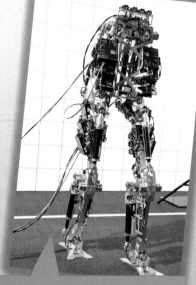

balance. The computer is programmed so the robot can perform tasks on its own without commands from a human operator.

《 A close-up of the gears in CHARLI-2's hip joints

FIREFIGHTER OF THE FUTURE

The same technology that was developed to make CHARLI-2 play a game of soccer is now being used to create another humanoid robot, called SAFFiR (Shipboard Autonomous Fire Fighting Robot), which will be used on Navy ships for fighting fires.

REDECORATED ROBOT

Ten things on this retro robot have changed. Can you spot them all?

Answers on page 216.

The Human Eye

Most people rely heavily on their sense of sight to get information about what is going on around them. But did you know that the images our eyes see are actually upside down? A person's eyes take in what they can see and send messages to the brain, but the lenses in our eyes produce images that are upside down. The human brain takes in that information and flips it around, so that we can understand the world around us. This image-flipping process is completely instinctual and unconscious. That is, we do not realize that it is happening.

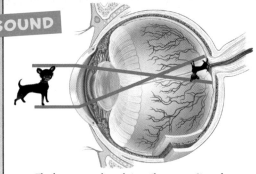

The human eye is an interesting organ. It works in a way that is similar to a camera.

BENDING LIGHT

Lenses, just like the ones in people's eyes, bend and redirect light. They are used in eyeglasses, contact lenses, microscopes, magnifiers, cameras, and many other things. There are two basic kinds of lenses: **convex** and **concave.**

⋛ CONVEX LENSES are thicker in the middle. They make light converge, or focus.

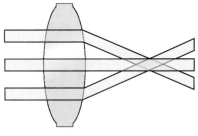

⋛ CONCAVE LENSES are thicker on the outsides. They make light diverge, or spread out.

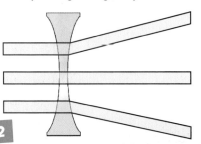

LIQUID LENSES

Many people suffer from one of two easily correctible eye conditions:

• **Hyperopia,** or farsightedness, which makes it difficult to see objects that are close by

• **Myopia,** or nearsightedness, which makes it difficult to see things in the distance

Scientists have created glasses and contact lenses to help people with these eye conditions see more clearly.

As people age, they sometimes have trouble seeing things that are both close up and far away. They may wear bifocals or progressive lenses. With these, the shape of the lens is different in different areas. For example, the wearer can look through the top of the lens to see far away and the bottom of the lens to see close up.

Recently, some companies have begun working with fluid-filled lenses for eyeglasses. The shape of the lenses could be changed by quickly shifting the fluid around, enabling people to entirely alter the focus of their glasses.

⌃ Notice the line in the lenses? That marks the place in bifocal lenses where the type of lens changes.

OPTICAL ILLUSIONS

An optical illusion occurs when there is a difference in what we expect to see and what we actually see. The receptors in the eyes take in information about the world at different rates. For example, the eye may take note of the shape of an object before taking note of the color. The tiny delay in processing this information may result in the brain coming to a conclusion about the object a person is looking at that differs from what the object really is. Some artists are very good at creating mind-boggling images that make the most of this difference. Take a look at some optical illusions.

What's wrong with this shape? Hint: look at the vertical lines.

Do you see a vase or two faces?

Is this an elderly person and a princess? Or two princesses?

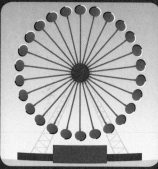

Is this wheel moving or still?

Can you see a butterfly? Can you see two flowers?

3-D MOVIES

Until the 1950s, most movies were only 2-D—they had height and width, but appeared on a flat screen and had no depth. Three-dimensional, or 3-D, movies use techniques that trick the audience into seeing depth. Early 3-D films used two projectors to show two slightly different pictures—one for each eye. Special red-and-blue glasses made sure that each eye saw only what it was supposed to. Then the brain perceived images in 3-D. But sometimes the jittery picture would give people headaches or make them feel like throwing up.

Recently developed technology has made watching films in 3-D much more pleasant—and much more intense. Digital projectors and special new glasses are used to make more realistic 3-D effects. *Hugo, The Adventures of Tintin,* and *Madagascar 3: Europe's Most Wanted* are just a few of the recent movies that have been released in 3-D. Today, consumers can even purchase televisions capable of creating 3-D experiences. Soon, gamers may be playing all of their video games in 3-D. The science behind moviemaking and 3-D imagery is constantly changing. Stay tuned for more cool scientific advances soon!

Make Some Noise!

Sound waves travel through the air just like waves move through water.

Sound is all about vibrations. All things, including air, are made up of molecules. When a person strikes a drum, the movement causes the molecules in the air to vibrate. The air closest to the drum vibrates, causing the air next to it to vibrate. In this way, the vibration passes through the air as a sound wave. Molecules do not travel from the drum to someone's ear. Instead, they move a little bit, which pushes the air next to them a little bit, which in turn causes more air to move, creating a ripple effect. This ripple effect can be expressed in a waveform (see below).

DO THE WAVE!

≋ The AMPLITUDE, or strength, of a sound, can be measured by looking at the height of a sound wave. Striking the drum harder or talking more loudly will amplify, or increase the amplitude of, a sound.

《 The WAVELENGTH is the distance between a point on the wave and the point on the same spot of the next wave.

≋ The FREQUENCY of a sound corresponds to the number of wavelengths that take place in a second. The more quickly a sound vibrates the molecules in the air, the higher the frequency of a sound wave. A sound with high-frequency waves sounds high-pitched to humans. One with low-frequency waves is low-pitched.

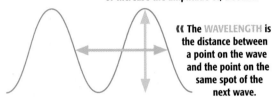

GOOD VIBRATIONS

When a sound wave reaches a person's ear, the vibrations move down the auditory canal, or ear canal, until they hit the eardrum, which is flexible and responds to sounds. It both protects the inner ear from loud noises and allows a person to focus on certain noises. For example, the eardrum reacts to loud noises in such a way that you can still hear a friend talking next to you when you are in the noisy gym at recess or at a rock concert.

Three tiny bones, commonly called the hammer, anvil, and stirrup, amplify the vibrations, making them more forceful, as they reach the cochlea. The cochlea is filled with liquid, and it requires more force to have the sound waves move through liquid than through air. Inside the cochlea are thousands of tiny hairs called cilia, which are moved by the sound waves. The movement of the cilia is transmitted to the auditory nerve, which takes the message to the brain. The brain interprets the impulses and reacts to the dog barking, the waves crashing, your mom calling you, or whatever else the sound might be.

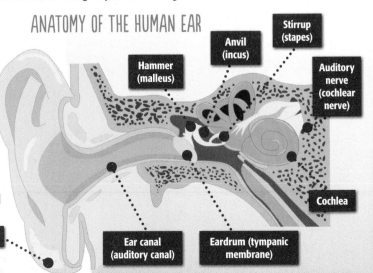

ANATOMY OF THE HUMAN EAR

Stirrup (stapes)

Anvil (incus)

Hammer (malleus)

Auditory nerve (cochlear nerve)

Cochlea

Earlobe

Ear canal (auditory canal)

Eardrum (tympanic membrane)

We live in a noisy world, and this isn't good for our ears. Tiny cells in the inner ear are damaged by noises that are too loud and that last for too long. This damage is permanent. Once you've lost some of your hearing ability, you'll never get it back. Get in the habit of protecting your ears. Here are some suggestions:

- Listen to music and TV at safe volumes.

- Wear earplugs or other hearing protectors in noisy environments—for example, when you mow the lawn or ride a dirt bike.

- Move away from loud sounds.

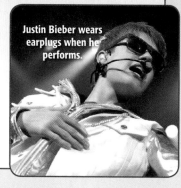

Justin Bieber wears earplugs when he performs.

≋ When a person speaks, his or her vocal folds (often called vocal cords) vibrate. These vibrations produce sound waves. That is why we hear the person's speech.

PIANO

Did you know that a piano is a string instrument, just like a violin or guitar? The inside of a grand piano contains around 230 strings of different lengths and tensions. It also contains small hammers. When a person presses a key, it causes a chain reaction that brings a hammer down on the strings. At the same time, a damper is raised off of the strings, allowing them to vibrate more. When the player releases the key, the damper presses against the string again, stopping the vibrations, which stops the sound.

The vibrating strings themselves aren't very loud, but their vibrations are transmitted to a large soundboard, made of a curved piece of wood, that magnifies the sound. It also gives a piano a unique sound. The quality and position of the wood is important to a piano's sound.

PEDAL POWER Most pianos also have three pedals (some have only two) with different functions. When a person steps on the right pedal, all the dampers are released from the strings, so the sound continues until you release it. The middle pedal allows a player to draw out only some notes. In this way, certain notes can ring out while others fade. The left pedal moves the hammers closer to the strings to make a softer sound.

Longer pianos with longer strings have a richer sound. That's why the strings are positioned diagonally in a piano, to allow for longer strings.

1876: Telephone

LIFE-CHANGING INVENTIONS

Even before 1800, many helpful tools and objects had already been invented. Insecticide, soap, the bow and arrow, steam power, chocolate, detergent, windmills, matches, chess, and toothpaste were all being used by the year 1000. By 1700, people wore eyeglasses, made books on a printing press, used the barometer to predict the weather, and even operated human-powered submarines. In the next 100 years, the steam engine, fire extinguisher, mercury thermometer, and cotton gin were put into action. Here are some more recent inventions that have changed lives around the world.

Rayon was the first human-made fiber ever developed. Made from wood or cotton pulp, it was originally known as "artificial silk." The name *rayon* was introduced in 1924.

1830 **Sewing machine**

1837 **Telegraph**

1839 **Rubber**

1830: Sewing machine

1851 **Refrigerator**

1856 **Plastic**

1858 **Rotary washing machine**

1866 **Dynamite**

Alfred Nobel invented dynamite. After his younger brother and four other people were killed in a factory explosion, Nobel wanted to find a safer way to handle explosives. When he died, the inventor left behind a fortune to provide yearly prizes for work in physics, chemistry, medicine and physiology, literature, and the promotion of peace.

1868 **Typewriter**

1873 **Barbed wire**

1876 **Telephone**

1877 **Microphone, phonograph (record player)**

In addition to inventing the phonograph, Thomas Edison made improvements to the telegraph and created the kinetoscope, which allowed people to see moving pictures.

1893 **Motion picture**

1894 **Rayon fabric**

1895 **X-ray photography**

1897 **Diesel engine**

1900 **Fingerprinting**

1901 **Safety razor, vacuum cleaner**

1903 **Airplane, safety glass**

1908 **Cellophane, Ford Model T car**

Henry Ford founded the Ford Motor Company, which built and sold the **Model T** for $950. This made owning an automobile much more affordable than ever before. He also developed the moving assembly line. Workers stood in front of a conveyor belt, and each completed one task on every car that passed by. Ford's method of mass production revolutionized car manufacturing.

1908: Ford Model T car

1910	Neon lamp		

1910 Neon lamp

1911 Air conditioning

1913 Stainless steel ●····

Harry Brearley invented stainless steel while looking for a way to improve the quality of gun barrels.

1914 Gas mask

1920 Self-adhesive bandage

1922 Insulin ●········

Insulin, identified by Canadian scientists in 1922, is a hormone created in the pancreas. It offers life-saving treatment for people who suffer from diabetes.

1923 Modern traffic light

1924 Frozen food ●

1927 Television

1928 Chewing gum, penicillin ●····

1931 Electron microscope

1933 FM radio

Alexander Fleming discovered penicillin ···· accidentally, after leaving a dish of staphylococcus bacteria uncovered and finding mold.

1935 Radar

1938 Nylon, photocopier, Teflon

1941 Silicon solar cell

1945 Atomic bomb, microwave ●······

1946 Tupperware

1948 Hologram

1952 Car air bag, polio vaccine

1955 Velcro

Percy LeBaron Spencer was experimenting with radar waves, when the waves melted a candy bar in his pocket without burning a hole in his pants. Spencer knew he was on to something. Today, the **microwave** allows people to cook all kinds of things very quickly and safely.

1956 Super Glue

1959 Modern seat belt

1924: Frozen food

1960 Bubble Wrap

1963 Computer mouse

Clarence Birdseye developed two methods for quickly **freezing foods** so that they would retain their flavor. This led to a whole new way of eating and transporting food.

1965 Smoke alarm

1971 Floppy disk, Kevlar (used for bulletproof vests)

1972 *Pong,* the first video game

1978 Global Positioning System (GPS)

1979 Mobile phone

1982 Compact disc

1982: Compact disc

1994 Genetically modified (GM) food

1996 Smog-eating cement ●·····

2001 Artificial liver, iPod, self-cleaning glass

Italian inventors spent 10 years developing **smog-eating cement** called TX Active. They say it cuts some pollutants by as much as 60%.

2007 iPhone

2008 flying wind turbines

2009 Kinect

2009: Kinect

177

FROM **TIME** FOR KIDS

Coolest Inventions of 2011

By the TIME and TIME FOR KIDS Staffs

Inventors find ways to make our lives easier, greener, and, sometimes, more fun. Check out the results of their creativity.

Guess what? The wheel was invented about 5,000 years ago, but it wasn't the first human invention. Sewing needles, woven baskets, fishing lines, boats, and flutes were all created thousands of years before wheels.

POWER PLANT

Every hour, enough solar energy strikes the Earth's surface to power the world for an entire year. What if that energy could be stored for later use? A professor at the Massachusetts Institute of Technology has found a way to do just that. He has invented an **artificial leaf.** Much like a real leaf, it can convert energy from the sun into energy that can be stored.

IT'S A BOAT! IT'S A PLANE!

For people who like to travel in style on both land and water, French designer Yelken Octuri has crafted the **flying yacht.** This gorgeous boat boasts four 133-foot-tall (41 m) masts. When it's time to take to the sky, the masts become wings. The yacht's dual propellers pull it through the air at 240 miles (386 km) per hour.

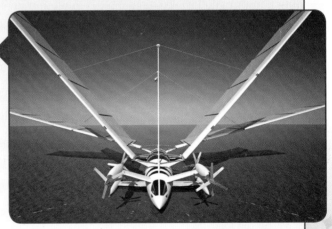

Take out trash now.

What can I help you with?

HELP AT HAND

Need to find the best nearby burger? Just ask **Siri,** a feature first found on Apple's iPhone 4S. Siri can also remind you to take out the garbage or do your homework. And it's better than past digital assistants that operate on voice recognition. You can speak naturally to Siri. There's no need to use special words in order to be understood. Ask away! Siri is ready to serve.

Guess what? Elisha Gray applied for a patent for a telephone just one hour before Alexander Graham Bell registered his own design. After many lawsuits, the Patent Office granted the patent to Bell.

THE WORLD'S FASTEST CAR

In 1997, Andy Green set a land-speed record of 763 miles (1,228 km) per hour. Now he's out to break that record with the **Bloodhound SSC.** He is shooting for 1,000 miles (1,609 km) per hour. This car is powered by both jet and rocket engines. The Bloodhound project is about more than speed. Green and his teammates hope to inspire a generation of scientists and engineers. Start your engines!

A BIRD'S-EYE VIEW

It looks and flies like a hummingbird. But don't be fooled. This tiny aircraft, called the **Nano Air Vehicle (NAV),** is a spying device. The remote-controlled, $4 million NAV has a built-in video camera. Because it is so small, it can go where humans can't. It can scout out safe spots in combat zones, search for earthquake survivors, and even locate a chemical spill.

POP-UP MAP

You don't need 3-D glasses to see this three-dimensional image. The **Urban Photonic Sandtable Display** is a full-color holographic map. To create the map, a laser sweeps across a landscape. Software does the rest. Buildings and land features can be displayed at heights of up to 1 foot (30.5 cm). The U.S. Department of Defense hopes to use the map for battlefield planning.

THE SWITCH IS ON!

The energy-wasting incandescent bulb will be outlawed by 2014. But many of the newer bulbs give off a harsh white light. So the race is on to create an energy-efficient bulb with a soft glow. The **Switch bulb** may be the answer. It gives off a yellow light and uses only a fraction of the energy that incandescents do. Each bulb costs $20 but lasts 20 years.

EASY ENERGY

Solar power is plentiful. But it takes a lot of solar panels—and space—to collect a usable amount of energy from the sun. That's where Ascent Solar's **thin-film solar panels** come in handy. The flexible sheets roll and unroll, and can be used in building materials. A roof or a wall can be made entirely of the thin-film panels, making it easier to soak up the power of the sun.

MILK DUDS

Moo-ve over, cotton. Now there's a fabric made from milk. Biologist and fashion designer Anke Domaske discovered a way to create clothes using sour milk. First, she extracts protein from the milk. Then she spins the protein into yarn. The result is a flexible fabric similar to silk. A dress or shirt can be made from about 1.5 gallons (5.7 L) of milk. The clothes range in price from $200 to $270.

Guess what?

Elias Howe, the inventor of the sewing machine, also invented the zipper. He registered this device, which he called a "clothing closure," in 1851, but he didn't pay much attention to it. Whitcomb Judson marketed a similar item 44 years later, and got credit for the invention.

DRUM PORTAL

UNICEF's (United Nations Children's Fund) **Digital Drum** is a solar-powered computer center preloaded with educational content. It helps get information about health, education, and other issues to rural communities in Uganda, in Africa, where access to resources is limited. It is made from low-cost metal oil drums and can hold up against the weather. The first Digital Drum was set up in March 2011 at a youth center in the Ugandan city of Gulu.

EAR EMOTIONS

Ever wish you could tell how people are feeling just by looking at them? Now you can, with this new product from Japanese company Neurowear. The **Necomimi** headband has a sensor on it. The sensor sends brain waves to the band's catlike ears. The ears drop when the wearer is relaxed. They stand straight up when she is concentrating. And when she is both? Then the ears perk up and wiggle wildly.

WHIZ KID WORD SEARCH

Some inventors really stood out from the pack. See if the names of some impressive inventors and helpful inventions stand out in the word search below.

L	Z	D	Y	N	A	M	I	T	E	Z	W
I	O	V	U	E	D	I	S	O	N	E	O
G	A	A	O	W	S	J	G	C	P	C	Q
H	G	C	A	T	V	C	Y	I	K	A	U
T	B	C	E	O	M	R	U	F	O	R	D
B	I	I	R	N	O	B	E	L	P	L	K
U	R	N	H	E	A	F	W	E	I	R	V
L	D	E	V	A	C	U	U	M	K	A	E
B	S	C	O	E	V	B	R	I	N	Y	L
D	E	A	I	R	P	L	A	N	E	J	C
M	Y	O	T	N	B	R	T	G	U	M	R
T	E	L	E	V	I	S	I	O	N	X	O

Airplane
Birdseye
Car
Dynamite
Edison
Fleming
Ford
Gum
Lightbulb
Newton
Nobel
Television
Vaccine
Vacuum
Velcro

TOP 5 DATED INVENTIONS

The gas-powered car is on its way out, according to a survey of 500 teens. Here are some other inventions they think are headed for the scrap heap.

1. Gas-powered car: 37%

2. Landline phone: 32%

3. Computer mouse: 21%

4. Other (includes books, DVDs, VCRs, and radios): 4%

5. Television: 3%
   I don't know: 3%

FROM TIME FOR KIDS

Ideas to Inspire By TFK Kid Reporter Linda Tong

Hip-hop music? Cockroaches? A gecko's sticky feet? Believe it or not, these things may be the way to spark creativity in inventions, product design, and engineering. At least that's what organizers of the first-ever TEDYouth event hope. TED is a nonprofit group that is dedicated to "ideas worth spreading." The event took place on November 19, 2011, in New York City.

The theme of TEDYouth was "play, learn, build, and share." More than 300 New York City students in grades 6 through 12 were selected to participate. There were 19 speakers, including world-famous scientists, TV hosts, authors, poets, educators, and entertainers. Author Steve Stoute spoke about how hip-hop music has influenced urban culture. Robert Full, a professor at the University of California at Berkeley, spoke about inventions that are inspired by nature. "TED allows kids to see the range of possibilities of what they can become in life," TEDYouth organizer Lara Stein told TFK. "I hope the speakers will inspire young people to try new things and to dream big."

IDEAS THAT STICK

Cockroaches and geckos make many people cringe. But not Robert Full, the University of California professor who spoke at the event. He has a love for these creatures. He inspired his students to figure out how a gecko sticks to a wall or surface, and that allowed them to discover new ways of making things stick. One student used what he learned about geckos to create a bandage that can be peeled off easily. Full is using the sticky technology to create the first search-and-rescue bot that can climb up walls.

Robert Full

Harry Kile, a middle school student, came up with a new type of car seat that doesn't need a safety belt. The car seat uses gecko-inspired technology to make a kid stick to the seat. Harry earned a real gecko at the event for his innovative idea. "You don't know what can't be done," Full said. "You could get even more than you could ever imagine."

Why is the first-ever TEDYouth event so special? Kids can't attend the adult TED conferences, but that doesn't mean they don't have dreams of changing the world too. "At TEDYouth Day, kids get the same opportunity to learn and to get inspired," 10-year-old Alexandra Frank told TFK.

CUTTING-EDGE SCIENCE

The World's Lowest-Density Material

In November 2011, HRL Laboratories announced that it developed the world's lowest-density material. The material is about 1,000 times less **dense** than water and 100 times lighter than Styrofoam. The secret—to both its light weight and its strength—is the material's latticelike structural organization. One of the engineers who created it likened it to that of the Eiffel Tower, in Paris, France. The lattice structure is made up of hollow tubes with walls that are 1,000 times thinner than a human hair.

This surprisingly squishy material is so lightweight that it can rest on the seed heads of a dandelion.

guess what?
The design of the Eiffel Tower was inspired by the complex structure inside of human bones.

THAT'S SO DENSE!

All materials are made up of molecules. In some materials, the molecules are packed tightly together. In others, the molecules are more spread out. An object's density describes how tightly packed the molecules are. For example, iron is incredibly dense. Styrofoam is not very dense at all. Mass is the measurement of density.

Gravity pulls down on all objects. That's why a dense object is heavier to lift than a less dense one.

Styrofoam: not very dense

Iron: very dense

Real-Life X-Ray Vision

A team of researchers from the Massachusetts Institute of Technology developed a device that can provide its operators with video of what's going on behind an 8-inch-thick (20 cm) concrete wall from 60 feet (18 m) away! This device sends out radio waves. A tiny amount of the radio waves manage to pass through the solid wall. An even smaller amount of those waves reach the person or thing on the other side and bounce back. After these radio waves pass back through the wall, they are read by a transmitter that indicates the movements of the person on the other side of the wall.

⌒ Researchers Gregory Charvat, left, and John Peabody stand in front of the solid concrete used in their experiment.

Guess what?
Engineering and technology are the fastest-growing fields in science.

Making Virtual Objects Feel Real

Imagine playing a video game where you can actually *feel* the virtual world in which your avatar lives! Scientists have gotten one step closer to making that possible. An international team of **neuroengineers** (scientists who design hardware for the brain) has developed a brain-machine interface that's bidirectional, meaning that a person with the implant could both control the movements of a virtual hand, and also "feel," or experience, the sensation of touching virtual objects. Someday in the near future, human patients who have lost arms or legs may take advantage of this technology. It may help them to move their prosthetic limbs and to sense when an object touches their prostheses.

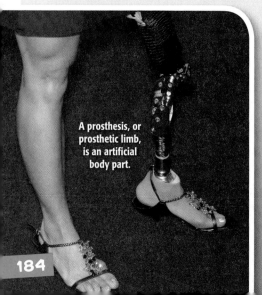

A prosthesis, or prosthetic limb, is an artificial body part.

Energy with Every Beat of Your Heart

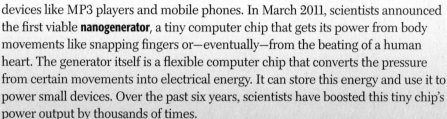

A nanogenerator made of tiny fibers

In a few years, a generator the size of a tiny microchip could replace batteries for small devices like MP3 players and mobile phones. In March 2011, scientists announced the first viable **nanogenerator**, a tiny computer chip that gets its power from body movements like snapping fingers or—eventually—from the beating of a human heart. The generator itself is a flexible computer chip that converts the pressure from certain movements into electrical energy. It can store this energy and use it to power small devices. Over the past six years, scientists have boosted this tiny chip's power output by thousands of times.

Zhong Lin Wang, the project's lead scientist said, "This development represents a milestone toward producing portable electronics that can be powered by body movements without the use of batteries or electrical outlets. Our nanogenerators are poised to change lives in the future. Their potential is only limited by one's imagination."

》 Some scientists are looking into using nanogenerators to harvest energy from the bending of car tires as they rotate. The part of a car's tire that touches the ground is squeezed between the force of the ground pushing up and the weight of the car pushing down. With a nanogenerator inside the wall of the tire, energy could be created each time the tire is squeezed.

A Super Fuel Cell!

Scientists in China have created a type of fuel cell that uses organic materials to sanitize water, making it clean and safe to drink. What makes this fuel cell truly groundbreaking is that it creates energy at the same time. In experiments, the cell removed such pollutants as perfumes, dyes, and medications from water. At

this stage, the system is just a prototype (a test model) and further research is needed before it can be put into practical use. One day, this wonderful invention might change the lives of many who need clean energy and safe drinking water.

《 More than 780 million people around the globe do not have easy access to clean, safe drinking water.

SPACE

According to the big bang theory, the universe began in an instant. It is enormous and filled with mysterious and interesting things, including galaxies, planets, stars, and nebulae. Asteroids, comets, meteoroids, and dust whiz through space at amazing speeds. Read about the solar system, the International Space Station, and the history of space exploration to get a better idea about what happens beyond Earth's atmosphere.

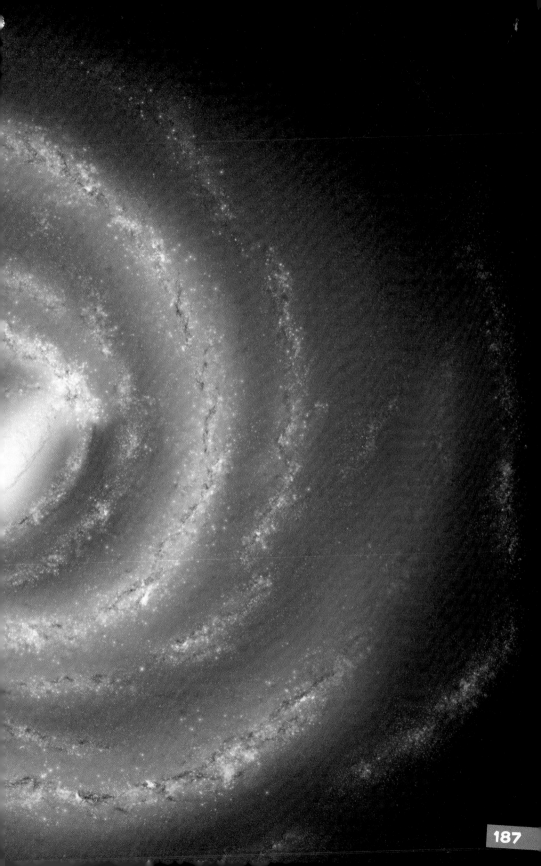

THE BIG BANG AND THE UNIVERSE

According to the big bang theory, the universe had a beginning. For a brief moment, it existed in an extremely dense and hot state—so dense that it could fit on the head of a pin. Then, about 13.7 billion years ago, it very rapidly expanded.

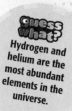

Guess What?
Hydrogen and helium are the most abundant elements in the universe.

As it expanded, the universe cooled down, creating elementary particles and the known forces of physics. Energy changed into particles of matter and antimatter, canceling one another out. When the universe was just seconds old, more stable particles, called protons and neutrons, began to form. About 300,000 years later, the universe had cooled enough to form atoms. It filled with hydrogen and helium gas.

TYPES OF GALAXIES

Spiral

Elliptical

Irregular

FROM GAS CLOUDS TO GALAXIES

As millions of years passed, denser areas with more gravity pulled together materials. First, they formed **gas clouds.** About 400 million years after the big bang, the gas clouds became hot and dense enough to form **stars.** Large clusters of stars became the first **galaxies.** They were closer together than they are now, so collisions were common. These collisions formed bigger galaxies, such as our **Milky Way galaxy.**

THEORY OR FACT?

The big bang is a well-tested scientific theory. It is the best explanation scientists have devised with the available evidence in astronomy and physics. They can detect traces of the big bang in the form of a faint glow that is the same in every direction. They believe that this radiation does not come from any star, galaxy, or other object. Instead, it is the heat left over from the big bang.

This image, taken by the Hubble Space Telescope, shows some of the oldest burned-out stars in the Milky Way galaxy. They are found in an area of space called the globular cluster M4. Some scientists refer to stars as the clocks of the universe, because knowing how old stars are helps us to calculate the age of the entire universe.

NEW TECHNOLOGY BRINGS NEW EVIDENCE

Scientists believe the universe is still expanding. In recent years, using the Hubble Space Telescope and powerful ground telescopes, astronomers have found and continue to find galaxies that were created about one billion years after the big bang. In 1998, astronomers made a shocking discovery: The universe was expanding at an increasing rate. Until then, it was believed that gravitational forces would slow down the expansion of the universe. The causes for this acceleration are the subject of much discussion.

The blue circles indicate ancient, dim white dwarf stars. NASA scientists believe these white dwarfs are about 12 to 13 billion years old.

Guess What?

It may look as though outer space has vast empty areas, but in fact, the gaps between stars and between galaxies are filled with huge amounts of thinly spread gas and dust, as well as many forms of radiation.

THE SUN

The sun is a star, a gaseous ball with no solid surface. Its energy comes from burning hydrogen into helium at its core, a process called nuclear fusion. (Fusion happens when lighter elements are changed into heavier elements.)

As stars go, the sun is a pretty common one. There are trillions more like it in the universe, many with their own systems of planets and moons. Studying the sun helps us to learn more about other stars and galaxies.

The gravitational pull of the sun keeps the planets in this solar system from flying out into space. It keeps the planets in orbit. The sun provides Earth with energy, enabling plants to grow and living things to thrive.

The sun determines the seasons and sleep cycles of all living creatures.

WHAT ARE SUNSPOTS?

Inside the sun is a magnetic field. When the magnetic field rises up to the surface, sunspots are formed. They appear darker, because they are cooler than the rest of the sun, but they are still hotter than 8,000°F (4,427°C).

SOLAR STATS

The average distance between the sun and Earth is about 93 million miles (150 million km).

The sun is about 4.5 billion years old. Like all stars, it was born in a vast cloud of gas and dust. It will burn for another 5 billion years before it runs out of fuel.

The radius of the sun (which is the length of a straight line from its center to any point on its surface) is 109 times bigger than the radius of Earth.

Radius

The sun's average surface temperature is 10,292°F (5,700°C). Earth's average surface temperature is 58°F (14°C).

The sun rotates on its axis. It takes an average of 27 days to complete a full rotation. Because the sun is a gaseous ball and has no solid surface, different parts rotate at different speeds.

SOLAR ECLIPSES

A solar eclipse occurs when the moon moves between the sun and Earth, blocking the sun from our view. When an eclipse takes place during the day, a bright, sunny day can take on the appearance of a dark, overcast day in an instant. The position of the moon relative to the sun and Earth can result in either a partial eclipse or a total eclipse. A total eclipse lasts only a few minutes.

SOLAR SAFETY TIP

Never look directly at the sun, even during an eclipse. It can cause permanent damage to the retina of the eye.

A partial eclipse as seen in China in 2010

TFK GAME

SUNNY ADVICE

A proverb is a short saying that often contains a bit of advice, wisdom, or a practical thought. Use the key below to decode a proverb from the Maori people of New Zealand about keeping a positive attitude. Fill in the blanks to solve the riddle.

A	B	C	D	E	F	G	H	I	J	K	L	M	N	O	P	Q	R	S	T	U	V	W	X	Y	Z

Answer on page 216.

191

Solar flare

SOLAR FLARES

The sun is changing constantly. During periods of high solar activity, the sun will shoot out massive amounts of magnetic energy. These are known as **solar flares.** Some solar flares are so large that the radiation they release can reach the Earth's atmosphere. This radiation can disrupt power grids, satellites, and other communication devices, affecting our cell phones, trains, and televisions.

NASA uses satellites such as the Solar and Heliospheric Observatory (SOHO) to predict these eruptions in order to give scientists, government officials, and others two or three days of warning to protect expensive equipment.

Guess What?
Solar eruptions occur in an 11-year cycle. Scientists expect the cycle to be at its most active phase in 2013.

Aurora borealis as seen from Norway

Light Shows

Solar flares can also interact with Earth's magnetic field, creating beautiful, natural light shows in the sky. These cool displays are known as the southern lights, or aurora australis (which can be seen in places including Antarctica, New Zealand, southern Australia, and southern Argentina) and the northern lights, or aurora borealis. The aurora borealis is sometimes visible in the northern areas of Greenland, Alaska, Siberia (in Russia), Sweden, Norway, and other places near the North Pole.

A view of aurora borealis from Alaska

Death of a Star

When a star runs out of material to burn in its core, we say that it starts to die. Some stars burn out slowly, eventually turning into clouds of gas and dust, while others explode violently in an instant.

Most stars die slowly, first becoming **red giants** and then **white dwarfs.** If a dying white dwarf is close enough to another star, it can steal energy and turn into a **supernova** in a sudden, violent explosion. A supernova can release more light in a few days than 100 million suns.

When a supernova collapses on itself, it can create a **neutron star,** which is an incredibly dense but small star, or a **black hole,** a place where a huge amount of matter is packed into a tiny space with a powerful gravitational pull. The pull is so strong that nothing—not even light—can escape a black hole. That's how it got its name!

In about 5 billion years, our sun will turn into a red giant. As a red giant, it will become cooler but grow in size and extend past Mars. Over time, the outer layers of gas will float away. The core will then become a white dwarf.

Gassy remnant of a supernova

Mira (*my*-ruh) looks like a comet but is actually a dying star, or red giant. As Mira burns out, it expands in size and releases dust that will help form other stars and planets.

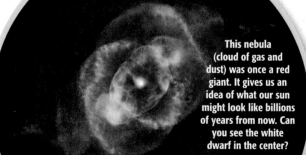

This nebula (cloud of gas and dust) was once a red giant. It gives us an idea of what our sun might look like billions of years from now. Can you see the white dwarf in the center?

THE PLANETS

The eight planets in the solar system orbit around the sun. Early astronomers were able to see the six closest planets to the sun simply by looking up, but Uranus and Neptune can be seen only by telescope. Mercury, Venus, Earth, and Mars are called the terrestrial planets, because they have solid, rocky bodies. The outer four planets are called the gas giants, because they do not have surfaces and are made up of gases.

VENUS

Venus is similar in size to Earth but it has no oceans. It's covered by a layer of thick clouds, which trap heat in its atmosphere.

HOW BIG IS IT?* With a diameter of 7,504 miles (12,077 km), it is a little smaller than Earth.

WHERE IS IT? About 67.24 million miles (108.2 million km) from the sun

HOW'S THE WEATHER? The average surface temperature is 867°F (464°C).

RINGS: 0

THE SUN

MERCURY

Because it's so close to the sun, Mercury can be seen only shortly before sunrise or just after sunset. At other times, it is hidden by the bright glare of the sun.

HOW BIG IS IT?* With a diameter of 3,025 miles (4,868.3 km), it is less than half the size of Earth.

WHERE IS IT? About 36 million miles (57.9 million km) from the sun

HOW'S THE WEATHER? The average surface temperature is 354°F (179°C).

RINGS: 0

EARTH

Earth is the only planet known to sustain life. Its atmosphere protects the planet from the worst of the sun's rays. About 70% of Earth is covered with water.

HOW BIG IS IT?* Earth has a diameter of 7,926.2 miles (12,756 km).

WHERE IS IT? About 92.9 million miles (149.5 million km) from the sun

HOW'S THE WEATHER? The average surface temperature is 58°F (14°C).

RINGS: 0

MARS

Mars is prone to dust storms that engulf the entire planet.

HOW BIG IS IT?* With a diameter of 4,222 miles (6,795 km), it is roughly half as big as Earth.

WHERE IS IT? About 141.71 million miles (228.1 million km) from the sun

HOW'S THE WEATHER? The average surface temperature is −82°F (−63°C).

RINGS: 0

SATURN

Known as the ringed planet, Saturn spins very quickly. It only takes 11 hours for the planet to rotate fully on its axis. Saturn's famous rings are made up of ice and rock.

HOW BIG IS IT?* With a diameter of 74,732 miles (120,270 km), it is 9$\frac{1}{2}$ times the size of Earth.

WHERE IS IT? About 885.9 million miles (1.43 billion km) from the sun

HOW'S THE WEATHER? The average surface temperature is −285°F (−176°C).

RINGS: Thousands

NEPTUNE

Neptune was the first planet located by mathematical predictions instead of observation.

HOW BIG IS IT?* With a diameter of 30,707 miles (49,418 km), it is four times bigger than Earth.

WHERE IS IT? About 2.8 billion miles (4.5 billion km) from the sun

HOW'S THE WEATHER? The average surface temperature is −373°F (−225°C).

RINGS: 9, made up of thousands of "ringlets"

JUPITER

Jupiter is the solar system's biggest planet. Four of its many moons are planet-size themselves.

HOW BIG IS IT?*
At 88,650 miles (142,668 km), its diameter is 11 times bigger than Earth's.

WHERE IS IT? About 483.9 million miles (778.8 million km) from the sun

HOW'S THE WEATHER? The average surface temperature is −238°F (−150°C).

RINGS: 3

URANUS

Uranus was discovered by William Herschel in 1781.

HOW BIG IS IT?* With a diameter of 31,693 miles (51,005 km), it is about four times the size of Earth.

WHERE IS IT? About 1.78 billion miles (2.86 billion km) from the sun

HOW'S THE WEATHER? The average surface temperature is −353°F (−214°C).

RINGS: 13

*This illustration is not drawn to scale.

EARTH'S MOON

1969 moon landing

As the sun shines on the moon, half of the moon is always lit and half is in darkness. But because the moon orbits the Earth, and the Earth orbits the sun, the amount of the sunlit moon that we see on Earth changes. These changing views are called the phases of the moon. When the moon waxes, the amount of the moon that is visible on Earth gets bigger. When it wanes, the visible amount gets smaller, until the cycle begins again.

Guess what?
Humans first landed on the moon in 1969. There have been five other manned U.S. landings since then and numerous unmanned landings.

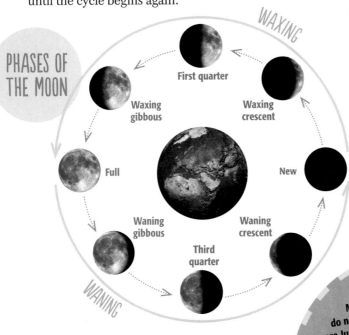

WAXING

PHASES OF THE MOON

First quarter

Waxing gibbous

Waxing crescent

Full

New

In a new moon, the moon is between Earth and the sun, and we can't see it.

THE SUN

Waning gibbous

Waning crescent

Third quarter

WANING

Guess what?
Most moons, like ours, do not have air. The exceptions are Jupiter's Io, Saturn's Titan, and Neptune's Triton. Io has more than 400 active volcanoes, which account for its thin, sulphur dioxide atmosphere. Titan has a thick atmosphere. Some of these moons are good candidates for future space missions. They are large enough to serve as space stations for human exploration beyond our solar system.

HOW MANY MOONS? Every year,
astronomers discover more moons in the far reaches of the solar system. But some of the smallest moons may actually be asteroids captured by the gravity of a planet. Mercury and Venus do not have moons. The other planets have the following number:

PLANET	NUMBER OF MOONS
EARTH	1
MARS	2
JUPITER	50 moons and 14 provisional moons*
SATURN	53 moons and 9 provisional moons*
URANUS	27
NEPTUNE	13

Jupiter's moon Ganymede looks tiny next to the giant planet, but it is the largest satellite in the solar system. In fact, this icy moon is larger than Mercury and about three-fourths the size of Mars.

*Provisional moons have not yet been confirmed.

Pluto Is a Papa!

By Michael D. Lemonick

At this moment, a spacecraft is aimed straight at Pluto, heading out toward the edge of the solar system at speeds faster than 50,000 miles (80,467 km) an hour. The New Horizons probe was launched in 2006. But even at that blistering speed, it won't arrive until 2015. Mission scientists have been scouting ahead with the Hubble Space Telescope to see if there's anything unusual to photograph. They are also looking for any hazards to avoid—rings, for example. If a space probe were to smash through a planet's rings at high speed, it could be damaged or even destroyed. In June 2011, they spotted P4, a moon orbiting Pluto that nobody knew about.

The New Horizons probe

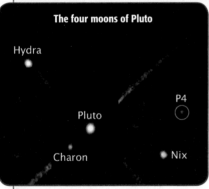

The four moons of Pluto

There's a good reason P4 escaped notice until now: Its small size makes it all but impossible to see from Earth. "We always knew it was possible there were more moons out there," says Alan Stern of the Southwest Research Institute, in Boulder, Colorado. Stern is the principal investigator of the New Horizons mission and a co-discoverer of the new moon. "Lo and behold, there it was," he says.

A CLOSE ENCOUNTER

Even though New Horizons will be flashing past Pluto at a blinding speed, the total encounter will last for weeks. "Lots of people think we're going to go by on a Tuesday or something," says Stern. But New Horizons will start getting better images than the Hubble—and thus the best ever taken of Pluto and its moons—starting 10 weeks before the flyby and lasting 10 weeks afterward. The probe's closest approach will happen on July 14, 2015.

NAMING A NEW MOON

Tiny P4 needs a real name. "We're tossing around some ideas," says Mark Showalter of the SETI Institute in Mountain View, California. "But the name has to come out of Greek mythology associated with Hades and the underworld." Underworld myths are the rule for moons of Pluto. The International Astronomical Union (IAU) has strict guidelines for the naming of heavenly objects. It has to formally approve all new names.

Guess what?
The IAU was also responsible for deciding, in 2006, that Pluto would no longer be considered a planet. Pluto, which is about half the size of Earth's moon, now has the status of dwarf planet.

197

Asteroids

Asteroids are rocky objects orbiting the sun that are smaller than planets but larger than meteoroids. Ceres, the first asteroid ever discovered, was spotted in 1801. Since then, people have learned more about these rocky worlds, and Ceres's classification has changed. Now scientists consider Ceres, which is a whopping 592 miles (952 km) in diameter, to be a dwarf planet, like Pluto.

Asteroids are most likely the leftover chunks of rock from the formation of the universe. They are usually irregularly shaped and covered with craters. Lots of asteroids can be found between Mars and Jupiter, in an area known as the asteroid belt, or main belt.

The asteroid Ida has its own moon, Dactyl. Dactyl is only 1 mile (1.6 km) across. Scientists call pairs like these binary, or double, asteroids.

Guess what? All asteroids are given a name and a number so that scientists can keep track of them.

Dawn

Guess what? The Dawn spacecraft, launched in 2006, is currently exploring an asteroid called Vesta in the asteroid belt. It took five years to reach Vesta. After Vesta, Dawn will head to Ceres.

FROM TIME FOR KIDS

A Close Call

By Jeffrey Kluger for TIME

Astronomers knew for several years that November 8, 2011, would end one of two ways: either uneventfully or with a massive impact that would leave a 4-mile (6.44 km) crater somewhere on the planet and unleash 70-foot-tall (21.34 m) tsunami waves on the world.

They even knew the exact time it would happen. It was the precise time at which asteroid 2005 YU55 was expected make its closest approach to Earth. Asteroid 2005 YU55 is a 1,312-foot (399.9 m) space rock that was discovered in December 2005.

Now the moment has come and gone. As the date got closer, astronomers knew there was nothing to fear. They calculated that the asteroid would miss Earth by 201,700 miles (324,605 km). It sounds like a lot. But on a cosmic scale, it was still a close call. The asteroid was a full 38,000 miles (61,155 km) closer than the moon is to us. That's a little like a car speeding down your street and touching your property with its tires. It is not enough to hurt you, but it is enough to make you uneasy.

Scientists were excited about the close call. Don Yeomans, manager of NASA's Near-Earth Object (NEO) Program, called it "an extraordinary opportunity" to learn more about

NEXT STOP: ROCKY LANDING

NASA has plans to send astronauts to an asteroid by 2025. Scientists hope that the samples they obtain will tell us more about the solar system's origins. And what NASA learns about how to land on or link a spacecraft to an asteroid may come in handy in the future if we ever have to deflect an asteroid heading toward Earth!

An artist's vision of an astronaut tethered to an asteroid

asteroids. It also gave scientists a chance to sharpen tracking and early-warning skills.

Asteroids are dangerous because there are so many of them. Scientists at the NEO Program are currently keeping their eyes on 19,500 rocks in the 330-foot to 3,300-foot (100.6 m to 1,006 m) range. Those are hardly the only asteroids of that size out there, but they're the ones near Earth.

Professional astronomers studied YU55 in detail as it passed by. They looked for the chemical signatures of carbon and water. Since asteroids are artifacts of the earliest days of the solar system, they might tell us something about how life got started on Earth and perhaps elsewhere.

Asteroids of this size—about 310 miles (499 km) in diameter—may have hit Earth in the far distant past. Fortunately, no asteroids this big threaten us now!

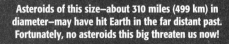

Comets

This amazing image of the center of Halley's Comet—which is approximately 9.32 miles (15 km) wide—was captured in 1986 by the European spacecraft Giotto.

Made up of frozen gas, rocks, dust, and ice, comets orbit the sun. They're like cosmic snowballs flying through space. Comets move in an elliptical—that is, an oval-shaped—orbit around the sun. Some comets take less than 200 years to complete an entire lap around the sun, while others can take thousands of years. When a comet gets near the sun, it heats up and parts of it begin to melt, leaving a visible tail of dust and gases that can be a few miles, a few hundred miles, or even a few hundred million miles in length. Because the paths of comets may take them deep into space before they come back toward the sun, some are seen only for short periods of time. Halley's Comet, for example, is visible from Earth for a short period every 76 years.

Comet Hale-Bopp was visible on Earth in 1996 and 1997. Spectators did not even need to use telescopes to see it.

Guess what?

The European Space Agency's (ESA) Solar and Heliospheric Observatory (SOHO) spacecraft is great at spotting comets. It has found more comets than any other person or spacecraft. Between December 2005 and December 2010, it located 2,000 comets.

Rosetta

Guess what?

The ESA's Rosetta mission is the first one designed to orbit and eventually land on a comet. Launched in 2004, Rosetta should reach the 67P/Churyumov-Gerasimenko comet by 2014.

Bull's-eye!

Space rocks and dust often crash into the moon. Unlike Earth, the moon doesn't have an atmosphere to protect it and turn a falling meteoroid into a pretty—and harmless—streak of light in the night sky. That's why the surface of the moon is marked with craters and holes—evidence of past impacts. On May 2, 2006, scientists watched through a telescope as a 10-inch-wide (25 cm) meteoroid struck the moon, where it left a crater approximately 45 feet (13.7 m) wide and 10 feet (3 m) deep. Researchers estimate that the meteoroid was traveling at 85,000 miles (136,794 km) per hour when it crashed!

Meteoroids

Meteoroids are hunks of rock or debris found in space. They are often fragments of comets or asteroids. When a meteoroid enters Earth's atmosphere, it usually burns up. If it does not, it is known as a **meteor**, or falling star. Meteors that hit the ground are called **meteorites**. An explosion in 1908 known as the Tunguska Event is believed to have been caused by a large meteorite. It destroyed 770 square miles (1,994 sq km) of forest in the Tunguska Basin, in Siberia, which is a large, cold region of central and eastern Russia. The largest single meteorite ever found was discovered in Namibia, in southwestern Africa. Known as the Hoba meteorite (named for the farmland it crashed into), it measures approximately 9 feet (2.7 m) wide. It is 3 feet (0.9 m) deep and weighs about 66 tons (60 metric tons).

Meteorite damage near the Tunguska River in Russia

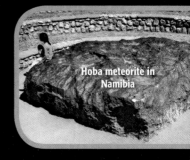
Hoba meteorite in Namibia

An artist's version of a meteoroid impact on the moon

Guess What?

Space dust is not like the harmless stuff you find under your carpet. Technically small meteoroids, space-dust particles can be just a few tenths of a millimeter. But because it whizzes through space at tremendous speeds—22,000 to 157,000 miles (35,406 to 252,667 km) per hour—space dust can damage satellites and other orbiting equipment.

Look closely at this photo and you can see streaks in the sky. They are part of a meteor shower. Meteor showers occur when Earth passes into a comet's path and pieces of the comet burn up in the planet's atmosphere.

SPACE JUNK

Humans have been traveling into space for only 50 years (see pages 202–205), but have already left behind lots of junk. There are old satellites, pieces broken off spacecraft, and objects dropped by astronauts. This space waste can be dangerous for astronauts. Even tiny particles can damage sensitive equipment. In June 2011, astronauts aboard the International Space Station (ISS) were forced to evacuate to the Russian *Soyuz* spacecraft docked to the station after spotting space junk heading their way. The orbiting debris missed the ISS by just 820 feet (250 m)!

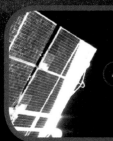
During a 2008 space walk, an ISS astronaut dropped a 30-pound (13.6 kg) tool bag. It drifted away in space.

OUT-OF-THIS-WORLD EVENTS

People have been studying space since ancient times. However, all of this exploration took place on the ground until the 1950s. Here are some of the many milestones in space exploration that have occurred since then.

1957: Laika

1958: Explorer I designers

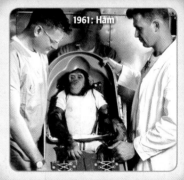
1961: Ham

1957

OCTOBER 4 The Soviet Union launches Sputnik 1, the first artificial satellite, into Earth's orbit.

NOVEMBER 3 Sputnik 2 carries a dog, Laika, into space.

1958

JANUARY 31 The U.S. launches Explorer 1, its first satellite, into Earth's orbit.

OCTOBER 1 National Aeronautics and Space Administration (NASA) is founded. It incorporates parts of an earlier group, the National Advisory Committee for Aeronautics (NACA) and other government organizations.

≋ 1959: Luna 2

1959

SEPTEMBER 14 The Soviet spacecraft Luna 2 slams into the moon, becoming the first human-made object to land on another celestial body.

≋ 1961: Yuri Gagarin

1961

JANUARY 31 A chimpanzee named Ham is launched into space as part of Project Mercury—the U.S.'s first manned spaceflight program.

APRIL 12 Soviet cosmonaut Yuri Gagarin becomes the first human in space. Aboard the *Vostok 1,* he makes a single orbit of Earth.

MAY 5 Piloting *Freedom 7,* Alan Shepard becomes the first American in space.

1962

FEBRUARY 20 John Glenn is the first American to orbit Earth.

MAY 25 President Kennedy, in a famous speech to Congress, urges the U.S. to put a man on the moon "before this decade is out."

1962: John Glenn enters the capsule of *Friendship 7* before his historic flight.

1965: Edward White

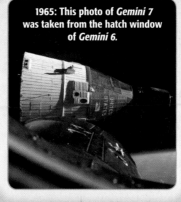
1965: This photo of *Gemini 7* was taken from the hatch window of *Gemini 6.*

1966: Surveyor 1

1963

JUNE 16 Soviet Valentina Tereshkova becomes the first woman in space, orbiting Earth in *Vostok 6.*

1964

OCTOBER 12 The Soviet *Voskhod 1* is the first mission to send multiple men into space.

1965

MARCH 18 Soviet cosmonaut Alexei Leonov exits the *Voskhod 2* and goes on the first space walk.

JUNE 3 Edward White, the pilot of *Gemini 4,* is the first American to go on a space walk.

DECEMBER 15 *Gemini 6* and *Gemini 7* fly within 1 foot (30 cm) of each other, marking the first "space rendezvous."

1966

MARCH 31 The unmanned Soviet probe Luna 10 is launched. It becomes the first spacecraft to orbit the moon.

MAY 30 The robotic spacecraft Surveyor 1 lifts off. It is the first spacecraft to make a soft landing on the moon. Surveyor 1 transmits photos and other information back to Earth.

1967

JANUARY 27 All three astronauts on the first *Apollo* mission die before takeoff when a fire breaks out in the cockpit. NASA makes numerous safety changes to their spacecraft.

1968

DECEMBER 21–27 *Apollo 8* completes the first manned orbit of the moon. The first pictures of Earth are taken from space.

1969

JULY 20 Neil Armstrong walks on the surface of the moon. He is the first human to do so. He is joined by Buzz Aldrin, and the pair spend 21 hours on the moon's surface.

1971

APRIL 19 The Russians launch Salyut I, the first space station.

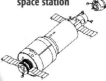
1971: Illustration of a spacecraft docking with the Salyut 1 space station

Guess what? Space suits provide oxygen for astronauts to breathe and pressurization to keep their blood from boiling in space. An astronaut's body heat is trapped inside a suit. To maintain a normal body temperature, the suit contains undergarments that keep cold liquid close to the skin.

Guess what? Temperatures in space vary greatly: from 248°F to −148°F (120°C to −100°C).

1968: Earth, as seen from *Apollo 8*

1975

JULY 17 A U.S. *Apollo* spacecraft docks with a Soviet *Soyuz* spacecraft, in the first joint mission between the two countries.

1976

JULY 20 NASA's Viking 1 lands on Mars.

1977

SEPTEMBER 5 AND AUGUST 20 NASA launches Voyager 1 and Voyager 2. Their mission: Visit Jupiter and Saturn and explore the outer reaches of the solar system.

Guess what? Although Voyager 2 was built after Voyager 1, it was launched first.

1978

NOVEMBER 16–20 NASA's Pioneer Venus Multiprobe spacecraft drops four probes to the planet's surface.

DECEMBER 4 NASA's Pioneer Venus Orbiter spacecraft begins a 14-year orbit of Venus, during which it maps the planet's surface by radar.

1979–1981

NASA's Voyager 1 passes Saturn and Jupiter, taking the first close-up pictures of these planets.

1981

APRIL 12 The first space shuttle, *Columbia,* is launched.

1983

JUNE 18 America's first woman astronaut, Sally Ride, travels into space aboard the space shuttle *Challenger.*

AUGUST 30 Guion S. Bluford, a mission specialist aboard the space shuttle *Challenger,* becomes the first African American in space.

1986

JANUARY 28 The space shuttle *Challenger* explodes during launch, killing all seven astronauts aboard, including Christa McAuliffe, the first teacher to participate in a space mission.

1983: Guion S. Bluford

Guess what? Astronauts have condiments—like ketchup and hot sauce—in space. Unlike at home, salt and pepper are available only in liquid form. If an astronaut tried to shake out the tiny salt grains or pepper flakes, they would drift all over the cabin!

1989

Voyager 2 passes Neptune.

❮❮ 1983: Sally Ride monitors control panels on the *Challenger*'s flight deck.

1979–1981: Voyager 1 took this photo of Jupiter on February 1, 1979—from 20 million miles (32.2 million km) away.

1981: Space Shuttle *Columbia*

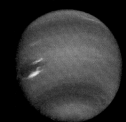

1989: Voyager 2 captured this image of Neptune at a range of 9.2 million miles (14.8 million km), on August 14, 1989.

1990: The Hubble Space Telescope circles Earth every 97 minutes, traveling at about 5 miles (8 km) per second.

1990

APRIL 24 The shuttle *Discovery* launches the Hubble Space Telescope into orbit above Earth. Hubble is the world's first space-based optical telescope.

1998

NOVEMBER 20 The first module of the International Space Station (ISS) is launched into orbit above Earth.

2000

NOVEMBER 2 The first manned expedition to the ISS docks. The U.S. and Russian crew lives and works aboard the ISS for four months.

≋ 2003–2005: This view of Mars's surface combined several different photos taken by Mars Odyssey between April 2003 and September 2005.

2001

FEBRUARY 12 The Near-Earth Asteroid Rendezvous (NEAR) Shoemaker spacecraft touches down on the asteroid Eros.

OCTOBER 24 After a 7¹/₂-month voyage, NASA's Mars Odyssey arrives at Mars and begins to map the planet's surface.

2003

OCTOBER 15 China launches *Shenzhou 5,* its first manned space mission.

2004

OCTOBER 4 *SpaceShipOne,* the first privately launched spacecraft, lifts off from Mojave, California, and makes a successful flight into space.

2008

OCTOBER 22 India launches Chandrayaan 1, its first unmanned moon mission.

≋ 1998: The ISS celebrated its 10th anniversary of having astronauts onboard continuously. At that point, it had completed 57,361 orbits of Earth. That's the equivalent of going around the sun eight times.

2009

MARCH 7 NASA's Kepler spacecraft begins its journey through space, tasked with identifying and collecting data on Earth-like planets.

For more recent space news and information about future missions, check out pages 206–215.

Guess what? In 2001, California businessman Dennis A. Tito became the first space tourist. His trip to the ISS lasted eight days and cost him $20 million.

2004: *SpaceShipOne*

A View from Space

In 1998, the first pieces of the **International Space Station** (ISS) were launched into orbit. Since 2000, the ISS has been continuously occupied by a rotating crew of astronauts and scientists. This high-tech space lab is a collaboration between NASA, the ESA (European Space Agency), and the space programs of Russia, Japan, Canada. While in orbit, astronauts from around the world perform scientific research and collect data about conditions in the Milky Way galaxy and beyond. Many of their experiments focus on humans' ability to live and work in space over long periods of time. They experiment with cells, tissues, and plants to see if they grow differently without gravity.

The ISS is also uniquely placed to observe Earth and collect data about weather patterns, the growth of cities, and the health of glaciers, coral reefs, fields, and forests. When they aren't working, performing experiments, or exercising, the astronauts aboard the station spend a lot of time looking out the windows and taking pictures of Earth. Here are some amazing photos snapped by ISS crew members.

Baitoushan Volcano in China and North Korea

Viedma Glacier in Argentina

Las Vegas, Nevada

Murzuq Desert in Libya

space workouts

When we walk around on Earth, the planet's gravity is pulling on us at all times. We need to exert force in order to lift a heavy box, to jump into the air, or even just to lift our arms and legs. In fact, our muscles get a little workout just by supporting our bodies. Living with very little gravity, the ISS astronauts have to be careful or their muscles and bones will weaken. To stay healthy, the astronauts work out for at least two hours per day.

≈ ISS astronauts attach themselves to straps while they run on treadmills. The straps pull down on them—kind of like gravity does back on Earth.

LIFE WITHOUT GRAVITY

The ISS is a noisy place. In addition to the sounds of the people working, there are many, many air-conditioning fans running, motors whirring, and machines buzzing. Some astronauts who have spent time at the station talk about how much they missed the simple sound of silence. Get the inside scoop on living in space with these 10 cool facts.

There is no laundry on the space station.

Astronauts strap themselves into bed so they stay in one place while they sleep.

There are Velcro patches, bungee cords, and foot restraints located all over the ISS. These are used for strapping down items (and people) to keep them from floating away and getting lost.

Astronauts try to make their sleeping quarters as cozy as possible. They hang up photos of their families and pets, and keep other personal belongings, such as books, gifts, musical instruments, and hobby supplies.

Without gravity and with the station constantly moving, any wall of a room could be considered the floor or the ceiling. So that the astronauts can have a frame of reference, they designate the deck, port, starboard, and overhead in each module. The words *starboard* and *port* are used on boats to refer to the right and the left when facing forward.

There is a water-purifying device that recycles wastewater (including urine!) and turns it into clean drinking water.

According to astronauts who've spent time on the ISS, space has a very distinct smell. One astronaut described it as "a mild version of the smell of an overheating car engine."

While in space, astronauts often grow 2 to 3 inches (5 to 8 cm).

In January 2010, the ISS got a software upgrade that gave astronauts personal access to the Internet for the first time.

Because the ISS is moving so quickly—about 17,500 miles (28,163 km) per hour—it orbits Earth every 90 minutes. That means that the astronauts witness a sunrise or sunset every 45 minutes.

SUPER SHUTTLE:
THE LAST MISSION

DAY 3 *Atlantis* coasts high over the Bahamas just before docking with the International Space Station.

On the warm summer morning of July 8, 2011, more than 1 million spectators gathered along the coastline near the Kennedy Space Center, in Florida, to witness the launch of STS-135: the 135th and final mission in the 30-year-old Space Transport System (STS, or space shuttle) program. On the launch pad, the orbiter *Atlantis*, loaded with supplies and parts for the International Space Station (ISS), waited for countdown. Finally, at 11:29 a.m., with just a minute to spare in the day's launch window, *Atlantis* and her four-person crew roared into the sky and into the history books.

DAY 1 *Atlantis* rockets into space. Two minutes after liftoff, the two boosters, their fuel spent, are dropped. The large external fuel tank empties after eight minutes and is also dropped.

Soyuz

Atlantis

DAY 4 *Atlantis* (see the nose of the spacecraft on the far right) is docked at the ISS, where it joined another visiting spacecraft, the Russian *Soyuz* (the T-shaped craft at far left).

DAY 5 NASA astronaut Mike Fossum takes a picture during a 6 1/2-hour space walk.

SHUTTLE FACTS

LENGTH (OF ORBITER):
122 feet (37.19 m)

WINGSPAN: 78 feet (23.77 m)

WEIGHT OF ORBITER:
178,000 pounds (80,739 kg)

WEIGHT AT LIFTOFF (ORBITER PLUS BOOSTERS AND EXTERNAL FUEL TANK):
4.5 million pounds (2.04 million kg)

WEIGHT OF FUEL BURNED DURING FIRST 8.5 MINUTES OF FLIGHT:
3.5 million pounds (1.59 million kg)

SPEED OF SHUTTLE, 8 SECONDS AFTER LIFTOFF: 100 miles (161 km) per hour

SPEED OF SHUTTLE, 1 MINUTE AFTER LIFTOFF: 1,000 miles (1,609 km) per hour

SPEED OF SHUTTLE, 2 MINUTES AFTER LIFTOFF: 3,000 miles (4,828 km) per hour

SPEED OF SHUTTLE, 8.5 MINUTES AFTER LIFTOFF: 18,000 miles (28,968 km) per hour

DAY 12 As *Atlantis* heads back to Earth, a crew member snaps this photo of the ISS.

DAY 13
Viewed from the ISS, *Atlantis,* returning home, is an arrow of light aimed at the clouds in Earth's atmosphere.

DAY 13 *Atlantis* touches down for the final time at Kennedy Space Center, at 5:57 a.m., on July 21, 2011. During STS-135, *Atlantis* orbited Earth 200 times, traveling 5,284,862 miles (8,505,161 km).

ROVING ROBOTS

BIG, BIGGER, BIGGEST!

To get a closer look at Mars, NASA has been sending robots on wheels into space. These traveling robots are called rovers. On November 26, 2011, the Curiosity rover launched into space aboard the Atlas V-541 rocket. After a nine-month journey covering more than 352 million miles (566 million km), Curiosity is expected to land and begin exploring the dry, dusty surface of Mars. Past explorations have found some evidence of water, and water is necessary to sustain living things. But Curiosity is not looking for humans or the kinds of aliens seen in movies. Instead, it is looking for environmental traces that suggest that microbes could ever have lived there. Microbes are microscopic organisms. Curiosity will use its many tools to look for other requirements for life, such as minerals like carbon.

The first rover to visit Mars was the 2-foot-long (61 cm) Sojourner. It landed on Mars in 1997 and explored the planet's surface for three months. The medium-size rover came next. Two of these machines, Spirit and Opportunity, went to the red planet in 2004. Opportunity covered 20 miles (32 km). The largest of the rovers, Curiosity, is 9 feet, 8 inches tall (3 m). See how it towers over the engineers in the photo below?

Curiosity can travel longer than earlier rovers. Its battery allows it to function year-round. The previous rovers ran on solar power and were forced to hibernate in the winter. Curiosity can roll over bigger obstacles and is equipped with powerful tools, including a drill.

➢ To make sure they do not introduce bacteria or other organisms to places in space, scientists build spacecraft and equipment in dust-free and bug-free areas called "clean rooms." Workers, likes these people assembling Curiosity, wear protective gear as well.

The actual versions of Sojourner, Spirit, and Opportunity are still on Mars. The rovers in this photo are the test versions that stayed on Earth.

CURIOSITY'S TOOLS

The **ChemCam** (short for Chemistry and Camera) instrument can shoot laser pulses to vaporize rocks up to 23 feet (7 m) away. A telescope and spectrometer can analyze the sparks that are released to figure out what chemical elements make up the rock.

Cameras, called **MastCams,** on the head of the rover offer an almost humanlike view from 6½ feet (2 m) above the ground. The right camera captures images near and far, using a telephoto lens that can greatly magnify objects. The left camera takes pictures of much wider expanses of landscape.

Three **antennas** allow Curiosity to transmit data and photos to spacecraft orbiting Mars and to scientists on Earth.

At the end of the **robotic arm** is a "hand" filled with instruments, including a drill, a brush, and a scooper.

Curiosity's **wheels** allow it to roll over rocks 30 inches (75 cm) tall.

The **Radiation Assessment Detector (RAD)** measures the amount of radiation, or subatomic particles, that reach Mars from the sun and other stars.

SIMULATING LOW GRAVITY

To train the astronauts of the future, the U.S. space agency created a project called NASA Extreme Environment Mission Operation, or NEEMO. Astronauts, engineers, doctors, and divers spend up to three weeks living in an underwater laboratory off the coast of Florida. Because people feel weightless underwater, they are able to practice with equipment in a way that is similar to what it might be like to work on the moon, on an asteroid, or even on Mars.

Guess what?
Mars is known as the "red planet" because a layer of iron oxide dust gives it a reddish appearance. Common rust is a type of iron oxide.

Infinity and Beyond

By Jeffrey Kluger for TIME

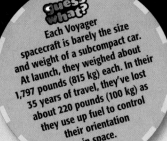

Guess what? Each Voyager spacecraft is barely the size and weight of a subcompact car. At launch, they weighed about 1,797 pounds (815 kg) each. In their 35 years of travel, they've lost about 220 pounds (100 kg) as they use up fuel to control their orientation in space.

When the two Voyager spacecraft launched in 1977, their mission was ambitious: Fly to Jupiter, then on to Saturn, and then maybe swing by Uranus and Neptune. Voyager 2 made that grand tour. It flew through the solar system and successfully visited Neptune in 1989. It is still the only spacecraft to have visited the outer planets, Uranus and Neptune. Voyager 1 visited Jupiter and Saturn, and spun past Saturn's methane-gas-covered moon, Titan. Then the craft's flight path flung it out toward the edge of the solar system.

The Voyagers' main mission was more successful than anyone could ever have expected. And it continues today. The creaky old spacecraft add 330 million miles (531 million km) to their journey every year. Each mile marks a new distance record for spacecraft. Now the Voyagers are set to pass at last from the outermost boundary of the solar system into uncharted regions of interstellar space. What will they find?

THE GREAT BEYOND

There's no way of knowing the exact point at which the solar system ends, but it is about 12 billion miles (19.3 billion km) from the sun. That is more than twice the distance from the

sun to Pluto. So scientists always knew there would be a lot of flying to do before the little ships crossed that distant threshold.

That threshold is approaching. Voyager 1 is about 11.2 billion miles (18 billion km) away from the sun. Voyager 2 is about 9.2 billion miles (14.8 billion km) away. "Since we travel a billion miles (1.6 billion km) every three years, it should be soon," says Voyager project scientist Ed Stone.

How have the Voyagers gone so far? It is a tribute to their tiny nuclear power plants. These are necessary for a deep-space mission, since spacecraft cannot rely on solar panels in a region where there is little sunlight. Scientists predicted that the power plants would be able to keep the ships going for 50 years. And power is expected to last until 2025. To make sure that it does, engineers have instructed both spacecraft to switch to thrusters that had not been used in flight. The thrusters control movement. The switch will save power.

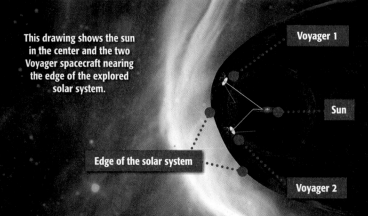

This drawing shows the sun in the center and the two Voyager spacecraft nearing the edge of the explored solar system.

Voyager 1

Sun

Edge of the solar system

Voyager 2

THE VOYAGERS

The two Voyager spacecraft are identical.
Check out a few of their features.

There are many instruments attached
to this boom, including wide-angle
and narrow-angle cameras.

This dish is used as an
antenna to communicate
with instruments on Earth.

The magnometer boom
senses magnetic fields
near the spacecraft.

The spacecraft gets its power
from generators that are like
tiny nuclear power plants.

The golden record

GREETINGS FROM EARTH

Eventually, the twin spacecraft will
fall silent. But their mission won't be
over. They will continue to serve as earthly
messengers. Attached to the ships are gold-plated
copper disks known as the golden records. The 12-
inch (30 cm) disks carry messages. Like time capsules, the
disks contain pictures, music from different cultures and eras, and greetings from Earth
in 55 languages. Because the disks were designed when the Voyagers launched, they
work like old phonograph records. In 1977, CDs were a thing of the future. If the golden
records are found one day, CDs, too, will likely be a thing of the long-distant past.

COMING UP SOON...

The Crab Nebula is made up of the remnants of a star that exploded in 1054. The explosion was so huge that Japanese, Chinese, and Native Americans noticed and recorded the event.

≋ Globular cluster M13 is a giant ball of more than 100,000 stars. These stars are so closely packed together that sometimes they collide and form new stars. M13 can be seen in the winter sky in the constellation Hercules.

THE HUBBLE SPACE TELESCOPE

The Hubble Space Telescope, a joint effort by NASA and the European Space Agency (ESA), was launched in 1990 and remains operational. During its lifetime, Hubble made discoveries that forced textbooks to be rewritten, and it captured brilliant images of such marvels as star births and two galaxies smashing together. Data collected by Hubble revealed that the universe is expanding faster than was previously thought. By measuring where distant galaxies are and how fast they are moving, Hubble also answered the question of how old the universe is: roughly 13.7 billion years.

Hubble is the only telescope that has to be repaired and maintained in space by astronauts. Between 1993 and 2009, five servicing missions were flown. In 2009, NASA and ESA decided to cancel future repair flights and let Hubble degrade until it no longer works. It is expected to function until 2014.

≋ The continuing aftermath of the collision of two galaxies. The bluish ring is matter pushing out from the center after first contact.

Hubble captured this photo of a dying star in 2009. What looks like colorful butterfly wings is actually a mass of incredibly hot gas. The gas is more than 36,000°F (19,982°C) and is moving through space faster than 600,000 miles (965,606 km) per hour.

This illustration shows Kepler-22b, the first planet that the Kepler mission confirmed orbits in a star's habitable zone. Kepler-22b is 2.4 times the size of Earth, but little more is known about it.

The Kepler spacecraft

THE KEPLER MISSION

Are we alone in the universe? The Kepler Mission is NASA's first attempt to answer this question. Launched in 2009, this space observatory seeks Earthlike planets that orbit other stars in our region of the Milky Way galaxy.

On its first flight, it studied 100,000 sunlike stars in search of planetary systems, like ours, that are in the habitable zone. This zone is a region where liquid water can exist on the surface of a planet. Where there's water, there can be life. This zone is not too close to a star, where it would be too hot, and not too far from a star, where it would be too cold. In other words, it is "just right." That's why the nickname for a planet in this zone is a "Goldilocks planet."

By early 2012, Kepler had identified 2,321 planet candidates. The Kepler Mission has been extended through 2016.

≍ JWST scientists stand before a full-scale model.

JAMES WEBB SPACE MISSION

The James Webb Space Telescope (JWST) is a collaboration between NASA, ESA, and the Canadian Space Agency.

Its goal is to search for the first stars and galaxies to form after the big bang and study their evolution. Unlike Hubble, which measures visible or ultraviolet light, the JWST will detect infrared wavelengths. This will allow it to "see" through dust and gas that can make it difficult to peer into deep space. This enormous telescope will be able to study relatively cooler objects that emit infrared radiation, including planets, brown dwarfs (which are like stars, only smaller and not powerful enough for nuclear fusion), and comets, as well as objects in the distant universe. According to the big bang theory (see page 188), the most distant objects are the youngest.

Originally planned for 2013, the JWST launch has been postponed until 2018.

Guess what?
A mirror on the James Webb Space Telescope will be 12.3 feet (3.7 m) wide. The telescope will feature a sun shield that is as big as a tennis court. The mirror and the sun shield will fold up inside a rocket during the launch and open up in space.

ANSWERS

PAGE 59:
WHO DOES WHAT?

1. h	6. b	11. a
2. d	7. e	12. i
3. m	8. l	13. c
4. k	9. j	
5. g	10. f	

PAGE 102:
PICK THE PATTERN

1. e
2. f
3. a
4. c
5. d
6. b

PAGE 105:
USE YOUR EAGLE EYES

PAGE 171:
REDECORATED ROBOT

PAGE 181:
WHIZ KID WORD SEARCH

L	Z	D	Y	N	A	M	I	T	E	Z	W
I	O	V	U	E	D	I	S	O	N	E	O
G	A	A	O	W	S	J	G	C	P	C	Q
H	G	C	A	T	V	C	Y	I	K	A	U
T	B	C	E	O	M	R	U	F	O	R	D
B	I	I	R	N	O	B	E	L	P	L	K
U	R	N	H	E	A	F	W	E	I	R	V
L	D	E	V	A	C	U	U	M	K	A	E
B	S	C	O	E	V	B	R	I	N	Y	L
D	E	A	I	R	P	L	A	N	E	J	C
M	Y	O	T	N	B	R	T	G	U	M	R
T	E	L	E	V	I	S	I	O	N	X	O

PAGE 191:
SUNNY ADVICE
Turn your face to the sun, and the shadows always fall behind you.

PHOTO CREDITS

FRONT COVER: Patrick Pleul/DPA/Getty Images (background); NASA/JPL-Caltech (Curiosity); AVAVA/Shutterstock.com (girl); ©iStockPhoto.com/Mads Abildgaard (body); Audrey Snider-Bell/Shutterstock.com (spider); Triff/Shutterstock.com (sun); Lucian Coman/Shutterstock.com (karate kid); Yellowj/Shutterstock.com (ladybug); mikeledray/Shutterstock.com (plants); Kevork Djansezian/Getty Images (dinosaur).

FRONT MATTER: 3: Nicku/Shutterstock.com (Newton); GeoM/Shutterstock.com (medicine); R_R/Shutterstock.com (plants); Tatiana Makotra/Shutterstock.com (iris); Falater Photography/Shutterstock.com (dancer); Kirsty Pargeter/Shutterstock.com (ribs). 4: Eric Isselée/Shutterstock.com (frog); HeinSchlebusch/Shutterstock.com (lions); ©iStockphoto.com/John Carnemolla (platypus); Ivancovlad/Shutterstock.com (magnet); PavelSvoboda/Shutterstock.com (geyser); Isabella Pfenninger/Shutterstock.com (rock formation). 5: AP Photo/AeroVironment Inc. (NAV); Diana Rich/Shutterstock.com (robot); NASA (Rosetta, Hubble); Petr84/Shutterstock.com (planet).

SCIENTIFIC CONCEPTS: 6–7: Andrey Burmakin/Shutterstock.com. 8: U.S. Department of Agriculture/Photo by Stephen Ausmus (all). 9: U.S. Department of Agriculture/Photo by Jack Dykinga (meteorologist); Lisa F. Young/Shutterstock.com (psychologist); RGtimeline/Shutterstock.com (engineer); michaeljung/Shutterstock.com (mathematician). 10: Stacie Stauff Smith Photography (beach); olly/Shutterstock.com (boy); Oleksiy Mark/Shutterstock.com (soda); Gelpi/Shutterstock.com (girl). 11: Skobrik/Shutterstock.com (chips); Elena Schweitzer/Shutterstock.com (bottles); Péter Gudella/Shutterstock.com (tire); Swapan/Shutterstock.com (pan); 3DDock/Shutterstock.com (computer); ©Aviahuismanphotography/Dreamstime.com (science fair). 12: ©Evgenyb/Dreamstime.com (girl); R_R/Shutterstock.com (plants). 13: ©Toseg/Dreamstime.com (girl); Ljupco Smokovski/Shutterstock.com (egg); optimarc/Shutterstock.com (box). 14: Image by NASA/Stockli, Nelson, Hasler Laboratory for Atmospheres Goddard Space Flight Center (Earth); Anne Kitzman/Shutterstock.com (girl); sonya etchison/Shutterstock.com (golfer). 15: daulon/Shutterstock.com (solar system); Rob Wilson/Shutterstock.com (car); njaj/Shutterstock.com (Jupiter). 16: Nicku/Shutterstock.com (Newton); Photo by NASA (rocket); cozyta/Shutterstock.com (Newton's cradle). 17: Vasilieva Tatiana/Shutterstock.com (Trinity); Valentina R./Shutterstock.com (apple); Image by Ian Spackman (plague doctor); VasikO/Shutterstock.com (books); andrea crisante/Shutterstock.com (metal); zentilia/Shutterstock.com (gold). 18: Levent Konuk/Shutterstock.com (TV); Petr Vaclavek/Shutterstock.com (atom); azaphoto/Shutterstock.com (power lines). 19: Georgios Kollidas/Shutterstock.com (Democritus); Library of Congress, Prints and Photographs Division (Einstein); Marina Aver/Shutterstock.com (cookie); atm2003/Shutterstock.com (house). 20: Molodec/Shutterstock.com (background); Marynchenko Oleksandr/Shutterstock.com (wires). 21: Fotokostic/Shutterstock.com (vest); R. Gino Santa Maria/Shutterstock.com (water); Chris Lenfert/Shutterstock.com (hydrogen peroxide); Aaron Amat/Shutterstock.com (salt). 22–23: charobnica/Shutterstock.com. 24: Mansell/Time Life Pictures/Getty Images (Mendeleyev); itsmejust/Shutterstock.com (X-ray); Marcio Jose Bastos Silva/Shutterstock.com (dinosaur). 25: Photos.com (Curie); Comstock/Photos.com (sunscreen). 26: GekaSkr/Shutterstock.com (match); el lobo/Shutterstock.com (bike); Steshkin Yevgeniy/Shutterstock.com (boy); AGphotographer/Shutterstock.com (ice);

Lisa S./Shutterstock.com (background). 27: Magone/Shutterstock.com (bread); Omer N Raja/Shutterstock.com (boy); Africa Studio/Shutterstock.com (cleaning supplies); R. Gino Santa Maria/Shutterstock.com (paint). 28: AP Photo/Damian Dovarganes (seismologist); U.S. Department of Agriculture/Peggy Greb (entomologist); National Oceanic and Atmospheric Administration/Commander John Bortniak, NOAA Corps (glaciologist); Emilia Stasiak/Shutterstock.com (mouse). 29: AP Photo/Science (art kit); The Center for Game Science, University of Washington (Foldit); Peter Waters/Shutterstock.com (roaches).

HUMANS: 30–31: Blend Images/Shutterstock.com. 32: Helder Almeida/Shutterstock.com (sweaty girl); Convit/Shutterstock.com (stomach cells). 33: Gl0ck/Shutterstock.com (red blood cells); Aleksandr Markin/Shutterstock.com (smile); AP Photo/University of Michigan, Gary Smith (stem cell); Maxim Kalmykov/Shutterstock.com (man). 34: alxhar/Shutterstock.com (body); Ocsi Balazs/Shutterstock.com (ear); Kirsty Pargeter/Shutterstock.com (ribs); andesign101/Shutterstock.com (foot). 35: alxhar/Shutterstock.com (body); Yurchyks/Shutterstock.com (eye); NatalieJean/Shutterstock.com (baby); sianc/Shutterstock.com (teen); goodluz/Shutterstock.com (senior); Goodluz/Shutterstock.com (adult). 36: Fedorov Oleksiy/Shutterstock.com (skin); Sergej Khakimullin/Shutterstock.com (hand); Blaz Kure/Shutterstock.com (eye). 37: Anita Potter/Shutterstock.com (diagram); H. Tuller/Shutterstock.com (graft). 38: alxhar/Shutterstock.com (body); ©iStockPhoto.com/John_Woodcock (heart); Reprinted with permission from Thoratec (pump). 39: alxhar/Shutterstock.com (body); Alex Luengo/Shutterstock.com (lungs); gemphotography/Shutterstock.com (bubbles); Maridav/Shutterstock.com (runner). 40: alxhar/Shutterstock.com (body); leonello calvetti/Shutterstock.com (stomach); ©iStockPhoto.com/gerenme (girl). 41: blambca/Shutterstock.com (vomit); Geordie/Shutterstock.com (bran); Sebastian Kaulitzki/Shutterstock.com (body); Peter zijlstra/Shutterstock.com (kidney bean). 42: alxhar/Shutterstock.com (body); Sebastian Kaulitzki/Shutterstock.com (nerve); CLIPAREA/Custom media/Shutterstock.com (brain); Jiang Dao Hua/Shutterstock.com (gymnast). 43: Milan Vasicek/Shutterstock.com (tongue); ociek666/Shutterstock.com (sick girl); omkar.a.v/Shutterstock.com (ice cream); iofoto/Shutterstock.com (reflex). 44: Alexander Raths/Shutterstock.com (thyroid); Jorg Hackemann/Shutterstock.com (acne); Waschnig/Shutterstock.com (sweat). 45: ©Gaby Kooijman/Dreamstime.com (feet); Lisa F. Young/Shutterstock.com (family). 46: Anton Prado PHOTO/Shutterstock.com (finger); bikeriderlondon/Shutterstock.com (freckles); Tomasz Parys/Shutterstock.com (curly hair). 47: BioPhoto Associates/Photo Researchers/Getty Images (chromosome); PRNewsFoto/FEI Company (Scanning Electron Microscope); Ivonne Wierink/Shutterstock.com (peanuts). 48: Cary Wollinsky/Aurora/Getty Images (scientist and chimpanzee); AP Photo/American Museum of Natural History (mural); AP-PHOTO/HO (Lucy). 49: AP Photo/Shekhar Srivastava (painting); AP Phoro/Remy de la Mauviniere (tools). 50: VikaRayu/Shutterstock.com (bread); Mark Herreid/Shutterstock.com (steak); oriori/Shutterstock.com (walnut); bergamont/Shutterstock.com (sunflower seeds); Darrin Henry/Shutterstock.com (girl). 51: matin/Shutterstock.com (blueberries); U.S. Department of Agriculture (MyPlate); fotohunter/Shutterstock.com (basil); Valeriy Lebedev/Shutterstock.com (boy). 52: olly/Shutterstock.com (muscular); Lucian Coman/Shutterstock.com (karate kid); Falater Photography/Shutterstock.com (dancer). 53: Anatoliy Samara/Shutterstock.com (basketball); aida ricciardiello/Shutterstock.com (sleeping). 54: Tischenko Irina/Shutterstock.com (bacteria); maximino/Shutterstock.com (girl). 55: Photo by CDC/Judy Schmidt (shot); Dave Thompson/PA Wire/Press Association via AP Images (chicken pox); kurt_G/Shutterstock.com (mosquito). 56: Photo by CDC/Brian Judd (sneeze); Matt Antonino/Shutterstock.com (grill). 57: GeoM/Shutterstock.com (medicine); giorgiomtb/Shutterstock.com (ear); Candace Hartley/Shutterstock.com (bloody knee). 58: GWImages/Shutterstock.com (Phoropter); The State/McClatchy-Tribune/Getty Images (ECG); Vince Clements/Shutterstock.com (food label); triocean/Shutterstock.com (inhaler). 59: Courtesy of Dr. Joseph Hahn (Hahn); Kenneth Man/Shutterstock.com (doctor). 60: Jiri Hera/Shutterstock.com (snail); AP Photo/Association for the Preservation of Virginia Antiquities (trepanation); Carlos E. Santa Maria/Shutterstock.com (mummy). 61: Bork/Shutterstock.com (acupuncture); DEA/G. DAGLI ORTI/De Agostini/Getty Images (Egyptian art); Image by Jacques-Louis David (painting); North Wind Picture Archives via AP Images (Pasteur); AP Photo/File (Fleming). 62: Galina Barskaya/Shutterstock.com (consoling);

Jeka/Shutterstock.com (sad girl). 63: AP Photo/*Houston Chronicle*, Karen Warren (bullying); Eric Isselée/Shutterstock.com (cat); Audrey Snider-Bell/Shutterstock.com (spider); Dmitry Lobanov/Shutterstock.com (blood); Iwona Grodzka/Shutterstock.com (puppet). 64: Zia Soleil/Iconica/Getty Images (sweaty boys); aliisik/Shutterstock.com (fingerprint); Kletr/Shutterstock.com (finger pad); Tatiana Makotra/Shutterstock.com (iris). 65: jcjgphotography/Shutterstock.com (boy); Dmitriy Shironosov/Shutterstock.com (woman); Blend Images/Shutterstock.com (fingernails).

ANIMALS: 66–67: littlesam/Shutterstock.com. 68: Mark Conlin/Oxford Scientific/Getty Images (whale); Sunny Forest/Shutterstock.com (plants); TSpider/Shutterstock.com (mushrooms); Photo by U.S. Department of Agriculture/Eric Erbe, Colorization by Christopher Pooley (bacteria); National Oceanic and Atmospheric Administration/Orange Coast College Biology Department (protists); Frederic B/Shutterstock.com (archaea). 69: Jordan Tan/Shutterstock.com (giraffe); liubomir/Shutterstock.com (turtle). 70: Jurie Maree/Shutterstock.com (lobster); oneo/Shutterstock.com (pig); Tatiana Belova/Shutterstock.com (polar bear); Ecoimages/Shutterstock.com (hyena); DG Jervis/Shutterstock.com (tiger); KA Photography KEVM111/Shutterstock.com (lioness). 71: Susan Schmitz/Shutterstock.com (eagle); Eric Isselée/Shutterstock.com (ladybugs); neelsky/Shutterstock.com (Bengal tiger); ©iStockphoto.com/pixonaut (Siberian tiger). 72: Melinda Fawver/Shutterstock.com (salamander); Four Oaks/Shutterstock.com (ostrich); Shawn Hempel/Shutterstock.com (peacock); Arto Hakola/Shutterstock.com (tern); Wild At Art/Shutterstock.com (jackal); Heiko Kiera/Shutterstock.com (knot). 73: Ryan M. Bolton/Shutterstock.com (rattlesnake); Krzysztof Odziomek/Shutterstock.com (whale shark); Eric Isselée/Shutterstock.com (bear, cow); Hugh Lansdown/Shutterstock.com (bat); ©iStockPhoto.com/Mark Dursetwitz (flying fish); Marty Wakat/Shutterstock.com (puffer fish); Paul Burdett/Shutterstock.com (koala); Jupiterimages/Photos.com (wood frog); Mayskyphoto/Shutterstock.com (crocodile). 74: riekephotos/Shutterstock.com (anemone); Videowokart/Shutterstock.com (clam); Dennis Sabo/Shutterstock.com (sponge); peappop/Shutterstock.com (slug); lavigne herve/Shutterstock.com (octopus); archana bhartia/Shutterstock.com (jellyfish); ECOSTOCK/Shutterstock.com (live scallop); Dima Kalinin/Shutterstock.com (scallop shells). 75: Galina Mikhalishina/Shutterstock.com (leeches); Undersea Discoveries/Shutterstock.com (urchin); Kokhanchikov/Shutterstock.com (earthworms); Stubblefield Photography/Shutterstock.com (brittle star); Harald Toepfer/Shutterstock.com (crab); Audrey Snider-Bell/Shutterstock.com (scorpion); Jason S/Shutterstock.com (molting). 76: Jason Maehl/Shutterstock.com (alligator); Naaman Abreu/Shutterstock.com (crocodile); Mircea BEZERGHEANU/Shutterstock.com (damselfly); iliuta goean/Shutterstock.com (dragonfly); Imaginechina via AP Images (ligers). 77: JacoBecker/Shutterstock.com (leopard); George Lamson/Shutterstock.com (cheetah); tubuceo/Shutterstock.com (dolphin); Jan Zoetekouw/Shutterstock.com (porpoise). 78: AP Photo (pidgeon); AP Photo/*The Journal-Standard*, Hilary Matheson (llama); U.S. Navy photo by Mass Communication Specialist 1st Class Bruce Cummins (dolphin). 79: Jocelyn Augustino/FEMA (dog climbing); Marvin Nauman/FEMA (dog barking); PRNewsFoto/National Disaster Search Dog Foundation, Michael Justice (seated dog). 80: ©iStockphoto.com/Duncan Walker (dodo); USFWS (mouse); Steve Maslowski/USFWS (bear); Roger Clapp/UFSWS (duck). 81: Houshmand Rabbani/Shutterstock.com (rabbits); AP Photo/Emilio Morenatti (fish). 82: AP Photo/*The Baxter Bulletin*, Kevin Pieper (bats); Ann Froschauer/USFWS (holding bat); AP Photo/Abu Dhabi Environment Agency (oryx). 83: AP Photo/Joydip Suchandra Kundu (tiger in net); AP Photo/Mahesh Kumar A. (tiger); AP Photo (tiger in water). 84: Jung Hsuan/Shutterstock.com (flatworm); StanOd/Shutterstock.com (jellyfish). 85: Tom McHugh/Photo Researchers/Getty Images (Cambrian); Studio-Chase/Photo Researchers/Getty Images (*Anomalocaris*); MarcelClemens/Shutterstock.com (trilobite); Colin Keates/Dorling Kindersley/Getty Images (nautiloid fossil); Laurie O'Keefe/Photo Researchers/Getty Images (nautiloid). 86: DEA/G. CIGOLINI/De Agostoni Picture Library/Getty Images (eurypterid fossil); Photo by Obsidian Soul (eurypterid); Zina Deretsky, National Science Foundation (*Tiktaalik*); Studio-Chase/Photo Researchers/Getty Images (Devonian). 87: Photo Researchers/Photo Researchers/Getty Images (Carboniferous); Joanne Kowne/Dorling Kindersley RF/Getty Images (*Hylomonus*); Dorling Kindersley/Dorling Kindersley/Getty Images (*Dimetrodon*); AP Photo/*Houston Chronicle*, James Nielsen (fossil). 88: Russell Shively/Shutterstock.com (ichthyosaur); Image by Mark Witton/

NSF (pterosaur); DM7/Shutterstock.com (T. rex model); Linda Bucklin/ Shutterstock.com (spinosaurus); Marques/Shutterstock.com (T. rex skull). 89: AP Photo/Eckehard Schulz (brachiosaur fossil); ©iStockphoto.com/Linda Bucklin (brachiosaur landscape); AP Photo/ Francois Mori (spinosaurus); AP Photo/Remy de la Mauviniere (triceratops); Andreas Meyer/Shutterstock.com (mosasaur); dezignor/ Shutterstock.com (asteroid). 90: Photo by NPS/Arvid Aase of James E. Tynsky specimen (horse); Photo by NPS (bird); AP Photo/Francois Mori (jaw); Jeffrey L. Rotman/Getty Images (teeth). 91: ©iStockPhoto.com/ Matthew Grove (mammoth fossil); Catmando/Shutterstock.com (mammoth painting); Noam Armonn/Shutterstock.com (kids). 92: C. Gaskin/Geology Museum, University of Otago (Kairuku); University of Otago (Kairuku fossil); Artwork by Meike Köhler (Nuralagus rex); Photo by Josep Quintana (foot bones). 93: Nicolle Rager Fuller/NSF (drawing); AP Photo/Science (fossil). 94: ©iStockphoto.com/Niko Guido (vicuña); William Attard McCarthy/Shutterstock.com (dragonflies). 95: Durden Images/Shutterstock.com (puffer fish); ©iStockphoto.com/Kevin Dyer (fiddler crab). 96: Neale Cousland/Shutterstock.com (termites); ©Paparico/Dreamstime.com (aardvark); EcoPrint/Shutterstock.com (social weaver nest); Dmitry Zamorin/Shutterstock.com (clownfish). 97: Stefan Fierros/Shutterstock.com (spawning); Eric Isselée/Shutterstock.com (tadpole, tadpole with legs, froglet, frog); Torsten Dietrich/Shutterstock. com (nymph); Micha Klootwijk/Shutterstock.com (grasshopper). 98: Scenic Shutterbug/Shutterstock.com (owl); HeinSchlebusch/Shutterstock. com (lions); Christopher Tan Teck Hean/Shutterstock.com (leaf). 99: David Aleksandrowicz/Shutterstock.com (octopus); John A. Anderson/ Shutterstock.com (cuttlefish). 100: Victor Malevankin/Shutterstock.com. 101: ecoventurestravel/Shutterstock.com (cheetah); Stephen Meese/ Shutterstock.com (jaguar); Galyna Andrushko/Shutterstock.com (leopard); Andy Poole/Shutterstock.com (ocelot); hightowernrw/ Shutterstock.com (serval); neelsky/Shutterstock.com (tiger); George Lamson/Shutterstock.com (cheetah spots). 102: Eric Isselée/Shutterstock. com (dart frog); vblinov/Shutterstock.com (beetle); Dirk Ercken/ Shutterstock.com (colorful dart frog); AP Photo/marinethemes.com, Kelvin Aitken (jellyfish). 103: ©Millermountainman/Dreamstime.com (Pogonomyrmex ants); Heiko Kiera/Shutterstock.com (black mamba); mrfiza/Shutterstock.com (mosquito); Johan_R/Shutterstock.com (crocodile); davidpstephens/Shutterstock.com (shark). 104: Wendy Nero/ Shutterstock.com (elephants); FikMik/Shutterstock.com (iguana). 105: Gerry Bishop/Visuals Unlimited, Inc./Getty Images (ants); Karen Gowlett-Holmes/Oxford Scientific/Getty Images (fish); Eagle game from left to right, top to bottom: FloridaStock/Shutterstock.com (eagles 1, 7, 10, 17), Eric Isselée/Shutterstock.com (eagles 2, 4, 5, 6, 12, 13, 15), Uryadnikov Sergey/Shutterstock.com (eagles 3, 8, 9, 11, 14, 16). 106: Visuals Unlimited Inc./Alex Wild/Getty Images (Dracula ant); ©iStockphoto.com/John Carnemolla (platypus); ©Halil I. Inci/Dreamstime.com (hummingbird); AP Photo/Vanderbilt University, Kenneth Catania (mole); J van der Wolf/ Shutterstock.com (cows). 107: Alexey Stiop/Shutterstock.com (firefly); Susan Montgomery/Shutterstock.com (dolphin); Robert Koss/ Shutterstock.com (frigate bird); Josh Anon/Shutterstock.com (Japanese cranes). 108: Graeme Shannon/Shutterstock.com (hawk); Kruglov_Orda/ Shutterstock.com (snake); D. Kucharski & K. Kucharska/Shutterstock.com (earthworms); CreativeNature.nl/Shutterstock.com (mice); Kirsanov/ Shutterstock.com (grasshopper); basketman23/Shutterstock.com (grass). 109: Balazs Justin/Shutterstock.com (spider); ©Christopher Moncrieff/ Dreamstime.com (owl); Brberrys/Shutterstock.com (crocodile); ©Orchidart/Dreamstime.com (trapdoor spider); Ron Hilton/Shutterstock. com (wolf); Hugh Lansdown/Shutterstock.com (bat). 110: Danita Delimont/Gallo Images/Getty Images (common poorwill); Rex Features via AP Images (bear); Nature Picture Library/Britain On View/Getty Images (dormouse); Norbert Rosing/National Geographic/Getty Images (snakes). 111: Lynn Human/Shutterstock.com (background); Charles Shapiro/Shutterstock.com (inset). 112: Photo by Marvin Moriarty/USFWS (bat); AP Photo/UCLA, Brian Curry (new frog). 113: AP Photo/Mick Ellison, American Museum of Natural History, Science/AAAS (microraptor, fossil); AP Photo/World Wide Fund for Nature, Lee Grismer (lizard).

EARTH: 114–115: Serg Zastavkin/Shutterstock.com. 116: Bychkov Kirill Alexandrovich/Shutterstock.com (volcano); Lukiyanova Natalia/frenta/ Shutterstock.com (diagram). 117: John Cancalosi/Age Fotostock/Getty Images (Mesosaurus); Itay Gal/Shutterstock.com (Andes); Photo by Adam Dubrowa/FEMA (hillside). 118: MilanB/ Shutterstock.com (like poles, opposite poles); Michael

Chamberlin/Shutterstock.com (girl with magnet); Ivancovlad/Shutterstock. com (magnet); discpicture/Shutterstock.com (compass). 119: Snowbelle/ Shutterstock.com (Earth); Rich Carey/Shutterstock.com (turtle). 120: Photo Courtesy of Michael Rampino (Rampino); Andrea Danti/Shutterstock. com (volcano). 121: NPS Photo (Devils Postpile); Mikhail Nekrasov/ Shutterstock.com (Great Pyramid); photobank.ch/Shutterstock.com (marble); Christina Tisi-Kramer/Shutterstock.com (diamonds). 122: Iakov Filimonov/Shutterstock.com (background); Ilya D. Gridnev/Shutterstock. com (horseshoe crab); ©LohKH/Dreamstime.com (cycad); Graeme Knox/Shutterstock.com (tuatara); Heinrich van den Berg/Gallo Images/ Getty Images (lizard); ©Minden Pictures/SuperStock (katydid). 123: Vitaly Titov & Maria/Shutterstock.com (tropical forest); hainaultphoto/ Shutterstock.com (camels); chris2766/Shutterstock.com (foot); jaana piira/Shutterstock.com (howler monkey). 124: TTphoto/Shutterstock. com (taiga); Nicola Destefano/Shutterstock.com (bear); Adam Cegledi/ Shutterstock.com (reindeer); Thorsten Schier/Shutterstock.com (temperate forest); Lumir Jurka "Lumis"/Shutterstock.com (hedgehog). 125: Romewo Koitmae/BigStockPhoto.com (tundra); JKlingebiel/Shutterstock.com (fox); Serg Zastavkin/Shutterstock.com (flowers); Eric Isselée/Shutterstock. com (grassland); ylq/Shutterstock.com (wildebeests). 126: mythja/ Shutterstock.com (background); Frontpage/Shutterstock.com (Nile); Map by Joe Lemonnier and Joe Lertola (map). 127: Alexei Novikov/ Shutterstock.com (trees); Steve Schwettman/Shutterstock.com (beach); ©Cecoffman/Dreamstime.com (mountains). 128: gopixgo/Shutterstock. com (dry, cracked earth); ©Vladimir Borodin/Dreamstime.com (rusting ship); Alita Bobrov/Shutterstock.com (glaciers). 129: AP Photo/Arctic and Antarctic Research Institute Press Service. 130: egd/Shutterstock.com (rain); suravid/Shutterstock.com (woman); DarkOne/Shutterstock.com (tornado); photobank.kiev.ua/Shutterstock.com (wind). 131: dubassy/ Shutterstock.com (city); Viktor Gladkov/Shutterstock.com (beach); My Portfolio/Shutterstock.com (fronts); NOAA (hurricane). 132: EuToch/ Shutterstock.com (thermometer); Gl0ck/Shutterstock.com (barometer); NOAA Photo Library (satellite, radar, balloon); T.W. van Urk/Shutterstock. com (anemometer); donvictorio@o2.pl/Shutterstock.com (hygrometer). 133: Artisticco/Shutterstock.com (forecast); Lisa F. Young/Shutterstock. com (meteorologist); Nicku/Shutterstock.com (radar). 134: ben bryant/ Shutterstock.com (ivy); Guinet/Shutterstock.com (General Sherman); Le Do/Shutterstock.com (samara); Jerry Horbert/Shutterstock.com (milkweed seeds). 135: Rigucci/Shutterstock.com (tree); Cheryl Casey/Shutterstock. com (girl); Dreamy Girl/Shutterstock.com (diagram); Nagel Photography/ Shutterstock.com (algae). 136: Maija/Shutterstock.com (deciduous); Dudarev Mikhail/Shutterstock.com (evergreen); HamsterMan/Shutterstock. com (pine needles); vesna cvorovic/Shutterstock.com (branch); Alexonline/Shutterstock.com (cell). 137: Cathy Keifer/Shutterstock. com (sundew, Venus flytrap); leungchopan/Shutterstock.com (pitcher plant); Jeff McMillian@USDA-NRCS PLANTS Database (bladderwort). 138: U.S. Department of Agriculture, Food Safety and Inspection Service, Kitchen Companion Image Library (seal); Fotokostic/Shutterstock.com (spraying); Gabriela Trojanowska/Shutterstock.com (girl). 139: Photo by U.S. Department of Agriculture/Bruce Fitz (scientist with hybrid); Nattika/ Shutterstock.com (potato); AP Photo/Alexander Merkushev (scientist with ancient plant); AP Photo/HO, the Institute of Cell Biophysics of the Russian Academy of Sciences (oldest plant). 140: ladyjane/Shutterstock. com (greenhouse); firedark/Shutterstock.com (illustration). 141: Dan Schreiber/Shutterstock.com (background); electra/Shutterstock.com (smoke); Vladislav Gurfinkel/Shutterstock.com (hurricane); Werner Goetz/Shutterstock.com (glacier); Ed Berlen/Shutterstock.com (drought); Brisbane/Shutterstock.com (flood). 142: Dudarev Mikhail/Shutterstock. com (background); Nataliya Hora/Shutterstock.com (smog); Artens/ Shutterstock.com (cars); risteski goce/Shutterstock.com (illustration). 143: AP Photo/BP PLC (robot); AP Photo/US Navy–Jeffery Tilghman (fire); Danny E Hooks/Shutterstock.com (beach). 144: Karoline Cullen/ Shutterstock.com (waves); USDA/NRCS (Dust Bowl). 145: Jarno Gonzalez Zarraonandia/Shutterstock.com (Grand Canyon); Maxim Petrichuk/ Shutterstock.com (desert); cholder/Shutterstock.com (dust storm). 146: Vadim Petrakov/Shutterstock.com (blue hole); AP Photo/Moises Castillo (sinkhole); kavram/Shutterstock.com (natural bridge); Darren J. Bradley/ Shutterstock.com (natural arch). 147: ©Annemario/Dreamstime.com (boiling lake); chbaum/Shutterstock.com (mud pool); nouseforname/ Shutterstock.com (fumarole); PavelSvoboda/Shutterstock.com (geyser). 148: Steve Bower/Shutterstock.com (Devils Tower); M.R./Shutterstock. com (fair chimney); nikidel/Shutterstock.com (fairy chimney inset);

Pecold/Shutterstock.com (Giant's Causeway); Josemaria Toscano/Shutterstock.com (Giant's Causeway inset). 149: CSLD/Shutterstock.com (Twelve Apostles); Jun Mu/Shutterstock.com (Stone Forest); N Mrtgh/Shutterstock.com (White Desert); sabella Pfenninger/Shutterstock.com (White Desert inset).

TECHNOLOGY: 150–151: 06photo/Shutterstock.com. 152: Robyn Mackenzie/Shutterstock.com (food); Vikulin/Shutterstock.com (coal); Elena Elisseeva/Shutterstock.com (girl); ©Hdconnelly/Dreamstime.com (rubber band); Lisa Rivali/Shutterstock.com (wrecking ball). 153: Jean Valley/Shutterstock.com (ball); Shebeko/Shutterstock.com (power lines); Roman Sigaev/Shutterstock.com (stove); Gelpi/Shutterstock.com (boy); Tomasz Trojanowski/Shutterstock.com (archer); Péter Gudella/Photos.com (arrow); daseaford/Shutterstock.com (target). 154: Sukpaiboonwat/Shutterstock.com (digging); kilukilu/Shutterstock.com (coal); Jezper/Shutterstock.com (oil rig); huyangshu/Shutterstock.com (oil pumps). 155: Oleg-F/Shutterstock.com (pipes); Meryll/Shutterstock.com (nuclear power plant); AP Photo/Mark Stehle (protest). 156: samotrebizan/Shutterstock.com (dam); Photo by DVIDS/Petty Officer 2nd Class Jonathan Chandler (turbine); AMA/Shutterstock.com (solar panels); atm2003/Shutterstock.com (solar-powered home). 157: majeczka/Shutterstock.com (wind farm); N.Minton/Shutterstock.com (geothermal); NASA (hydrogen); AP Photo/Damian Dovarganes (Honda). 158–159: hansenn/Shutterstock.com (background). 158: Photo by U.S. Department of Agriculture/Scott Bauer (switch grass); Tramper/Shutterstock.com (wood stove). 159: Nagel Photography/Shutterstock.com (algae); ©iStockPhoto.com/Christophe Heylen (cow); ©Priya Patel/Dreamstime.com (cow pies); Artter/Shutterstock.com (ocean). 160–161: Anettphoto/Shutterstock.com (background). 160: dedMazay/Shutterstock.com (eel); JacquelineSouthby/Photos.com (static); sutsaiy/Shutterstock.com (toaster); Elena Elisseeva/Shutterstock.com (surge protector). 161: cobalt88/Shutterstock.com (computer); Library of Congress, Prints and Photographs Division (Edison, Tesla). 162: baldyrgan/Shutterstock.com (battery); MilaLiu/Shutterstock.com (lightbulb); tuulijumala/Shutterstock.com (light switch). 163: Peter Tambroni/Shutterstock.com (plug); Roman Sotola/Shutterstock.com (sign); ©Simon Greig/Dreamstime.com (frayed wire); ilker canikligil/Shutterstock.com (battery). 164: MilanB/Shutterstock.com (magnet); nui7711/Shutterstock.com (toothbrush); taelove7/Shutterstock.com (camera); Joel Arem/Photo Researchers/Getty Images (magnetite). 165: Doug Martin/Photo Researchers/Getty Images (homemade electromagnet); Clive Streeter/Dorling Kindersley/Getty Images (electromagnet); Wessam Eldeeb/Photos.com (teacher); donatas1205/Shutterstock.com (paper). 166: Hal_P/Shutterstock.com (cell tower); akiradesigns/Shutterstock.com (kid, grandma); Bloomberg/Getty Images (first mobile phone); ©iStockPhoto.com/Brett Gage (iPhone); Jiri Hera/Shutterstock.com (tin cans). 167: DoD photo by Staff Sgt. James V. Downen Jr., U.S. Army (satellite phone); Zern Liew/Shutterstock.com (satellite); Brad Wynnyk/Shutterstock.com (girl); maryo/Shutterstock.com (Earth). 168: Photo by Jack Cook, Woods Hole Oceanographic Institution (Nereus); THP/Tim Hester Photography/Shutterstock.com (Mount Everest). 169: AP Photo/Mark Thiessen, National Geographic (*Deepsea Challenger*); NOAA/Archival Photography by Steve Nicklas, NOS, NGS (*Trieste*); Imaginechina via AP Images (Cameron). 170: Photo by John McCormick/Virginia Tech (all). 171: Photo by John McCormick/Virginia Tech (Charlie hip); Photo by Logan Wallace/Virginia Tech (SAFFiR); Diana Rich/Shutterstock.com (robot); Brian Michael Thomas/Our Hero Productions (game). 172: Felixdesign/Shutterstock.com (eye); Basheera Designs/Shutterstock.com (dog); Brian Michael Thomas/Our Hero Productions (lenses); ©Juan Moyano/Dreamstime.com (glasses). 173: valdis torms/Shutterstock.com (shape); Ye/Shutterstock.com (vase or faces); Peteri/Shutterstock.com (old man or princess); Barry Barnes/Shutterstock.com (wheel); Kamil Hajek/Shutterstock.com (butterfly or flowers); Danie Nel/Shutterstock.com (3-D glasses). 174: luchschen/Shutterstock.com (water); mmutlu/Shutterstock.com (ear). 175: AP Photo/Thibault Camus (Bieber); jocic/Shutterstock.com (listen); mast3r/Shutterstock.com (yell); fotoret/Shutterstock.com (piano). 176: Antonín Vodák/Shutterstock.com (sewing machine); Hemera Technologies/Photos.com (typewriter); Library of Congress, Prints and Photographs Division (car, telephone): Photo Courtesy of New York Public Library (airplane). 177: Hemera Technologies/Photos.com (gas mask); Library of Congress, Prints and Photographs Division (bomb, frozen food); Vladyslav Danilin/Shutterstock.com (CDs); AP Photo/Nell Redmond

(Kinect). 178: Photo by MIT/Dominick Reuter (artificial leaf); Yelken Octuri/Octuri.com (flying yacht); AP Photo/Eric Risberg (iPhone). 179: Image by Curventa and Siemens (Bloodhound); AP Photo/AeroVironment Inc. (Nav); Photo by DARPA (Urban Photonic Sandtable Display); Photo by James Wade Photography (Switch bulb). 180: Photo by Ascent Solar Technologies (thin-film solar panels); Photo by Anny CK Photography (fabric); ©UNICEF/UGDA2011-00100/Yannick Tylle (Digital Drum); Photo by Neurowear (Necomimi). 181: Le Do/Shutterstock.com (phone); urfin/Shutterstock.com (mouse); oksana2010/Shutterstock.com (TV). 182: saicle/Shutterstock.com (background); Hung Chung Chih (boy); DDCoral/Shutterstock.com (gecko); Thomas Libby-CiBER (Robert Full). 183: Photo by Dan Little ©HRL Laboratories, LLC. (lowest-density material); optimarc/Shutterstock.com (Styrofoam); Fokin Oleg/Shutterstock.com (iron); prochasson frederic/Shutterstock.com (Eiffel Tower). 184: Photo by MIT/Melanie Gonick (scientists); Featureflash/Shutterstock.com (prosthetic limb); AP Photo/Georgia Tech University (nanogenerator); Lisa A/Shutterstock.com (tire); AP Photo/Anupam Nath (women getting water).

SPACE: 186–187: NASA/JPL-Caltech/R. Hurt [SSC-Caltech]. 188: NASA, ESA, and The Hubble Heritage Team [STScI/AURA] (spiral); NASA, ESA, and the Hubble Heritage [STScI/AURA]-ESA/Hubble Collaboration (elliptical); NASA, ESA, the Hubble Heritage Team [STScI/AURA], and A. Aloisi [STScI/ESA] (irregular). 189: NOAO/AURA/NSF (globular cluster M4); NASA and H. Richer/University of British Columbia (close up); NASA, ESA, G. Illingworth [UCO/Lick Observatory and the University of California, Santa Cruz], R. Bouwens [UCO/Lick Observatory and Leiden University], and the HUDF09 Team (space). 190: SOHO [ESA & NASA] (sun, sunspot); prudkov/Shutterstock.com (girl); Simon Bratt/Shutterstock.com (windows); Iryna1/Shutterstock.com (Galileo); Vertes Edmond Mihai/ Shutterstock.com (sun illustration). 191: NASA/Hinode/XRT (solar eclipse); Imaginechina via AP Images (partial eclipse). 192: NASA/SDO/AIA (solar flare); Walter S. Becker/Shutterstock.com (aurora borealis in Alaska); agrosse/Shutterstock.com (aurora borealis in Norway). 193: NASA/CXC/STScI/JPL-Caltech/UIUC/Univ. of Minnesota (supernova); ESA, NASA, HEIC and The Hubble Heritage Team [STScI/AURA] (nebula); NASA/JPL-Caltech (Mira). 194–195: zzoplanet/Shutterstock.com. 196: NASA (astronaut); zzoplanet/Shutterstock.com (sun); Tristan3D/Shutterstock.com (moons); Elenaphotos21/Shutterstock.com (Earth); NASA/Johns Hopkins University Applied Physics Laboratory/Southwest Research Institute/Goddard Space Flight Center (Jupiter). 197: NASA, ESA, and M. Showalter [SETI Institute] (New Horizons, Pluto's moons); Chimponzee/Shutterstock.com (Hades). 198: NASA/JPL-Caltech (asteroids, Dawn); NASA/JPL/USGS (Ida). 199: NASA (astronaut); Don Davis/NASA (impact). 200: Halley Multicolor Camera Team, Giotto Project, ESA (Halley's comet); NASA (Rosetta); AP Photo/Alastair Grant (Hale-Bopp). 201: Universal Images Group/Getty Images (Tunguska Event); Pichugin Dmitry/Shutterstock.com (Hoba); NASA/MSFC (moon impact); AP photo/Mike Riddell (meteor shower); NASA (space junk). 202: AP Photo/NASA (Laika); NASA (Explorer 1, Ham, John Glenn, Luna 2); AP Photo (Yuri Gagarin). 203: NASA (Edward White, *Gemini 7*, Illustration, Earth); Photo by NASA/JPL-Caltech (Surveyor 1). 204: NASA (Bluford, Sally Ride, *Columbia*); NASA/JPL (Jupiter, Voyager 2). 205: NASA (Hubble, *ISS*); Courtesy of Scaled Composites, LLC (*SpaceShipOne*); NASA/JPL-Caltech/ASU (Mars). 206: NASA (View, Libya, Vegas, volcano, glacier); NASA/Paolo Nespoli (*International Space Station*). 207: NASA (all). 208: NASA (day 3); NASA/Tony Gray and Tom Farrar (day 1). 209: NASA (Day 4, Day 5, Day 12, Day 13 reentry); NASA/Kim Shiflett (Day 13 lands). 210: NASA/JPL-Caltech (scientists, rovers); NASA (Orion). 211: NASA/JPL-Caltech (Curiosity); NASA (underwater). 212: NASA/JPL-Caltech. 213: NASA (Voyager); NASA/JPL-Caltech (golden record). 214: NASA, ESA, J. Hester and A. Loll]Arizona State University] (nebula); NASA, ESA, and the Hubble Heritage Team [STScI/AURA] (Globular cluster M13); NASA, ESA, the Hubble Heritage [STScI/AURA]-ESA/Hubble Collaboration, and A. Evans [University of Virginia, Charlottesville/NRAO/Stony Brook University] (cosmic collision); NASA, ESA, and the Hubble SM4 ERO Team (butterfly). 215: NASA/Kepler mission/Wendy Stenzel (Kepler); NASA/Ames/JPL-Caltech (Kepler-22b); NASA (JWST).

BACK COVER: Lightspring/Shutterstock.com (brain); Zern Liew/Shutterstock.com (satellite); peappop/Shutterstock.com (slug); Ian Scott/Shutterstock.com (volcano).